UNLOCKING
THE POWER OF
NETWORKS

D0093983

INNOVATIVE GOVERNANCE IN THE 21ST CENTURY

This is the fourth volume in a series that examines important issues of governance, public policy, and administration, highlighting innovative practices and original research worldwide. All titles in the series are copublished by the Brookings Institution Press and the Ash Institute for Democratic Governance and Innovation, housed at Harvard University's John F. Kennedy School of Government.

Decentralizing Governance: Emerging Concepts and Practices
G. Shabbir Cheema and Dennis A. Rondinelli, eds. (2007)

Innovations in Government: Research, Recognition, and Replication
Sandford Borins, ed. (2008)

The State of Access:
Success and Failure of Democracies to Create Equal Opportunities
Jorrit de Jong and Gowher Rizvi, eds. (2008)

UNLOCKING THE POWER OF NETWORKS

Keys to High-Performance Government

STEPHEN GOLDSMITH

DONALD F. KETTL

editors

ASH INSTITUTE FOR DEMOCRATIC GOVERNANCE AND INNOVATION
John F. Kennedy School of Government
Harvard University

BROOKINGS INSTITUTION PRESS
Washington, D.C.

Copyright © 2009
ASH INSTITUTE FOR DEMOCRATIC GOVERNANCE AND INNOVATION
HARVARD UNIVERSITY

Library of Congress Cataloging-in-Publication data
Unlocking the power of networks : keys to high-performance government / Stephen Goldsmith and Donald F. Kettl, editors.
    p.   cm. — (Innovative governance in the 21st century)
Includes bibliographical references and index.
Summary: "Explores the potential, strategies, and best practices of high-performance networks while identifying next-generation issues in public sector network management. Employs sector-specific analyses to reveal how networked governance achieves previously unthinkable policy goals, including natural resource protection by Interior, California's greenhouse emissions policy, Chesapeake Bay cleanup, and the fight against antiterrorism"—Provided by publisher.
    ISBN 978-0-8157-3187-0 (pbk. : alk. paper) 1. Public-private sector cooperation—United States. 2. Central-local government relations—United States. 3. Public administration—United States. I. Goldsmith, Stephen, 1946– II. Kettl, Donald F. III. Title. IV. Series.
    JK421.U59 2009
    352.3—dc22
                                                  2008052341

1 3 5 7 9 8 6 4 2

Typeset in Adobe Garamond

Composition by R. Lynn Rivenbark
Macon, Georgia

Printed by R. R. Donnelley
Harrisonburg, Virginia

Contents

Acknowledgments

The editors acknowledge the following individuals for their important contributions to this book: Roy Ash, whose service and accomplishments in many sectors of government, for profit, and philanthropic, represent the very best in American citizenship; Christina Marchand, who led the support effort at the Ash Institute for Democratic Governance and Innovation; editor Kathleen Lynch, whose comments and suggestions gave consistency to the chapters; and Chris Kelaher and Janet Walker from the Brookings Institution Press for their editorial advice. At the University of Pennsylvania's Fels Institute of Government, Allison Brummel coordinated a team of staff and students whose support proved invaluable: Anthony Hollingworth, Anna Wallace, and Andrew Gooch. Finally, we are grateful to the many practitioners who shared their experiences on the power of networks. Their insights powerfully shaped the book's analysis and conclusions.

UNLOCKING
THE POWER OF
NETWORKS

1

The Key to Networked Government

DONALD F. KETTL

Even the most casual look at how government programs actually operate raises big questions about orthodox theories of public policy. Translating big ideas into reality requires collaboration among many players. Government social service programs ripple out through a huge collection of nonprofit community-based organizations, and these organizations typically blend funding from federal, state, local, foundation, and voluntary contributions. Airport security is a complex partnership among airlines, airport authorities, and federal, state, and local governments. Attacking issues such as climate change requires global partnerships. Doing important things typically means bringing together a big collection of players. That, at its core, is the meaning and puzzle of networked government: gathering the players, coordinating their work, and ensuring that the result promotes the public interest.

The power of networked government lies in its pragmatism. Its proponents begin with the assessment that most classical theories fall short in describing how public programs actually work, and they seek to lay out a straightforward explanation policy implementation. As soon as anyone points out the interconnections among the programs citizens encounter every day, the more apparent such connections become everywhere. But networked government raises a problem. It provides an explanation for the way much of government operates, but the explanation is a long way from the theories that guide thinking about how government *should* work. The basic theory of government holds that policymakers delegate power to administrators to do good things and hold them accountable for how well administrators do them. This generations-old theory has proved remarkably robust, as scholars adapt it to changing governmental strategies and tactics, and thus has allowed policymakers to give government administrators more power in exchange for a process that holds them accountable. The problem has come as government's ambition has grown, with more government power extending into more nooks and crannies of civic life, more players with a role in exercising that power, and more hands responsible for how well public programs work.

The mismatch between academic theories and operating realities is more than just an arcane puzzle for academics. A fundamental puzzle for governance in the twenty-first century is the question: How do you make government effective enough to get its job done while holding its officials accountable in their exercise of power? In the late nineteenth century, the Progressives tackled this ageless dilemma by making a quiet deal: give government more power to do progressive things, and they would build institutions and processes to ensure that the bureaucrats exercising that power did not run amok. The institutions and processes they created presumed a chain of command from citizens to elected officials to bureaucrats. The Progressives could license the bureaucrats with great power because they believed that the system would hold the bureaucrats accountable. This approach became enshrined both in the theory of how government ought to work and in the practical understandings under which elected officials operated.

As public policies developed throughout the twentieth century, two big problems emerged with this theory. First, more public programs involved more players, so it was hard for elected officials to hold any single person or agency accountable for results. That posed big problems for accountability, because policymakers often puzzled over who was responsible for what. Second, the tools that elected officials used to track and control these programs did not keep up with the changing strategies and tactics. Growing partnerships made programs more complex and harder to manage and control. More players with weaker links to policymakers combined to create a twin dilemma: big performance problems along with weakened accountability.

That did not necessarily mean that effective and responsive government was doomed. Out of the expansive programs and complex partnerships came individual leaders who concentrated on the job at hand and worked to figure out how to get it done. By focusing on the immediate mission, many of them have proved remarkably effective in moving their programs forward. But how this works, and how the individual leadership might be integrated into a broader model for how to approach networked government, is an unanswered question. Among academics there is no consensus about whether networks are a theory, an approach, a phenomenon, a pattern, or a relationship.[1] Recognition of the importance of

1. For a review of the academic literature on networked government, see the bibliography.

networks has been growing since the end of the twentieth century, but just what they are is anything but clear.

Instead of adding high-level conjecture to this debate, the authors of this book took a different tack. Each author chose a policy area of clear importance and sought to describe the policy arena—who did what, and how well it worked. The methodology was deep immersion and thick description. Some authors shadowed public officials to get a sense of how their programs worked. Others convened day-long sessions of intense interviews about the issues the managers faced. Some gleaned important insights from often-neglected sources. Together, the authors present seven detailed cases about how networked government actually operates. The cases are wide-ranging: a cooperative conservation initiative, by William Eggers (chapter 2); climate change, by Barry Rabe (chapter 3); wetlands protection, by Paul Posner (chapter 4); changes in eligibility for governmental programs, by Steve Goldsmith and Tim Burke (chapter 5); coordination of national intelligence, by G. Edward DeSeve (chapter 6); port security, by Anne M. Khademian and William G. Berberich (chapter 7); and even "dark networks" such as al Qaeda, by H. Brinton Milward and Jörg Raab (chapter 8). The disparate cases provide clues to a basic question: How do the politics and management of public policy in the twenty-first century actually work? Networked government has become more prevalent and more important. What implications does it have for governance?

The Roots of Networked Government

Traditional approaches to public policy, especially the strategies framed by the nation's founders and the Progressives, are fundamentally *structural*. The founders put their faith in "separated institutions sharing power," as Richard Neustadt put it.[2] The Progressives built new regulatory agencies, the Federal Reserve, and new management processes, such as the executive budget. They sparked a century of lively debate by promoting separation of policymaking from policy administration, but that separation really attempted to solve one important problem: how to increase government's reach and power while holding government administrators accountable for the exercise of that power. The founders' and Progressives' solutions were structural and procedural: granting power but constraining it, within government organizations and through tough management accountability rules. The approach was boundary based. Elected officials were the principals; government administrators were their agents.

During the twentieth century those boundaries were breached. When private and nonprofit programs could not handle the overwhelming burden of responding effectively to the Great Depression, Franklin D. Roosevelt's New Deal vastly expanded government's reach, working through an alphabet soup of federal agencies

2. Neustadt (1964, p. 42).

and new partnerships with state and local governments. World War II magnified the organizational challenge. Faced with a two-front war, the federal government could have nationalized war production or operated its own armament factories. No one wanted to admit the possibility of a large permanent military establishment and, in any event, creating a government-owned and government-run military-industrial complex would have taken a long time. Instead, defense planners relied on private contractors so that the war mobilization effort could be dialed up and down as needed. The government signed huge deals with contractors such as Boeing, Northrop, and Kaiser to produce the needed military materiel and equipment.[3] In response to the crisis, Howard Hughes built his Hughes Aircraft Company from a tiny outfit employing just four people into an 80,000-person leviathan.[4]

The Roosevelt administration set a course of providing public funds, through incentives and direct finance, for private construction. A combination of special depreciation deals and outright construction grants created the facilities. Government contracts paid for supplies and equipment. The strategy became known simply as "GOCOs," for government-owned, contractor-operated facilities. In some cases private companies simply expanded their own operations, with government financial help, to meet the wartime demand. It was a war-fighting strategy born of pragmatism, but it had profound implications for the distribution of government power. Private companies became important, indeed indispensable, agents of governmental policy. They also became independent sources of influence that prompted Dwight D. Eisenhower to warn famously in his farewell address at the end of his presidency: "In the councils of government, we must guard against the acquisition of unwarranted influence, whether sought or unsought, by the military-industrial complex. The potential for the disastrous rise of misplaced power exists and will persist."[5] Not only were the government's private partners important to the pursuit of public goals, but they were also becoming important independent sources of political power.

Similar partnerships grew in other areas. New space technologies, spun off from the World War II research and development effort, led to the creation of a large ballistic missile program to launch nuclear weapons. That in turn led to the manned space program. By the early years of the twenty-first century, private contractors were responsible for 90 percent of all the spending in the space shuttle program. The interstate highway system, launched in 1956 as the National System of Interstate and Defense Highways, gave the states federal money to build a new national road network. It was irresistible to the states—the federal government paid 90 cents

3. U.S. Army, *Mobilization: The U.S. Army in World War II–The 50th Anniversary* (www.history.army.mil/documents/mobpam.htm).

4. U.S. Centennial of Flight Commission (www.centennialofflight.gov/essay/Aerospace/Hughes/Aero44.htm).

5. Dwight D. Eisenhower, "Military-Industrial Complex Speech, January 17, 1961" (http://coursesa.matrix.msu.edu/~hst306/documents/indust.html).

for each dollar spent on highway construction, and private contractors did most of the work. At the local level, the federal government helped cities tear down derelict neighborhoods in a major urban renewal effort, in the hope that large plots of developable land would spur new investment and revitalize neighborhoods. For decades critics have argued about the success of these strategies, but there is no mistaking their two fundamental impacts. First, they transformed the temporary pragmatism of the public-private partnerships that helped win World War II into a permanent policy strategy. Second, these partnerships moved well past the boundary-based strategies for expanding but controlling government power that the Progressives had envisioned. The ultimate impact of these gradual shifts might not have been clear, but they cast a long enough shadow for Eisenhower to register his concern.

Following the creation of permanent public-private partnerships in the 1950s, the floodgates of innovation opened wide in the 1960s. The space and interstate highway programs vastly expanded. So did the military establishment, nurtured by the cold war and then the war in Vietnam. Lyndon B. Johnson's War on Poverty expanded federal grants to local governments, and the rise of the administration's Model Cities Program spread federal cash to nonprofit neighborhood organizations. The Medicare and Medicaid programs extended health care programs for older and poorer Americans through extraordinarily complex arrangements with for-profit and nonprofit health care providers and private companies that managed reimbursement. Regulatory programs grew through similar partnerships, ranging from efforts to improve environmental quality to broad-based strategies to improve the health and safety of workplaces.

The privatization movement of the 1980s, championed by Ronald Reagan during his presidency, sought to rein in government and return more power to the private sector. In fact, it scarcely (if at all) reduced government's role but significantly expanded the array of services that government contracted out. From cafeterias to maintenance services, governments at all levels sought private providers of support services. Politicians of both parties—Reagan in the 1980s and Bill Clinton in the 1990s—accelerated the contracting-out movement. Politicians continually pledged to rein in government's reach into the private lives of citizens, but regulations expanded, covering everything from the safety of children's car seats to that of supermarket spinach.

A complex array of cross-cutting forces prompted the growth of these partnerships. Political demands for more government solutions to big problems balanced by political opposition to expanding government employment to do the job led to reliance on nongovernmental partners. So, too, did the rise of complex problems, from putting astronauts into space to managing tens of millions of Medicare transactions. Relying on private partners was far easier for government than building its own internal expertise to accomplish these goals.

The federal government has long had an official policy of encouraging such partnerships. In 1955 the Bureau of the Budget (now called the Office of Management and Budget, OMB) issued circular A-76, requiring the federal government to buy goods and services from the private sector whenever it was proper and cost-effective to do so. Contracting out was proper for functions that were not "inherently governmental," that is, functions that were not intrinsically tied to the government's basic responsibilities and power.

However, as government contracting spilled into more areas, setting the "inherently governmental" standard became ever more difficult. In fact, Stephen Goldsmith argues in chapter 5 of this book, there are few functions that government can do better than the private sector and no functions that truly are inherent to government. If anything can be contracted out, is there anything that should not be? This question lies at the core of a sharp ideological divide between conservatives and liberals, but it also raises a tough question for networks: Since networks are about effective bridges over boundaries, are there any boundaries that networks should not bridge?

The cost-effectiveness standard likewise proved hard to define. As the so-called A-76 movement evolved, a basic principle emerged: whenever government had a job to do, it should be done by whoever (in either the private or public sectors) could do it most cheaply. Over the years, the rules gradually changed to favor contracting out even more, and conservatives seized on circular A-76 to back up their privatization initiatives. Employees of government agencies regularly complained that the playing field was never level when they competed for contracts. They said that the competitions were often rigged against them: because the government pays relatively generous benefits while private competitors often skimp on benefits, contractors frequently low-balled the price to get the work. Government employees at all levels won a surprising number of these competitions, but contractors competed ever more aggressively, with substantial help from the Reagan and both Bush administrations.

Pragmatism, policy, and politics—together these forces further blurred the boundaries between government and its private and nonprofit partners. Networks emerged as a form of adaptive behavior, an effort to find ways to solve problems under tough political and substantive constraints. How should a spacecraft be built and launched to put astronauts into space and bring them back via a plane-like landing? How should lakes be made swimmable and rivers drinkable again? How should greenhouse gases be reduced or management of national intelligence improved? How should the transportation system be strengthened or health care improved? Other nations, especially in Europe, have answered these questions through an expansion of the welfare state. The special nature of U.S. federalism, coupled with Americans' deep-rooted love-hate relationship with government, made that impossible. The government's response to the financial meltdown in 2008 further blurred the neat boundaries around government programs and the agencies assigned to manage them. Bit by bit, Americans have jury-rigged a system of enormous complexity, adapting governmental structures and processes to new problems by tacking on new partnerships as the problems demanded.

Networked government, in fact, is something like the networked brain. Many of the brain's basic functions are hard-wired. Neural networks adapt to new stimuli, and new patterns of interconnection emerge as needed to help the brain solve fresh problems. The brain's learning is adaptive behavior. Government's networks likewise have learned to adapt to fit and solve the shifting patterns and growing expectations of public policy. Networked government has emerged as a strategy to help government adapt and perform in the changing policy world.

The closest that the U.S. government has come to embracing networked government as an explicit strategy is the A-76 process of encouraging contracting out. But networked government extends far past the mandate of circular A-76. State and local governments' contracting out has expanded into virtually every function, from libraries to fire protection. Welfare reform has been built on a network of contracts with private and nonprofit social service and job placement organizations.[6] For-profit and nonprofit organizations deliver most community social service programs, and the connections among them rival the most intricate neural map of brain activity. Most local governments have mutual assistance agreements with their neighbors for large public safety problems. For instance, in Virginia, Arlington County's response to the attack on the Pentagon was an intricate ballet performed by federal, state, regional, and local agencies.[7] State governments work with each other to improve the quality of the rivers and streams they share. Networked government is like an anthill. It might not look like much on the surface, but the deeper one scratches, the more intricate interconnections one finds.

Some networks connect government and the private and nonprofit sectors. Some are between government agencies at a single level of government, while others are within government but across its levels. Some stretch across international boundaries and, like the international space station, past the boundaries of earth itself. These networks are all pragmatic efforts to adapt existing organizations, through practical partnerships, to pursue public purposes. The very nature of these networks makes it difficult to assess how large they are, but their role and importance are unmistakable. The deeper one scratches below the surface, the more important the network phenomenon becomes.

Central Questions

Establishing the importance of networked government is one thing. Assessing its role in governance is quite another. In fact, the rise of networked government

---

6. See, for example, Sanger (2003).
7. Arlington County (2001).

raises a host of difficult issues, which constitute the central questions discussed in this book.

Is Networked Government New?

The role of networked government is inescapable. But is it really new—or just newly noticed? After all, governments have relied on contractors for millennia. An essential element in Caesar's campaign to extend the reach of the Roman empire was to ensure a steady supply of provisions for his army. Ill-fed troops make unreliable warriors. Napoleon, too, worried about creating and sustaining a supply network to feed his troops. He is widely credited with the adage "an army travels on its stomach." Both had to rely heavily on a complex chain of local suppliers to keep their troops moving.

Networked government is nothing new. Moreover, much networked government is ad hoc and out of sync with the conventional view of how government operates. Governments tend not to keep their books in a way that makes it easy (or even possible) to assess the full measure of the private sector's contribution to the public sector's work. The Federal Procurement Data System tracks federal contracts, but it has struggled to capture all federal contracting activity, and long-term analysis is extraordinarily difficult.[8] In 2006 Barack Obama cosponsored the creation of the website www.USASpending.gov, which is a database that tracks where federal grant and contract dollars go, making it possible, for example, to identify how many dollars flow to each community or congressional district. There is no similar database for state and local governments, although they have relied extensively on these indirect tools of government as well.

Table 1-1 shows estimates from USASpending.com of total federal spending, broken down by the type of fiscal tool used to administer the funding: contracts, grants to state and local governments, loans, insurance, direct payments (such as Social Security and Medicare), and others. The time period is short and the data are raw, but there is no escaping the expansion of networked government just from fiscal year 2000 through 2007, a period in which the volume of contracting out increased from 11.5 to 16.0 percent of all federal spending and grants grew from 16.2 to 18.7 percent. Getting a clear and consistent measure of networked government is extremely difficult, but two things are clear: it is large, and it is growing. If historical data were available for the pre–World War II years and we could compare them to the postwar years, there is no doubt that the conclusion would be dramatic: we would see that contracting expanded significantly and that the twenty-first-century U.S. government is vastly more networked than were Caesar's and Napoleon's.

---

8. See the Federal Procurement Data System website (www.fpds.gov).

Table 1-1. *Government Spending*
U.S.$ billions

	FY 2000	FY 2001	FY 2002	FY 2003	FY 2004	FY 2005	FY 2006
Contracts	208.84	219.80	259.60	298.51	341.88	382.12	419.89
Grants	294.51	330.74	406.15	493.28	449.61	441.02	488.52
Loans	107.98	141.81	216.76	210.83	154.78	118.78	95.39
Insurance	431.32	492.21	556.59	567.21	603.89	653.23	771.28
Direct payments (for example, Social Security)	768.25	839.65	841.51	947.94	965.48	1,004.07	1,092.67
Other	2.82	2.68	0.23	0.66	0.38	0.30	3.85
Total	1,813.72	2,026.89	2,280.83	2,518.45	2,516.02	2,599.51	2,871.59

Source: See www.usaspending.gov.

Through the fiscal tools mentioned previously, the true size of government has expanded (see table 1-1).[9] In the decades since World War II, the reach and impact of government at all levels has unquestionably grown significantly, breaking down the very boundaries that the Progressives created to license but restrain bureaucratic power. Eisenhower was prescient when he warned of the specter of a military-industrial complex. The twenty-first-century complex stretches far past the military into virtually every cranny of the U.S. government. In short, the government has become ever more networked, through a collection of collaborations that has materialized to get the work done, as often on an ad hoc basis as by design.

Is Networked Government the Product of Conscious Design?

Another reason why analyzing networked government is difficult is that it takes such different forms and follows no consistent model. In fact, it stands in stark contrast to the organizational strategies of the Progressives. They strengthened government by constraining its power within clear boundaries and held it accountable through tough processes. Networked government, by contrast, developed to escape the constraints imposed by the Progressives' design. Where the Progressives focused on holding power within organizational structures, networked government seeks to reach across political and organizational boundaries. Where the Progressives sought to hold power accountable through a variety of finance-based mechanisms, networked government pragmatically focuses on how best to solve the problem at hand. In short, the traditional model of policy and politics seeks consciously to design the system in advance. Networked government evolves in

9. See Light (1999).

response to problems, and solutions emerge that seem best to fit the problem, sometimes ad hoc and sometimes following previously used models.

This gives networked government enormous flexibility, but it also makes building a theory to explain what it is and how it works far more difficult. The Progressives had an inward approach, a straightforward, structure-based model that provided not only a road map for building a government but also a theory about how their model of government would work. Networked government, by contrast, is outward looking. Because the nature of the policy problem defines the role of the players and their interactions, it is far more difficult to generalize about what networked government is or how it works. The traditional system framed by the Progressives is indeed a product of intelligent design. Networked government is evolutionary. That is its strength, in helping government adapt to new problems, but it is also its conceptual fragility. Its adaptive nature has made it easy to posit the approach to networked governance as "we know it when we see it," but it has also made it that much harder to build a theory that describes what it is, how it works, and how it can be deployed.

In Networks Is Government Just One Player among Many?

The adaptive nature of networked government helps it evolve to fit new problems, but it also creates opportunities for new political games. The nature of policy problems defines the players in networks; stakeholders in a problem are the ones most likely to gather around it. For instance, the question of how best to clean up a bay brings together a coalition of the governmental units responsible for the bay's environmental health, the commercial interests that might have to pay a price for cleanup, and the citizens most likely to benefit from cleaner water and better-protected wildlife. National security and climate change debates bring together completely different coalitions of players. Networked government thus not only is a tactic for administering public policies, but it also creates its own tremendously varied political ecology, a pluralism in which different policies define different politics.

Moreover, networked government not only defines the nature of the political game but also creates a game in which the government is one player among many. Most theories of pluralism put government at the center of competing demands by external players, each involved in cross-cutting battles to influence government's decisions. In networked government, government itself is often one of the players, sometimes only a bit player in a far larger drama, and sometimes the central mover. Sometimes the players are governments at different levels of the intergovernmental system, governments abroad, different agencies with varied stakes in the policy outcome, interest groups and companies, citizens and neighborhood associations. Sometimes government convenes, stimulates, or controls the network. In national security policy, for example, a handful of relatively anonymous agencies are the prime movers. Sometimes, as with climate change, government is one player among many and seeks to nudge the others in a way that matches its preferred course. Sometimes other members of the network try to nudge government, in a process more like well-known versions of pluralism.

What all of these approaches to networked government share is that they differ sharply from traditional approaches to politics. Governmental decisionmakers are not so much the focus of competing external forces as part of an intricate web, defined by the policy at play, in which individual governmental decisionmakers are but one player among many. Traditional pluralism, by putting government at the center, makes governmental decisionmakers the principal focus, whereas networked government, by making government one among many players, creates a far more complicated process in which power is far more widely distributed—and in which government sometimes is not even the prime mover or the most powerful player. Left unanswered is the question of who convenes the network.

That leads to an important question: If complex cross pressures shape interactions, and if the outcome of the game is more a product of these interactions than of the decision made by any one player (including a government official), and if it is not clear who convenes the network, who is in charge when power is so broadly shared? The rules of the governance game provide no clear answer because in many cases there are no rules. This version of pluralism on steroids allows the system tremendous flexibility in adapting to new challenges. Indeed, as seen earlier, networked government emerged because boundary-based systems often reacted sluggishly to change. It also allows governmental players to bring in a vast array of other governmental and nongovernmental partners, thereby broadening the political base for public action.

This pragmatic flexibility can, however, also compromise the pursuit of the public interest. If no one is clearly in charge—if government officials are not necessarily the prime movers of the network and if, within government, public responsibility is fuzzy—how does accountability work? Who is responsible for defining, pursuing, and achieving the public interest? Or have the worst fears of pluralism's critics come home with a vengeance? Has the government's role in defining public policy weakened? Are policies being shaped increasingly by the interplay of private forces as government's voice has faded?

The cases in this book explore this question from a wide array of perspectives. One answer they give is that within each network, individual governmental leaders often emerge to define and shape public goals. They subtly work to redefine accountability away from the Progressives' focus on process to a shared focus on making the program work. In the eyes of many of these leaders, the networks are good and accountable in the degree to which they accomplish the programs' goals, not the degree to which the players simply follow the rules. The cases explore the puzzle about how this shift in accountability works—and whether it works well enough to ensure the responsible exercise of government's power in accordance with the wishes of policymakers and citizens. Is this an effective strategy for accountability?

In the case studies, one element is especially important to track. The cases are stories not only about cutting-edge public policy problems that increasingly are managed through networks but also about individual leadership, about governmental leaders who rose to the challenge of solving difficult and complex problems, picked up the flag, and sought to frame a consensus and coordinate network actions. The book's contributors did not commit themselves to a common methodology but rather to a shared mission: to identify important examples of networked government and examine how the networks operated. Thus, the rise of key leaders in each case was not the product of conscious design but signaled the emergence of a pattern that flows across all the cases.

The case studies are instructive at three levels: the emergence of complex policy problems that require response from many actors; the processes that knit together, sometimes well and sometimes badly, the behavior of these actors; and the role of individual leaders in trying to coordinate and focus the work of the network. These levels in turn frame several alternatives to the puzzle of creating effective and accountable government. Could accountability be the product of many actors contributing to the pursuit of a public goal? In this approach, is it the goal that defines accountability? Could accountability be the product of processes, some governmental and some from the private and nonprofit sectors, that nudge network participants in a similar direction? In this approach, is it the joint action that defines accountability, like geese flying in formation? Could it be that it is the role of individual leaders to define accountability? In this approach, it is the power of personal leadership that frames a logic of coordinated work. But in all these alternatives, the central puzzle—the central question of the book—is whether networked government helps or hinders the effective and responsible pursuit of *public* goals. The complexity of policy problems might well make networked government irresistible and inevitable. But how well does it advance the public's work? And if individual leaders emerge as the central drivers of networked government, what licenses their role? In a system where power is broadly shared, how do some leaders become more central than others? That is the central puzzle of the place of the public interest in networked government.

Is "Networked Government" an Empirical Description or a Normative Prescription?

These puzzles lead to the last question posed by the cases. In these accounts of government's role and behavior, does networked government emerge as a thick description for the way much policy implementation operates, or is it more a normative prescription for ensuring effective action in response to complex problems that extend beyond the boundaries of individual government entities, agencies, and programs? On the descriptive side, the cases chart the remarkably interwoven strategies and tactics used by network members to frame coordinated action. On the normative side, the cases hint at an answer. If networked government is not the most desirable strategy for dealing with issues from environmental protection to national security, what would work better?

In the worlds described by the cases, policy problems define processes, goals drive interactions, and leaders coordinate across multiple boundaries. The interactions described lie far beyond the realm of government as conceived by the Progressives. Their purposefulness in pursuing public goals makes them more than just another example of incentive-based, market-driven behavior. Scholars and analysts have long identified politics and markets as the basic alternatives for social action.[10] The Progressives framed the approach to politics that predominated for more than a century. They clearly meant their approach as a guide to frame public action. The market-based approach is just as clearly a normative guide, for it posits that competition in the marketplace produces the most efficient use of resources and the most satisfied consumer behavior. But what happens when neither the Progressives' nor the market approach to government suffices to deal with basic policy problems? The contributors describe how networks arise—sometimes in a halting fashion and sometimes ill formed. As these networks develop, they also raise the more fundamental question, implicit in each case, about whether networked government *should* be the preferred form of response to complex public problems? If so, how should it work? And if not, what are its limits?

Lurking behind the analyses of effective networked government is the specter, raised by H. Brinton Milward and Jörg Raab (chapter 8), that not all networks create positive forces. They powerfully argue that al Qaeda and other terrorist organizations, which they call "dark networks," grew from network-based patterns of behavior; now these networks threaten the stability of nations. Countering them poses big challenges. G. Edward DeSeve's discussion of networks in the intelligence community (chapter 6) suggests that it may take a "bright" network to counter a "dark" one. Most important, however, the specter of dark networks—networked interactions that seek to undermine, not support, the broad goals of nation states—paints a cautionary tale regarding prescriptive thinking on networks.

Finding the Key to Networked Government

This book is an effort to learn how modern governments can address and solve complex problems that challenge existing patterns of governance. When difficult issues arise that fit neither the Progressives' traditional model of structure- and process-bound government nor the economists' traditional model of market competition, what should governments do? The cases describe how governments have tackled this dilemma. Each case is a tale of adaptation. In no case did a prime

10. See, for example, Lindblom (1980).

mover leap out of the primordial policy soup to declare boldly, "Let's create a network!" Instead, in each case policy leaders arose with a clear focus on problems that needed solutions and designed strategies and tactics to advance their goals. Unlike the Progressives, they did not seek a fundamental structural or procedural reform before moving ahead. Unlike market-based theorists, they did not try to reshape the private market to produce better results. Instead, they sought to cobble together effective action from the resources at hand. Their tales of accomplishment are often remarkable. So, too, are the potholes that sometimes broke their axles along the way. Mark Moore's concluding contribution (chapter 9) charts the big questions that networked government, sometimes intentionally and sometimes not, raises about the future of U.S. government.

Together, the case studies focus a strong light on the alternative of ad hoc adaptation to structural reform in responding to cutting-edge policy problems. They also provide important input on setting standards by which network behavior should be judged—and on how the ability of these networks to advance the people's work can be assessed in an era in which tough policy problems increasingly challenge democratic institutions.

References

Arlington County (Va.). 2001. *After-Action Report on the Response to the 9/11 Terrorist Attack on the Pentagon.* Arlington, Va.: 2001 (www.arlingtonva.us/Departments/fire/edu/about/docs/after_report.pdf).
Light, Paul C. 1999. *The True Size of Government.* Brookings.
Lindblom, Charles E. 1980. *Politics and Markets: The World's Political Economic Systems.* New York: Basic Books.
Neustadt, Richard E. 1964. *Presidential Power.* New York: Wiley, 1964.
Sanger, Mary Bryna. 2003. *The Welfare Marketplace: Privatization and Welfare Reform.* Brookings.

2

From Conflict to Collaboration: Lessons in Networked Governance from the Federal Cooperative Conservation Initiative

WILLIAM D. EGGERS

One day in 1948, a convoy of Michigan sportsmen drove their pickup trucks to Lansing to dump piles of dead, oil-soaked ducks on the lawn of the state capitol.[1] Oil slicks on the Detroit River killed waterfowl every winter, but with a toll of 11,000, 1948 had seen the worst carnage ever.[2]

With its numerous islands and marshes and its vast variety of birds and fish, the Detroit River constitutes a vital ecosystem in the Great Lakes region of North America. Although the duck drop got the government's attention, environmental problems continued to plague the Detroit River watershed over the ensuing decades.

In the 1960s the heavily industrialized Rouge River, a tributary of the Detroit, actually burst into flames.[3] In 1970 mercury contamination forced wildlife officials to halt fishing on several major waterways, including all of the Detroit River and western Lake Erie.[4] A 1996 study of the Detroit River found toxic substances

Substantial research for this chapter was contributed by graduate students from the Maxwell School of Government at Syracuse University as part of their Master's in Public Administration Capstone Project. The student researchers were Kevin DePodwin, Kevin Johnson, Agrita Kiopa, and Theresa Miller. Dr. Alasdair Roberts was the faculty adviser.

1. Hartig (2003, p. 74).

2. Detroit River–Western Lake Erie Basin Indicator Project, "Oil Pollution of the Detroit and Rouge Rivers," U.S. Environmental Protection Agency (www.epa.gov/med/grosseile_site/indicators/oilspills. html).

3. Hartig (2003, p. 87).

4. John H. Hartig, author interview, September 5, 2007.

such as mercury, oil, lead, and PCBs still contaminating the river.[5] Throughout the decades, industrialization and sprawl kept eating away at this crucial habitat for scores of fish and bird species.

Only in the late 1990s did business and community leaders finally start to get serious about reclaiming the river for wildlife and public use. The costs of in-action—including potential long-term litigation and difficulty attracting new employees into a region widely known as a polluted wasteland—finally forced the area's leaders into action. The result: the Detroit River International Wildlife Refuge, a partnership of government, industry, and not-for-profit groups in the United States and Canada that is transforming this region from an industrial sewer into a haven for wildlife observation, recreation, and education.

Representative John D. Dingell (D-Mich.) and Peter Stroh, CEO of the Stroh Brewery Company, championed and helped launch the effort by asking interested groups to articulate a future vision for the wildlife refuge. Formed by an act of Congress in 2001, the refuge is a defined area of federally owned or managed lands bounded by forty-eight miles of shoreline and administered by the U.S. Fish and Wildlife Service. The law allows the secretary of the interior to acquire more land for the refuge through donations, to purchase land with donated or appro-priated funds, and to make exchanges of lands, waters, or interests in them within the refuge boundaries.[6] On the other side of the river, Canadian agencies also col-laborate on refuge activities.

Industry played a major role in the refuge from the start. Earlier, however, the relationship between local business and federal environmental agencies had not been so harmonious. Companies and government agencies had often faced off as adversaries on environmental issues, which made it hard to develop the trust that a partnership requires.

"It was a command-and-control mindset: 'We in government are going to issue permits to control your pollution and control you,'" says John Hartig, manager of the Detroit River International Wildlife Refuge. Taking a new approach, the partnership forged relationships with top executives in local cor-porations and got them involved in projects that would demonstrate the power of a public-private partnership.[7]

DTE Energy, for example, contributed 656 acres at its Fermi 2 Power Plant in Monroe County to the refuge. DTE still owns the land, but the company and the U.S. Fish and Wildlife Service manage it together. "We're bringing money to the

---

5. Jennifer Mitchell, "Detroit River Cleanup Plan Back in Action," (Detroit) *News-Herald*, March 15, 2005 (www.thenewsherald.com:80/stories/031605/loc_20050316024.shtml).

6. Detroit River International Wildlife Refuge Establishment Act, Public Law 107-91, December 21, 2001 (www.fws.gov/midwest/detroitriver/documents/DRIWRestablishmentAct.pdf).

7. Hartig interview.

table, they're bringing money to the table, and we're doing things differently than we did in the past—restoring wetlands, managing grasslands," Hartig says. DTE's example inspired other companies to put acreage under the refuge's management.[8]

Today, other corporate partners in the refuge include Ford Motor Company, General Motors, Daimler-Chrysler, the chemical company BASF, and U.S. Steel. Among the many other partners are the State of Michigan, the City of Detroit, Wayne County, Environment Canada, the Ontario Ministry of Natural Resources, the Nature Conservancy, the Trust for Public Land, Ducks Unlimited, and the Metropolitan Affairs Coalition.

One notable accomplishment of the partnership is the ongoing transformation of BASF's 1,200-acre Fighting Island from a brine disposal site into a wildlife sanctuary.[9] The chemical company actually started rehabilitating the island in the mid-1980s, for example, by adding yard leaves to improve the composition of the soil and planting 140,000 trees.[10] Now BASF is collaborating with U.S. and Canadian partners to build a sturgeon-spawning reef in Canadian waters off the island.[11]

The partnership also encouraged Ford Motor Company in its effort to use "green design" principles as it renovated its aging Rouge River plant in Dearborn. One technique the architects employed was to use plantings on the grounds, and even on the facility's roof, to soak up storm water that used to run off and carry toxins into the Rouge River. Another was to create gardens with certain native species that could break down toxins in the soil.[12] In the five years from 2001 to 2006, the refuge preserved 4,985 acres, completed more than twenty-five engineering projects to replace concrete infrastructure with "soft shore" habitats, and leveraged more than $11 million in conservation projects.[13]

The Larger Story

The Detroit River International Wildlife Refuge is just one of dozens of similar stories playing out from the coast of Maine to the valleys of Ohio to the rocky shores of Northern California.

The Blue Skyways consortium, a public-private partnership between business and ten local and state governments, seeks to reduce air pollution in a region

8. Ibid.

9. Cooperative Conservation America, "Detroit River Conservation Partnerships," Cooperative Conservation Case Study (www.cooperativeconservationamerica.org/viewproject.asp?pid=643).

10. BASF Corporation, "BASF's Fighting Island Hosts Kickoff for Wildlife Refuge Celebration," press release, September 29, 2003 (www.basf.com/corporate/news2003/newsinfo_9-29-03_fightingisland.html).

11. Hartig interview.

12. William McDonough and Michael Braungart, "Restoring the Industrial Landscape," green@work, September–October 2002 (www.mcdonough.com/writings/restoring_industrial.htm).

13. Dingell (2006).

stretching from Texas to Canada. In 2007 the consortium granted $1.35 million to support projects designed to slash diesel emissions from school buses in ten states.[14]

In Ohio, a partnership between the National Park Service and local farmers promotes sustainable agriculture on farm properties within the Cuyahoga Valley National Park by granting farmers sixty-year leases on the land. In exchange for the leases, farmers must promise to use environmentally friendly techniques such as organic farming.

The U.S. Fish and Wildlife Service manages the Gulf of Maine Coastal Program (GMCP), which coordinates partnerships between local, state, and federal government agencies and nonprofit organizations, community groups, and industry groups to protect and restore fish and wildlife resources. In 2003 GMCP worked with the Maine Coast Heritage Trust to purchase Flag Island, home to a large eider duck nesting colony, in order to place it under federal protection. Maine Coast Heritage Trust used privately raised funds to purchase the island before it could be developed, giving GMCP some time to obtain the federal grants it needed to buy the island.[15]

All of these disparate examples illustrate a new model of land management called cooperative conservation, which is carried out within a framework of networked governance. The breadth and depth of this cross-agency, cross-government, and cross-sector initiative make it a compelling case study of governing by network in action.

All Roads Go through Washington, D.C.

Twentieth-century environmentalism got its start in the 1960s. The growing conviction at the time that all was not well in the landscape spawned many major federal statutes on environmental issues: the Clean Air Act (1963), the Endangered Species Act (1973), the Safe Drinking Water Act (1974), and the Resource Conservation and Recovery Act (1976). The list is long.

The statutes from this era shared several characteristics:[16]

—*They took a piecemeal approach,* attacking each environmental problem in isolation. A regulation would focus on one air pollutant while ignoring all others, or deal with waste issues without looking at related water issues.

—*They focused heavily on process,* concentrating attention on simply following the rules instead of on the real benefits the rules were intended to provide.

14. David McQuiddy (Blue Skyways coordinator), author interview, July 2007.

15. Stewart Fefer (project leader, Gulf of Maine Coastal Program, U.S. Fish and Wildlife Service), author interview, May 2006.

16. Lynn Scarlett (deputy secretary, Department of the Interior), author interview, September 19, 2007.

—They relied on motivating constructive human actions through the threat of a fine or fee for negative actions. Generally, the statutes failed to reward positive deeds or help businesses and other entities benefit from good environmental citizenship.

—They were overly prescriptive. "My way or the highway" was the general tone of these laws. If the regulation said an electric utility had to have a smoke stack scrubber, or cattle on public lands could graze only to a four-inch level, that was exactly what had to happen. People affected by these rules had little opportunity to suggest alternatives that could work better.

Essentially, for three decades most major environmental and government land-use policy was made inside the Beltway. That policy tended to be very prescriptive, an outgrowth of the assumption that people who wanted to preserve the environment and those who wanted to use it would be locked in perpetual struggle. The laws evolved thus in part because command, control, and conflict were the tenor of the times. Lawmakers also leaned heavily on process and punishment because they had few effective ways to monitor outcomes—for example, to find out whether a particular measure actually produced cleaner air or helped an endangered species recover.[17]

Limitations of Command and Control

As the United States moved through the twentieth century and into the twenty-first, policymakers started to realize that this approach had several limitations.

First, nature itself knows no boundaries. From cleaning up air and water to protecting species that live on land to restoring a complex river habitat, environmental problems transcend boundaries between government agency jurisdictions. The challenge of protecting endangered wildlife does not belong solely to the U.S. Department of the Interior (DOI) nor a state department of environmental conservation. The country needed to develop a more holistic approach to its environmental challenges. In response to that need, the DOI started looking for ways to manage conservation efforts at a landscape scale—what some people call an ecosystem scale.

Second, requiring a permit or applying a punishment is not always the best way to remedy local environmental problems. It is one thing to require the small number of electric utilities operating across the country to obtain permits before building facilities. Environmental problems that result from the actions of thousands of individuals, however, call for a very different approach. For example, when a stream is polluted, much of the problem can be traced back to thousands of residents' rinsing ordinary household chemicals down their drains or fertilizers

17. Ibid.

and animal wastes' running off farmlands. Meeting such challenges requires that an agency form partnerships with interested parties and provide education and promote best practices to engage them in the conservation effort.

Third, the old permitting process and prescriptive approach got people's backs up. Landowners and businesses alike felt compelled, rather than inspired, to do things for the sake of the public good. If an endangered species turned up on your land, that was bad news. Before you knew it, regulators would start coming around telling you what you could and could not do on your own property: "Don't dig here, don't build there, and don't you dare drain that swamp!" That is not much of an inducement to engage in conservation to attract those species to your land.

This approach also created tense relations with local government stakeholders. Federal agencies, far removed from the locality, held significant influence over many land-use decisions. A perception emerged among local governments and landowners that federal land agencies considered themselves the sole "experts" capable of making the best decisions for the public interest.

This attitude hurt the cause of conservation in two ways. By failing to solicit input from local authorities on land conservation decisions, federal agencies lost the chance to benefit from the authorities' intimate knowledge of the region. Also, federal managers missed the opportunity to form bonds with people who could have served as important allies in their cause. Instead, they isolated themselves, breeding resentment and escalating tensions between federal agencies, citizen landowners, and environmentalists.[18]

So as the twenty-first century approached, reformers began to ask: Is there a different way to look at the world? Are there other tools we need in the environmental and conservation toolkit?

From Conflict to Cooperation

This was the environment when Gale Norton was confirmed as George W. Bush's interior secretary in 2001.

Norton and her leadership team at the DOI soon discovered that more than just the psychological landscape had changed over the past few decades. The physical landscape also had altered—dramatically. Developers were chopping large properties into small parcels. Cities and suburbs were sprawling across the previously wide-open West. Where once, in the course of an hour, you might have seen one cowboy and a few cows, you now saw thousands of people out for a day of fun with SUVs, pickups, and mountain bikes.

During most of the twentieth century, national parks were located in remote locations. Now millions of Americans live in what was once wild land, not far

18. Charles Wise, "Property Rights and Regulatory Takings," in Durant, O'Leary, and Fiorino (2004, pp. 289–90).

from national parks. Also, park infrastructure was aging, and there was not enough money to fix it.

To work effectively in this changed world, the new leadership at the DOI believed the department needed fresh tools based on a spirit of collaboration and local knowledge. It needed methods for turning people from adversaries into allies. It needed new strategies for managing land use. And it needed to stop looking inward and start looking outward.

Norton outlined a vision of a new environmentalism "based on communication, consultation, and cooperation all in the service of conservation (the 4C's)." In this vision, government works to protect the environment while recognizing people's need to make a living. Instead of dictating policy from on high, the federal government works with state and local officials and landowners to figure out how they can utilize land while protecting natural resources. Ultimately, she said, the government's role is to "empower the people to take conservation into their own hands."[19]

A principal architect of this vision was Lynn Scarlett, Norton's assistant secretary for policy, management, and budget (she later served as deputy secretary and acting secretary of the department). Scarlett had been writing and speaking on the new environmentalism for close to a decade from a perch at the Reason Foundation, a Los Angeles–based think tank where she had worked for two decades, eventually becoming its president. Her powerful intellect and search for common ground made her one of the few individuals in environmental policy who was respected by many leaders from both the business and the environmental communities.

The new environmentalism she outlined focused on local ideas, incentives, and innovation. The goal: to create a context in which companies, organizations, and individuals are inspired to become citizen stewards and where people make decisions in an integrated fashion. A key component of this approach was a belief in local expertise. Although some of the knowledge needed to manage environmental problems can come from academic training, the thinking went, many solutions reside in the practical knowledge of the people who actually live and work on a farm, on a ranch, and in each community. "These individuals come with all kinds of different perspectives, skills, and institutional knowledge," says Scarlett. "Success requires systematically tapping into this knowledge."[20]

To illustrate the concept, Scarlett tells the story of how endangered short-tailed albatrosses feeding too close to fishing vessels in the waters off Alaska were getting caught on the fishermen's hooks. The lines then dragged the birds under water, where they drowned. Under the traditional model, the government would have told the fishermen, "Thou shalt not fish." Instead, agency officials sat down with the fishing community and discussed the problem.

19. U.S. Department of the Interior, "Conservation in the 21st Century: A New Environmentalism," remarks prepared for Secretary Gale Norton, National Press Club, Washington, February 20, 2002 (www. doi.gov/news/020225.html).

20. Scarlett interview.

Combining local understanding with scientific knowledge, the two groups came up with several solutions, such as weighting the fishing lines to sink the hooks below the surface, where they would not snag the birds. The win-win solution, based on cooperation and local knowledge, allowed fishing to continue while protecting the albatross. This model stands in stark contrast to the traditional "Washington knows best" approach, which often devalued input from local authorities and ignored local landowners.

Norton and Scarlett soon discovered that public-private collaborations like the one in Alaska were occurring throughout the department at the local level. For example, in 1998 the Gettysburg Foundation and the National Park Service partnered to build a new museum and visitors' center at the Gettysburg National Battlefield.[21] In 1997 the Bureau of Land Management began working with tribal and county governments and the University of New Mexico to jointly manage the Kasha-Katuwe Tent Rocks National Monument in New Mexico.[22] In Nebraska, the Bureau of Reclamation and the Fish and Wildlife Service collaborated with the Platte River Endangered Species Partnership to conserve habitat for the whooping crane, piping plover, interior least tern, and pallid sturgeon, while allowing for new and existing water uses in the Platte River Basin.[23]

These examples, though powerful, were often isolated and sporadic. The challenge lay in institutionalizing this approach as the standard way of doing business throughout the Interior Department. "We recognized that our real challenge was not how do we create something out of whole cloth, but how do we encourage it?" explains Scarlett. "How do we foster it, facilitate it, nurture it, turn it from being an incidental practice to the central way we do business?"[24]

A Three-Pronged Strategy

Money, policy, and management were the three principal prongs of the approach Norton and Scarlett used to encourage the 4C's (later termed cooperative conservation) and their new environmentalism strategy. The first prong, money, was the easiest to deploy. The DOI operated several grant programs it could use as catalysts to bring people together to work on common projects. To sweeten the pot, the department added substantially more money to these cooperative conservation grant programs.

As for policy, DOI leadership started looking into the Endangered Species Act of 1973 , the National Environmental Policy Act of 1970, and other major land-

21. National Park Service, "Gettysburg National Battlefield Museum and Visitor Center" (www.nps. gov/partnerships/gettysburg.htm).

22. Bureau of Land Management, "Partner Case Study: Kasha-Katuwe Tent Rocks National Monument" (www.blm.gov/partnerships/case_studies/ktrnm.htm).

23. Platte River Endangered Species Partnership home page (www.platteriver.org)

24. Scarlett interview.

use laws to see if they contained policies that encouraged (or discouraged) cooperation. "We asked ourselves, do we have the right policies?" Scarlett says. "And we recognized that the answer was no. We could produce some enhancements that were more aligned with cooperation."[25]

Looking at the Endangered Species Act, for example, they asked how they could assure landowners who take steps to conserve endangered species on their lands that they would not be punished for their actions. They borrowed, and further strengthened, some tools introduced during the Clinton administration. One was the tool of "safe harbor." This is an agreement that a landowner signs with the Fish and Wildlife Service, saying in effect, "If I do good deeds that really attract endangered species to my land, and they flourish and grow, I won't be held responsible for maintaining the species at that higher level. I simply will have to assure that I will never let the species fall below the level where it stood when I began." This allows landowners to make real improvements to their land without having to worry about the government's encroaching on their ability to use their property.

It was, however, in the third area, management and administration, that the DOI really broke new ground. The management approach to drive cooperative conservation through the department in some ways itself mirrored the basic philosophy of cooperative conservation. It was bottom up and decentralized, relying on career employees with local knowledge of the situation, and it created incentives to engage in cooperative conservation.

The DOI leadership assembled cooperative conservation working groups that would give a prominent role to people from the field who understood their programs best, recognized the constraints they faced, and knew which systems and management tools they had available and which they lacked. Scarlett explains the approach: "All policy and all management are fundamentally about the interface of people and ideas. Where do you want to go? What do you want to do? What do you want to accomplish? And then you try to motivate folks who are the feet on the ground, the hands on the levers, to actually join together to move forward and advance the idea."[26] By engaging an assortment of officials who represented the views of different DOI bureaus and views within the department their goal was to stimulate a sense of involvement and ownership. It would show officials in the field that this new initiative was not simply something baked in Washington.

The 4C's Team

The plan to encourage grassroots participation took on flesh and bones in April 2003, when Norton formed the "4C's team," headed by Bob Lamb, senior policy

25. Ibid.
26. Ibid.

adviser at the DOI.[27] Its mandate was to study the barriers to using the new approach to manage natural resources.[28] (Future spinoffs included the Interagency Cooperative Conservation Team and the Partners and Cooperation Team.) Lamb was well suited to the job; with three decades of federal experience, he had developed particularly profound insights about federal employees and the federal workplace.

Lamb deliberately set out to populate the team not just with the Washington crowd but also with people from the field who had diverse professional backgrounds. Participants included procurement officers and environmental systems managers drawn from the Bureau of Land Management, the Fish and Wildlife Service, and the National Park Service, as well as field managers from the various national parks and refuges.

"I could never all by myself have thought of all those leverage points," says Scarlett. "Many minds are always better than one. They bring multiple perspectives and multiple knowledge bases."[29]

The 4C's team looked at barriers and best practices. Members embarked on a series of projects to improve the DOI's administrative capacity in planning, budget, and procurement. The team also examined all the DOI training programs and identified programs that would benefit from training employees in mediation, negotiation, facilitation, or cooperation.

Talent Show

A key question arose early in the team's work: Is the DOI staff on the ground prepared to do this kind of work? After all, collaborating with outside stakeholders can be difficult. To be successful, a project leader would need three important strengths: a strong scientific and technical base, the capacity to create and operate partnerships, and the ability to negotiate the maze of his or her own internal bureaucracy.

Soon it became clear that implementing cooperative conservation across the DOI would require a fundamental transformation of the department's human capital. The department would need more people with strong collaboration skills, and it would have to revamp its human resources systems to serve this

27. The original 4C's team was composed largely of DOI headquarter and field staff, with representatives from the Forest Service and the U.S. Army Environmental Corps of Engineers. Gradually representatives were added from the EPA, the Natural Resources Conservation Service, and the National Oceanic and Atmospheric Administration. The 4C's team became the Interagency Cooperative Conservation Team after the White House conference. In fall 2006, the new Partners and Cooperation Team was formed within the Department of the Interior to focus on internal efforts.

28. U.S. Department of the Interior, "Advancing Cooperative Conservation," PowerPoint presentation to the Management Initiative Team, U.S. Department of the Interior, February 10, 2005 (www.doi.gov/partnerships/4csTeam_Briefing%20_Feb05.ppt).

29. Ibid.

need. "HR strategic planning had been a bean-counting exercise," says Scarlett. "We decided to step back and ask the question: In the twenty-first century what is our mission and how does that affect what capacities and skill sets we need at the department?"[30]

One of the first things the department had to change was some of the criteria used in the hiring process. In the past, job classifications focused mostly on technical qualifications, but not on management capabilities. If a fish and wildlife refuge needed a new biologist, it would hire the candidate with the most degrees, experience, and publications. Partnering skill sets were rarely part of the discussion.[31]

In this new age of partnership, however, department officials realized that creativity counted as well. As one DOI manager noted, "It takes a creative mind to do partnership work. If it [were] easy, it would . . . already [have] been done."[32] The department's Interagency Cooperative Conservation Team set about identifying competencies ultimately to be used in job descriptions and performance evaluations, starting with leadership and senior executive service positions. The work was slow and methodical. Eventually they decided to use already established Office of Personnel Management competencies to avoid "reinventing the wheel."[33]

A key insight was that employees working at ground level needed not only a knack for collaboration and the confidence to carry it out but also specific leadership skills. The team identified eight Office of Personnel Management (OPM) leadership competencies, described in table 2-1, as the ones that were necessary to further collaboration: partnering, influencing and negotiating, interpersonal skills, creativity and innovation, external awareness, entrepreneurship, problem solving, and conflict management. These OPM competency definitions were then used across the department to maintain consistency.[34]

Until recently, formal job descriptions at the DOI did not include these competencies. The department then took steps to include negotiation, problem solving, conflict management, and other such skills among the criteria used to hire new employees.

Another critical human capital issue identified by the DOI was professional development.[35] Most employees did not know all the ins and outs of making cooperative conservation approaches successful. Both new and old employees needed training.

30. Ibid.

31. Fefer interview.

32. William Hartwig (director, National Wildlife Refuge System, U.S. Fish and Wildlife Service, retired June 2, 2006), author interview, May 5, 2006.

33. Kathleen Wheeler (deputy chief human capital officer, U.S. Department of the Interior), author interview, May 31, 2006.

34. Department of the Interior (2006).

35. Wheeler interview.

Table 2-1. *Fundamental Competencies Required of Cooperative Conservation Personnel*

Competence	Underlying skills and abilities
Partnering	Develops networks and builds alliances; engages in cross-functional activities; collaborates across boundaries; and finds common ground with a widening range of stakeholders. Uses contacts to build and strengthen internal support bases.
Influencing and negotiating	Persuades others; builds consensus through give and take; gains cooperation from others to obtain information and accomplish goals; facilitates "win-win" situations.
Interpersonal skills	Considers and responds appropriately to the needs and feelings of different people in different situations; is tactful, compassionate, and sensitive, and treats others with respect.
Creativity and innovation	Develops new insights and applies innovative solutions to make organizational improvements; creates a work environment that encourages creative thinking and innovation; designs and implements new or cutting-edge programs and processes.
External awareness	Identifies and keeps up-to-date with key national and international policies and economic, political, and social trends that affect the organization; understands near-term and long-range plans and determines how best to be positioned to achieve a competitive business advantage in a global economy.
Entrepreneurship	Identifies opportunities to develop and market new products and services within or outside the organization. Is willing to take risks; initiates actions that involve a deliberate risk to achieve a recognized benefit or advantage.
Problem solving	Identifies and analyzes problems; distinguishes between relevant and irrelevant information to make logical decisions; provides solutions to individual and organizational problems.
Conflict management	Identifies and takes steps to prevent potential situations that could result in unpleasant confrontations. Manages and resolves conflicts and disagreements in a positive and constructive manner to minimize negative effects.

Source: Based on Department of the Interior (2006).

Recognizing this, the DOI leadership first approached administrators at DOI University and other departmental training programs about creating specific cooperative conservation training programs. The response from the training community surprised them. They suggested an even broader approach—infusing modules on cooperation into all of the department's training programs. Training directors then inventoried all the training programs to see which ones already covered mediation, negotiation, and partnering, and which ones would benefit from the addition of such material.

As of November 2008, most training courses within the DOI try to incorporate some training on partnership skills. The department uses the Fish and Wildlife

Service's National Conservation Training Center in Shepherdstown, West Virginia, as a department-wide resource for cooperative conservation training.[36] The courses are available at minimal cost to personnel throughout the department.[37]

Another way DOI leadership sought to develop talent was to send employees to work in locations that excel at collaboration. For example, over time dozens of National Park Service employees were detailed to the Golden Gate National Recreation Area to learn about the park's innovative partnering practices.

The ultimate goal of creating the new competency models and training opportunities was to achieve a cultural shift at the DOI—to make partnering a "way of life at the department."[38] Although such a culture shift does not come easily, the DOI has made steady progress.

From Initiative to Movement

As the Department of the Interior was launching its cooperative conservation initiative in earnest, similar efforts were also under way at the Environmental Protection Agency (EPA), the Department of Agriculture, and the Army Corps of Engineers. To harness this momentum and bring more coherence to the individual departmental initiatives, in August 2004 President Bush issued executive order 13352, Facilitation of Cooperative Conservation. The order directed four cabinet-level departments—Interior, Commerce, Defense, and Agriculture—and the EPA to emphasize local decisionmaking when they acted on behalf of the federal government in land-use and wildlife issues and mandated the creation of the President's Task Force on Cooperative Conservation.[39] It also announced a plan to hold a White House conference on cooperative conservation the following year.

In August 2005, 1,300 representatives from federal, state, local, and tribal governments and from local community groups, nonprofit organizations, and industry journeyed to St. Louis from all over the United States to attend the first White House conference on cooperative conservation. The conference provided a forum for people who were doing cooperative conservation in the field to share best practices and identify their key challenges. Organizers hoped that as participants shared stories of their programs, they would inspire new initiatives and benefit from the cross-fertilization of ideas.

Another goal of the conference was to raise the profile of the many efforts going on in the field. By articulating the term "cooperative conservation" and

36. Ibid.; Dale Hall (director, U.S. Fish and Wildlife Service), interview, June 2, 2006.

37. Hall interview.

38. Marcia Marsh (senior vice president of operations, World Wildlife Fund), author interview, May 26, 2006.

39. George W. Bush, "Facilitation of Cooperative Conservation," executive order, August 26, 2004 (www.whitehouse.gov/news/releases/2004/08/20040826-11.html).

gathering disparate programs across the country under one umbrella, the administration had made a good deal of useful progress, but the concept had not yet taken root in the public mind as a new way of thinking about the environment and public lands.

By bringing together more than a thousand practitioners in one place, the conference, pulled together by the President's Task Force on Cooperative Conservation, provided a way to shine a brighter light on the concept of cooperative conservation and show how individual efforts formed part of a broader pattern. Practitioners swapped ideas and identified opportunities to help one another. Their conversations publicized the notion that people could work to conserve the environment in a spirit of cooperation rather than conflict.

The task force had two main goals in organizing the conference: to establish a set of guiding principles for successful cooperative conservation efforts, and to provide a vehicle for interagency collaboration. Using feedback obtained during the conference, the task force developed an action plan for assisting collaborative efforts nationwide. Since that time it also has gotten involved in several interagency efforts to institutionalize cooperative conservation programs and establish best practices.

Several pieces of legislation were introduced as a result of the task force's work, including, in 2007, the Cooperative Conservation Enhancement Act, to "enable federal agencies to work in closer cooperation, generate improved opportunities for funding of nongovernmental partnerships on conservation projects and increase flexibility to resolve disputes through collaborative problem solving."[40]

Meetings held during the conference and afterward highlighted the need for a "one-stop shop" across the federal government where employees could get information on subjects ranging from best practices to funding opportunities. To satisfy this demand, the task force created a federal Cooperative Conservation website, www.cooperativeconservation.gov. This has proved to be a valuable resource for "what works" and for identifying potential partnership members.

Perhaps the most important communications strategy employed by the task force was simply to listen. The Council on Environmental Quality and several federal agencies played host to twenty-five listening sessions on cooperative conservation nationwide to exchange ideas and compile concerns and lessons learned. All sessions featured high-level federal officials from the cooperative conservation agencies. For example, Dirk Kempthorne, who succeeded Norton as the interior secretary in 2006, personally attended seven listening sessions across the country.

The listening sessions proved an effective way of giving the grassroots a strong voice in this movement. The host agencies received more than 30,000 comments on discussion topics ranging from the partnership skills required for cooperative

40. Ibid.

conservation to how the federal government can facilitate more interagency and inter-entity cooperation.

Challenges

The DOI hit plenty of bumps on the road to implementing this new way of doing business. Of the myriad challenges faced by the DOI, the EPA, and other agencies in implementing cooperative conservation, there are three principal ones that offer important lessons for other governments as they move toward more networked models of governance.

Breaking through the Middle

As they tried to develop and carry out cooperative conservation initiatives, frontline staff and senior officials confronted many obstacles—legal requirements, procurement and financial assistance rules, and ethics regulations, to name just a few. Under the weight of rules and regulations put in place to serve a hierarchical operating model, collaborative initiatives frequently got stuck in the middle layers of the bureaucracy. Support often "falls down with the administrative officer, with the contracting officer, with the people that are the gatekeepers for money," says Chris Jarvi of the National Park Service, who has been involved with the Southern Nevada Area Partnership, which includes four federal agencies.[41]

Consider procurement rules. Contracting regulations require free, open, and frequent competition that produces contracts of fixed, usually short, length. Many of the most successful partnerships, however, depend on more flexible and long-term relationships. One point of contention: some of the department's partners wondered why they had to apply for competitive grants in order to enter an agreement with the DOI for cooperative projects involving the landowners' own property. On the other side, administrative officials were encouraging maximum competition—via a national website, Grants.gov—for all federal financial assistance awards.[42]

Risk management also proved particularly thorny from multiple perspectives. True partnerships usually require shared risk. However, the notion of shared risk is still a fairly new concept in government. The traditional strategy is to shift as much risk as possible to the private partner. So when DOI officials sent contracts to their lawyers for legal review, the documents invariably came back with language insisting that the private or nonprofit partner assume nearly all the risk for the project. The argument was that the federal government cannot assume any risk on behalf of a private entity. Needless to say, this often did not sit well with potential partners who balked at such unbalanced risk allocation.

41. Chris Jarvi, author interview, June 2006.
42. Olivia Barton Ferriter, author interview, October 4, 2007.

Friction also arose when middle management tried to discourage field managers from taking on the risk that might arise when working with community members. "Concerns about risk have been one of our biggest problems when you are talking about the middle-management level," says Rich Whitley, national stewardship and partnership coordinator for the Bureau of Land Management.[43]

These challenges demonstrate the need to revise rules geared more toward a command-and-control model of government and to develop new tools to better conform to today's networked environment. "Our institutions and instruments haven't kept up with the reality on the ground," explains Olivia Barton Ferriter, the career civil servant who coordinates cooperation conservation policy for the Department of the Interior. "We've evolved to the point where there need to be new instruments that describe an activity of mutual benefit to an agency and to an outside partner. These kinds of conservation activities may cross public-private jurisdictional lines or engender deep commitments to conservation on public lands."[44]

Aligning Incentives

How do you reward employees who are skilled connectors? What incentives can you provide to encourage staff to cultivate partnerships? These questions seem relatively simple, but the answers are anything but.

Traditional government performance systems do a poor job of measuring collaborative work. Instead, they measure how well employees complete specific technical activities. There are no systems for measuring goodwill, greater cooperation, and enhanced public participation—the very outputs that collaboration seeks to produce.

In fact, existing structures often discourage field managers and field office staff from participating in community-based collaboration. Initially, fear of personal liability was a barrier, as was the fact that community meetings often take place outside of office hours. Government representatives who participate in those meetings often must do so on a purely voluntary basis, paying for their own expenses. Resolving these issues required changes in ethics and personnel policies.

One option for encouraging collaborative activities has been to make them a factor in an employee's annual review. When effective collaboration opens the door to promotions and pay increases, many employees respond accordingly.[45] The department has incorporated collaboration and partnering standards in senior executive service performance plans. For example, the DOI has developed performance measures to gauge how well the bureaus and employees performed in the areas of partnering and cooperation. One of them measures the number of projects that involve local involvement; another measures the number of organi-

43. Richard Whitley (national stewardship and partnership coordinator, Bureau of Land Management), author interview, May 30, 2006.
44. Ferriter interview.
45. Marsh interview.

zations that have employees trained in collaboration and partnering skills. These kinds of performance measures are then cascaded down into the performance plans of individual employees.

Consider a partnership created to manage federal assets. To evaluate the output of the DOI manager who works with an outside organization, one might look at how much expertise the manager has been able to leverage. In other words, measure the performance of field personnel by tracking how much progress they make toward certain established goals or forming partnerships that produce positive results.

The DOI also presents "4C's" awards to recognize successful cooperative conservation efforts.[46] Since the first annual awards were given in 2004, fifty-eight awards have been granted to partnerships and collaborations involving hundreds of organizations and individuals inside and outside the federal government. Managers who support collaboration win promotions to leadership positions in the National Park Service and other agencies.

Accountability versus Flexibility

A third area where tension arises when implementing networked government is at the boundary between flexibility and accountability. A good example is the DOI's policy toward park superintendents. The DOI has tried to give superintendents a high degree of freedom. "You can't ever completely dictate what shape or form or direction the partnership will take," says Scarlett, "but you have to trust that the wisdom of the many folks out there will shape and mold it in a constructive direction."[47]

Still, DOI officials are accountable to the greater public and to Congress, not to mention responsible for carrying out specific policies of the administration. John Debo, superintendent of Cuyahoga Valley National Park, explains:

> There is an interesting tension that exists in the National Park system. It relates to the need to agree upon common policy versus the need to promote and encourage entrepreneurial behavior by people out in the field. There is definite tension between a policy framework and developing a culture and set of values that afford managers at the local level an opportunity to be entrepreneurial. What you are always striving for, is to try to maintain the right balance point. It's easy to become overly directive with policy.[48]

The way to strike a balance between entrepreneurship and accountability is to spell out the hard-and-fast rules and then clearly define the areas where participants may get creative (often called "loose-tight" management). Well-articulated

---

46. Wheeler interview.
47. Scarlett interview.
48. John Debo (superintendent of Cuyahoga Valley National Park), interview, June 2, 2006.

expectations for all parties involved in a project are indispensable building blocks for subsequent evaluation. As the DOI works to equip its workforce to design collaborative initiatives, most likely it will also get better at drafting program charters.

In some cases, field employees already have the resources to write strong agreements. For example, the Bureau of Land Management provides partnership mentors to guide site staff through the process of designing collaborative arrangements. Formal agreements within the DOI can take a variety of forms, ranging from a simple memorandum of understanding to a more complex contract, grant, or cooperative agreement that includes a transfer of funds.[49] Efforts like this play an important role in maintaining an acceptable level of transparency and accountability. They also offer some protection to the government if partners fail to keep up their end of the bargain.

Conclusion

The Department of the Interior is working to implement many of the principles associated with collaborative governance. The mission of the DOI makes it particularly well suited to employ the tools of networked governance, because the organization's physical resources are scattered throughout the country, surrounded by land belonging to others. Over time, DOI officials have learned that engaging the department's neighbors, and the public at large, offers a powerful approach for resource stewardship.

The DOI leadership recognized the changes afoot in the world and realized that these changes demanded different ways of achieving conservation goals. They connected the dots between the driving forces and the cooperative conservation vision.

By articulating this new vision, they helped people see a pattern. Until then, people had heard of a cooperative conservation initiative here or there. Norton, Kempthorne, and Scarlett gave those disparate efforts coherence by demonstrating that they were part of a larger trend.

At the ground level, many employees understand the need to cooperate with organizations that believe in the ideals of conservation. They also recognize the benefits of proactively engaging parties with sometimes conflicting goals.

Governments trying to move from a hierarchical approach to a networked model face one important dilemma. Although collaboration usually delivers a bigger payoff, it is typically harder to do well than one that follows the old top-down structure. A collaborative program also poses greater risks. It demands that executives find new ways to reward performance that aligns with the agency's

---

49. U.S. Department of the Interior, "Partnerships at the Department of the Interior; FAQ's" (www.doi.gov/partnerships/faqs_beginning_stages.html).

goals. The DOI cooperative conservation initiative shows that with the right leadership at the political and career levels, the challenges can be overcome.

References

Department of the Interior. 2006. *A Common Sense Approach to Collaboration and Partnering at the U.S. Department of the Interior: A Plan of Action for the years 2006–2010.* Washington: March 31.

Dingell, John D. 2006. "Building Our Refuge—2006." In *Annual Progress Report of the Detroit River International Wildlife Refuge and the International Wildlife Refuge Alliance.* Detroit.

Durant, Robert F., Rosemary O'Leary, and Daniel J. Fiorino, eds. 2004. *Environmental Governance Reconsidered: Challenges, Choices, and Opportunities.* MIT Press.

Hartig, John H. 2003. *Honoring Our Detroit River: Caring for Our Home.* Wayne State University Press, 2003.

3

Governing the Climate from Sacramento

BARRY G. RABE

The conventional wisdom of a decade ago tagged climate change as a straight-forward public policy problem. The science was indeed complex, but virtually all scholarly analysis suggested that the global scope of the problem would necessitate a global response. It was commonly expected that nations would join forces in an international accord, ushering in a world governing authority that would allocate greenhouse gas (GHG) reduction targets to developed and developing nations alike. After a marathon diplomatic binge in December 1997, the birth of the Kyoto Protocol was heralded as the official launch point for an international climate regime.

This new world order of climate governance was based on policy learning from two environmental policy cases, ozone depleting chemicals and sulfur dioxide emissions, a decade earlier. Any global climate regime was expected to emulate experience with those two cases. The ozone case had entailed formal collaboration among the main producer nations while preparing for a transition toward chemical alternatives that could be shared with every nation. It was widely heralded as the greatest international environmental policy triumph of the modern era. In the second case, the U.S. experience with utilizing an emissions cap-and-trade program for sulfur dioxide pollutants was seen as transferable to the international stage, allowing considerable flexibility in the search for the most cost-effective emission reductions. Combining lessons from these two environmental success cases, a hierarchical model of international climate governance could be established through a multinational pact (à la ozone) and implemented through flexible, market-like mechanisms (à la sulfur dioxide). Such an approach would leave no real roles for state and local governments, much less for networks cutting across governmental levels. Instead, all of the action would involve nation-states jockeying for position in an international regime. Once that deal was cut, it was assumed that the policy could self-execute via emissions trading monitored by global authorities, with periodic tinkering to adjust for new developments. The prevalence of such thinking may explain why public management scholars have essentially ignored the issue of climate policy, and the dominant scholarly voices have emerged instead from international relations and microeconomics.

Well before the ink on the Kyoto Protocol had dried came hints that crafting climate policy would be far more complicated. The ozone experience, though a promising model for international collaboration, may be hard to replicate. In that instance, alternative chemicals were moving rapidly toward marketability, and the mechanisms for sharing information and products were fairly straightforward. The sulfur dioxide experience continues to attest to the promise of market-based solutions, but the successful U.S. use of this tool was confined to fewer than 200 coal-burning power plants for which emissions had already been reliably measured, a range of prior emission controls were already in place, and abundant quantities of low-sulfur coal were readily available for use. In contrast, climate change poses an infinitely more complex policy puzzle. Greenhouse gas sources, most notably carbon dioxide and methane, are ubiquitous, generated by virtually every form of human activity in every polity on the globe. Many sources are difficult to measure with any degree of exactitude. And there are no immediate alternatives to oil, coal, and other fossil fuels, which account for the dominant share of greenhouse gas emissions in most nations amid growing global demand. Transitional work is under way in the electricity, transportation, and industrial sectors, but there is little evidence of a rapid shift to even the most promising alternatives.

Signs of this extraordinary complexity were already evident during the Kyoto negotiations. Alongside the predictable contributors to the deliberations, other participants came from "an unexpected array of fields including defense contracting, construction, transportation, forestry, biodiversity, health, fire services, religion, heritage protection, indigenous communities, unions, gender research, and manufacturing" (Orr 2006, pp. 152–53). This diversity was also reflected in the U.S. contingent, which included surprisingly large representation from municipalities and states, from California to New Hampshire. Other multilevel governmental systems, such as Australia, Canada, and some members of the European Union, demonstrated comparable diversity, although formal bargaining roles were confined to officials at the national and international levels.

More than ten years after Kyoto, the hopes for a global climate regime are in tatters. The United States' refusal to ratify Kyoto is well known, but fundamental flaws in the accord's design are perhaps more significant. There is no international system for emissions reporting and monitoring, many official Kyoto participants are failing to reach their pledged reduction targets, and a number of promising tools such as the European Emissions Trading Scheme have faced difficulties in the early stages of implementation. Proposals are floated periodically to jump-start the international negotiation process, but there is no clear model or obvious next step for somehow moving "beyond Kyoto."

Evaluating the past decade of climate policy demands more than simply revisiting Kyoto's foibles. Many negotiators began to consider ways to reduce emissions unilaterally. Other policymakers have since entered the scene who focus on a particular sector or unit of government. Collectively they constitute a virtual army of climate policy entrepreneurs, influential in designing and launching an ever-increasing set of climate initiatives. In the United States, this type of activity has proved particularly intensive at the state government level. Some states were experimenting with greenhouse gas emission reduction programs even before Kyoto, and their pace of engagement has only intensified. By late 2008, more than one-half of the states had enacted some combination of the following policies: mandate increasing levels of renewable electricity and transportation fuel; introduce a cap-and-trade system for carbon dioxide emissions from major industries; reduce vehicular emissions of carbon dioxide; petition the federal government to recognize carbon dioxide as an air pollutant under its existing statutory authority; and establish formal statewide emission reduction targets for 2010 and subsequent decades (Rabe 2008a, 2008b). Many of these policies set ambitious reduction requirements and collectively may help explain why U.S. greenhouse gas emissions have been somewhat more modest than expected in recent years. Such subnational engagement and variation is not unique to the United States, as it is also evident in varying degrees in other systems that have ratified Kyoto such as Australia, Canada, and the European Union.

Consequently, it is not accurate to say that either the world or the United States lacks policies to reduce greenhouse gas emissions. Instead, those policies are infinitely more complex and diverse than had been envisioned a decade ago, however limited in likely global impact. They may indeed suggest an enduring role for multilevel governance strategies as opposed to a single, unified global authority. As Stephen Goldsmith and William Eggers have written, "In many ways, 21st century challenges and the means of addressing them are more numerous and complex than ever before. Problems have become both more global and more local as power disperses and boundaries (where they exist at all) become more fluid" (Goldsmith and Eggers 2004, p. 7). It is hard to imagine a policy problem that more clearly fits this pattern than climate change, where innumerable policy options exist and potential involvement cuts across all governmental levels and units.

Some of the complexities of climate change governance are confronted in this chapter, with heavy reference to U.S. experience in the past decade. The argument builds on earlier work that outlines the role of policy entrepreneurs, particularly individuals who work at or near the "mezzo level" of state government agencies, most commonly one and two levels below political appointees (Carpenter 2001; Rabe 2004). But it also acknowledges the dramatic expansion and intensification of entrepreneurial activity in many states in very recent years. This necessitates a more elastic definition of "entrepreneurship" than confinement to one or a handful of upper-level bureaucrats in a state capital. Instead, the definition includes a range of elected officials, agency and department heads, and a cavalcade of other individuals from foundations, consulting firms, environmental groups, and industry that perceive (then seize) opportunity to influence the shape of climate policy for a given jurisdiction. This activity increasingly cuts across traditional boundaries—of an agency, state, or region. An attempt "to account for the gradual replacement of hierarchical interactions with horizontal ones" will reveal growing connectedness between governmental units, relevant interests, and even jurisdictions normally depicted as rivals, preoccupied with protecting their turf (Montpetit 2003). Alongside this proliferation of entrepreneurs, policy networks, and emergent climate policies comes the challenge of securing successful policy implementation and acknowledging that climate change will likely constitute a multilevel governance problem for decades, even generations, to come.

Perhaps no jurisdiction on the globe epitomizes this phenomenon better than the state of California, the primary case examined in this chapter. California has surpassed every other U.S. state in the sheer range of climate policies enacted and the boldness of its overall emissions reduction plan. The state can lay credible claim to "world leadership" on this issue. Even if it were removed from North America and deposited into the European Union, its policies and emission reduction goals would surpass those of most of its newfound neighbors. California's unique political and economic contexts have generated innumerable opportunities for policy entrepreneurship. These extend well beyond the highly visible role of the state's governor to include other elected officials in both the executive and legislative branches, officials from numerous state departments, agencies, and commissions, and a horde of interest group representatives.

California thus constitutes a valuable case study to begin to consider the larger challenges of addressing climate change as an issue of multilevel governance. This study begins with a look at policies to date and factors that have prompted such unilateral collective action. This sets the stage for an analysis of early lessons from California on the viability of a single state's attempting so much policy on its own at one time. This discussion includes an analysis of some of the leading challenges of translating multiple California policy commitments into greenhouse gas reductions, moving this climate case from the realm of optimal policy design into the arena of public management. Particular consideration is given to the significant challenges of governance that follow a massive political exercise in "climate credit claiming," which call for reconciliation of divergent views of various entrepreneurs, coordination across multiple departments and agencies, and collaboration with neighboring states, since a high level of emission-generating activity crosses state boundaries.

A State Aspires to Global Leadership: The California Climate Odyssey

California formally staked its claim to the role of "world leader" on climate change on September 27, 2006. At a ceremony on Treasure Island in San Francisco Bay, Governor Arnold Schwarzenegger, surrounded by international celebrities from the worlds of politics, industry, and entertainment, signed into law Assembly Bill 32, the Global Warming Solutions Act. This step was proclaimed a "first-in-the-world comprehensive program" to combat climate change as well as "the most radical climate policy in the world." Such claims constitute more than Hollywood hyperbole and have a basis in empirical reality, comparing favorably with the claims of international leaders on climate policy such as the United Kingdom and Germany. Assembly Bill 32 outlines a range of strategies to reduce the state's greenhouse gas emissions to 1990 levels by 2020, despite considerable economic and population growth projected over this period. Moreover, it sets reduction targets beyond 2020, with an ultimate commitment to cut emissions to 80 percent below 1990 levels by 2050.

Perhaps more remarkable than the passage of this legislation is the body of policy and emissions stabilization upon which it is built. Decades of aggressive efforts to promote energy efficiency and alternative energy as well as to reduce conventional air emissions from fixed and mobile sources have combined to give California one of the lowest rates of greenhouse gas emissions per person of any U.S. state. In fact, California's per capita emissions profile more closely resembles those of smaller, energy-conserving European nations such as Denmark and Sweden than those of most other U.S. states. According to the 2005 California Energy Plan, "For the past 30 years, while per capita electricity consumption in the United States has increased by nearly 50 percent, California electricity use per capita has been approximately flat" (State of California 2005, p. 3). The state's overall greenhouse gas emissions increased only 7 percent between 1990 and 2005, about 40 percent of the national average. Such a rate is matched only by states experiencing much less population and economic growth, such as Louisiana, Michigan, and Pennsylvania. California emissions growth during this period would be negligible were it not for the transportation sector, which was the target of path-breaking legislation signed by Schwarzenegger's predecessor, Gray Davis, in 2002.

Consequently, California has an extensive history with policies that have the effect of suppressing greenhouse gas emissions. Some of these were enacted several decades ago, long before global climate change entered the U.S. vernacular, and all set the stage for the Global Warming Solutions Act (Assembly Bill 32) in 2006. California's first explicit climate change legislation was enacted in 1988, when Governor George Deukmejian signed into law Assembly Bill 4420, which called upon the California Energy Commission to assess the likely impacts of climate change on the state's economy, energy and water supplies, and agricultural activity (Brown 2005). The following section offers an overview of some of the prominent policies that the state has since enacted.

A California Climate Policy Sampler

The tapestry of California climate policies is intended to address all of the sectors that generate significant emissions. The policies blend a variety of traditional and alternative policy approaches, including command-and-control regulations, regulatory mandates, emissions trading across sources, direct and indirect subsidies for new technologies, and tax incentives (Fiorino 2006). Many are applied at the institutional level, such as setting emission caps for individual electricity-generating plants. Others operate at the individual or household level, such as incentives for purchasing a low-emission vehicle or installing solar panels on a roof. As California Environmental Protection Agency administrator Linda Adams noted in 2006, "We're using probably all of the tools in the toolbox to address the problem." Any attempt to review all of these policies would constitute an encyclopedic undertaking, far beyond the scope of this chapter. Collectively, they are intended to work in an integrative manner and enable California to attain the emission reduction targets given in Assembly Bill 32 for 2020 and 2050. Some of the most prominent policies are highlighted here to show the scope of what is being undertaken in California.

Establishing an Economy-wide Cap

The Global Warming Solutions Act is best-known for its bold emissions-reduction targets, but perhaps more significant is its creation of a cap that cuts across sectors to achieve these mandated reductions. The legislation includes mandatory rules for reporting greenhouse gas emissions and calls for enforceable penalties for noncompliance. It also requires adoption of a "list of discrete early action" measures that could be rapidly implemented. While these early action measures are moving forward, annual benchmarks for development of regulations will determine "how emissions reductions will be achieved from significant GHG sources," what policy tools will be employed, how equity will be ensured across regulated constituencies, and how any emission reductions will avoid having a disproportionate impact on low-income communities. Finally, the legislation creates a "safety valve" whereby any future governor can suspend the policy "in the event of extraordinary circumstances, catastrophic events, or threat of significant economic harm" (Assembly Bill 32).[1]

If all goes according to plan, all components of the legislation will be in force by the beginning of 2011. What remains largely unclear is the exact shape much of this will take. The legislation is unusually brief, considering its scope; its text fills just seventeen pages and provides remarkably little detail. For example, there is no specific discussion about how the cap would be implemented and whether an emissions-trading component could or should be developed for some portion of the overall reductions required. This omission reflected considerable tension between the legislative and executive branches over the acceptability of adding the words "and trade" to the cap, and led to the deferral of the decision.

Curbing Tailpipe Emissions

California first laid claim to global leadership on climate change in 2002 legislation, through Assembly Bill 1493, that established statutory caps on carbon emissions from vehicles. Transportation has continued to contribute more than two-fifths of the state's greenhouse gas emissions and about a third of the national total. Other nations and member states of the European Union have struggled with an array of voluntary and incentive programs, but California's was the first, and is still the most ambitious, legislative effort to mandate vehicular emissions reduction. The legislation did not prescribe the technology for achieving the emissions reduction but prohibited such options as tax increases, mandatory vehicular weight reduction, mandatory vehicular use reduction, or restricted sale of certain types of vehicles. Instead, it called for development of an alternative series of approaches that would begin to take hold in 2009 and would reduce carbon dioxide emissions from vehicles sold after that year by about 20 percent.

California has since launched an arduous process to determine what it will require of vehicle manufacturers by 2009 while trying to secure federal authorization to proceed. Established federal law cedes control over vehicle fuel economy to Washington, D.C. In contrast, states have greater input on conventional air emissions, and California has long held unique power to request a waiver from federal oversight under the Clean Air Act if it wants to exceed federal standards (McCarthy 2007). A 2007 Supreme Court decision, *Massachusetts et al. v. U.S. Environmental Protection Agency,* opened the possibility that the federal government might declare carbon dioxide an air pollutant and grant California its waiver. Fourteen states representing more than 40 percent of the U.S. population have formally backed the California position and pledged to implement any California regulation if a waiver is granted.

---

1. For the text of the bill see www.arb.ca.gov/cc/docs/ab32text.pdf.

The future of this initiative remains shrouded in uncertainty, however, since the U.S. Environmental Protection Agency rejected California's waiver request. This denial was based in part on 2007 federal energy legislation that included the first increase in federal fuel economy standards in decades. This allowed federal officials to contend that a national strategy was already being put into place, albeit with more modest goals than the California approach. This decision has been denounced in Congress, which held repeated hearings in 2008 to determine why EPA administrator Stephen Johnson rejected the extensive staff consensus in support of granting the waiver. The EPA decision has in turn been condemned in Sacramento and the capitals of allied states, leading to added rounds of litigation. At the same time both Senators John McCain and Barack Obama indicated during the 2008 presidential campaign that they would grant the waiver in the event that they were elected. Amid all of this uncertainty, the process of interpreting the 2002 legislation continues in Sacramento with the assumption that implementation will go forward.

Mandating Renewable Energy

Perhaps the most popular climate policy tool among the U.S. states is the renewable portfolio standard (RPS), which requires utilities that operate within their state boundaries to increase the amount of electricity provided from renewable sources. Twenty-eight states that represent well over half of the U.S. population have established RPSs. California is a leading player in this area through its 2002 enactment of Senate Bill 1078, which required the state's three major investor-owned utilities to increase their use of renewables from about 10 percent in 2002 to 20 percent by 2017. Like many other states, California categorizes a wide range of possible technologies as renewables, although it excludes large hydro and nuclear sources. The state has struggled mightily to approach its expansionist renewables goals, having been eclipsed by Texas as the largest source of wind energy among the American states. California established a very complex regulatory oversight process that may have encouraged prospective developers to look elsewhere. Some early renewable projects collapsed at the contract stage, and the state is struggling to rebuild transmission capacity to fit the decentralized nature of renewables generation. Consequently, its renewables inventory has increased only modestly since 2002. Nonetheless, in legislation enacted in 2005, the state decided to set a more ambitious target that maintained the 20 percent target but advanced the deadline to 2010. The state's RPS moves forward alongside a dizzying array of continuing programs designed to promote expanded development of renewables, including tax breaks and utility rebates. California is also designing a "low-carbon fuel standard," which will establish a similar mechanism to promote transition toward renewable sources of transportation fuel. This program will be far more complex than more familiar state and federal mandates for a specific alternative fuel, most commonly corn based ethanol.

Decoupling Electricity Pricing

Under traditional electricity regulation, utilities have incentives to produce and sell as much electricity as possible to maximize their profits, even though the environmental consequences may be adverse. California recognized this "throughput-incentive" dilemma a quarter century ago and has systematically pursued "decoupling." This process allows utilities considerable opportunity for recovering costs when they produce and sell less electricity as a result of their energy efficiency initiatives. California is expanding this program, providing a set of financial incentives that would enable utilities not only to recover costs but also to derive extra profits through expanded commitment to energy efficiency (Swope 2007).

Performance Standards

California has increasingly turned to the question of using various policies to prod neighbors into reducing greenhouse gas emissions by literally extending the reach of its regulatory arm beyond its borders. In the case of electricity, California imports approximately one-quarter of its current supply, but nearly half of the carbon emissions generated by the electricity that it uses come from these sources because of their heavy reliance on coal (California Air Resources Board 2008, p. 7). This reality has raised the concern over "emissions leakage" and prompted California's efforts to impose similar emissions controls on all electricity used within its boundaries, regardless of source. Invariably, this raises concerns over possible violation of the Commerce Clause of the U.S. Constitution, which restricts any policy that thwarts the movement of commerce across state boundaries. This has not, however, deterred California from erecting a series of "emissions performance standards" that impose California carbon emission requirements on any electricity-supply contracts that provide power for California residents. This step was formalized at about the same time that the Global Warming Solutions Act was signed into law, but through a separate provision, Senate Bill 1368, that applies to both investor-owned and publicly owned utilities.

Climate Policy Formulation Versus Implementation

A series of factors have converged to create abundant opportunities for a wide range of entrepreneurs to conceptualize and secure political support for the policies just described and other climate policies. Indeed, California may constitute a perfect storm for climate policy formulation, driven by an unusual confluence of factors. First, surveys of Californians consistently demonstrate strong concern over the potential ramifications of climate change on the state and, at a broad level, support for unilateral action to reduce state emissions and to attempt to influence other jurisdictions as well (Petek and Baldassare 2007). Second, the state has begun to experience a cascade of adverse climate effects, including dramatic proliferation and intensification of wildfires, elevated temperatures in portions of the state, drought in some key agricultural zones, and declining productivity from large dams that produce more than 15 percent of the state's electricity. Certain industries, such as agriculture, are concerned about potential threats to their viability from accelerated climate change. Third, California has long provided a political venue receptive to taking a lead role among states and has offered incredible staging for credit-claiming among political officials who play some role in one or more of the pieces of climate policy described in the previous section. Invariably the dramatization that has accompanied Governor Schwarzenegger's every move on this issue comes to mind, from signing new legislation to jetting around the nation or the world negotiating new bilateral agreements. But other elected officials, such as Assembly Member Fran Pavley, then assembly speaker Fabian Núñez, Attorney General Edmund Brown Jr., Secretary of State Debra Bowen, and former state treasurer (and Schwarzenegger gubernatorial rival in 2006) Phil Angelides, among many others, have attempted to claim some credit for advancing state climate policy and have attained statewide (and, in some cases, national) recognition for their efforts.

Fourth, political support for aggressive unilateral action has been bolstered by the common argument that these policies are good not only for the environment but also for California's economy. Given its relatively limited base of heavy manufacturing and coal-fired power plants, California has an unusually diverse economy, one that already claims national and international leadership in many areas of technology that could be in high demand in a carbon-constrained economy. The actual economic ramifications of aggressive climate regulation are highly debatable, but it has become common practice across partisan and institutional lines in California to argue that what is good for the climate is also good for California's economic development. "I say unquestionably it is good for business," proclaimed Schwarzenegger in signing the Global Warming Solutions Act into law. "Not only large, well-established businesses, but small businesses that will harness their entrepreneurial spirit to help us achieve our climate goals." State government documents and reports have long emphasized such mutually enforcing goals (California Climate Action Team 2006). Moreover, given the state's relatively low rate of per capita emissions and considerable climate policy expertise, it could stand to play a dominant role in any future development or implementation of national or international climate policy. This might provide California with an unusually strong bargaining position to deliver benefits to the state, whether through selection of policy tools where the state has considerable expertise, endorsement of emissions reduction technologies that are manufactured within the state, or formal credit for low levels of per capita emissions or early reductions in emissions (Rabe 2008b).

With so many forms of climate policy moving forward simultaneously, much of it unique among the governments of North America and the rest of the world,

Sacramento has emerged as a haven for climate entrepreneurs. Some have characterized California climate policy as being in the midst of a "feeding frenzy" that affords agency officials, environmental advocacy group leaders, and industry representatives uncommon access to a highly charged policymaking process, each player attempting to use his particular expertise to influence the crafting of laws and executive orders. No two policies have followed identical paths or created identical entrepreneurial opportunities. In the case of the 2002 vehicle emissions legislation, an environmental advocacy group, the California Bluewater Network, drafted the legislation for a first-term sponsor, Assemblywoman Pavley. In contrast, much of the more recent policy development, including the evolving initiatives in the electricity sector, have provided abundant opportunity for entrepreneurs within established agencies and commissions. At the same time the governor has assembled a high-profile team of senior advisers and agency heads, subject to periodic reshuffling, who play a lead role on various aspects of climate policy.

But the enactment of a new policy and any political credit-claiming is invariably followed by the difficult work of implementation. For some entrepreneurs this is of little concern. Given the stringency of term limitations in California and the long-term nature of many emissions reduction commitments, virtually all of the elected officials in either the executive and legislative branch will have left office long before policies are finalized and placed into operation. Just as ex-governor Gray Davis is not being held accountable for any delays in implementing the 2002 California carbon emissions program for vehicles, it is unlikely that Governor Schwarzenegger or former speaker Fabian Núñez will be held accountable after leaving office for the state's ability to hit its 2020 or 2050 reduction targets. They can instead bask in an immediate wave of positive media attention and any political boost that it provides. Similarly, advocacy groups pushing for a particular policy in 2008 or 2009 will not be held accountable for the performance of that policy in 2015 or 2020 but can claim credit for influencing pioneering action in the interim and use that to burnish their own reputations (Bosso 2005).

Lack of Successful Governing Models

The realities are quite different, however, for officials within state agencies who may have played an active role in policy development and will also be responsible for interpreting legislation and executive orders and putting them into operation over an extended period of time. As was the case earlier in the decade when the United States began to consider the governance of "homeland security," no single department or agency in California holds exclusive jurisdiction over "climate" (Kettl 2007). No superagency exists in any national or subnational government on the planet, and climate change is by definition so expansive that it calls for collaboration across literally innumerable units of government. Many of these units have traditionally been divided by rivalries, including long-standing battles between lead units for energy development and environmental protection. Others—for example, transportation and agriculture—have barely had any semblance of a working relationship. Actual experience with "climate governance" is limited at best, and early efforts around the world have generally struggled. Carbon cap-and-trade programs in the European Union and among a consortium of ten northeastern U.S. states have proved considerably more difficult to put into operation than anticipated. They have yet to demonstrate significant ability to reduce emissions, much less do so cost-effectively (Rabe 2008a).

Jurisdictions that set ambitious emission reduction targets before California did have generally been unsuccessful in meeting them. In the European Union, Germany and the United Kingdom have been the most successful members in achieving significant reductions, although how much of this success is due to adept policy in contrast with the economic collapse of the former East Germany in the 1990s and the massive British shift from coal to natural gas for electricity remains unclear. Many other EU members have struggled to meet but are unlikely to approach their Kyoto targets by the end of the current decade. In Canada, Manitoba, the most supportive province of Kyoto ratification, unveiled a far-reaching set of policy efforts between 2001 and 2004. Yet its emissions have grown at a rate greater than that of California and many other states since 1990. Virtually none of Manitoba's much-heralded policies have been put into operation, and the interministerial network established to guide policy development and implementation has essentially imploded.

Among U.S. states, New Jersey laid claim to national leadership on climate change before California. Each New Jersey governor, from Thomas Kean in the late 1980s through Jon Corzine in 2008, has signed climate legislation, and state officials have long expressed concern about such climate threats as elevated sea level. This issue reached particular salience under Governor Christine Todd Whitman in the late 1990s, leading to an executive order that pledged statewide greenhouse gas emission reduction consistent with the level that would have been required under U.S. ratification of Kyoto. The state developed a comprehensive plan to attain these targets under the umbrella of the 2000 New Jersey Sustainability Greenhouse Gas Action Plan, which set forth an array of policies involving virtually every state government agency that oversaw activity linked to the generation of significant levels of greenhouse gases (Rabe 2004). Less than a decade later the plan was in disarray. The interunit work group that was to be coordinated by the Office of Innovative Technology and Market Development in the Division of Science, Research, and Technology lacked the authority to sustain necessary collaboration. Whether the work group faced an impossible challenge or simply lost favor after Whitman left office in 2001 remains unclear. Instead of following the downward emissions trajectory pledged under Whitman, New Jersey's emissions have increased more than twice as fast as California's during this period. Ironically, in July 2007 Governor Corzine signed into law the New Jersey Global Warming Response Act. This calls for California-like levels of emissions reductions by 2020 and 2050 and proposes broad collaboration in policy development between essentially the same set of agencies that had been given a similar task seven years earlier. This version, however, places the commissioner of the Department of Environmental Protection in more of a lead role, with a responsibility for advancing policy recommendations to meet the targets while weighing related economic benefits and costs. However, many of the initial duties imposed on the department and its partners resemble measures that were supposed to have been completed long since through the 2000 Action Plan.

Inventing a Climate Governance Network for California

California thus moves forward with the most ambitious set of climate policies of any government on the globe but no clear models of successful governance from other states or nations. Much of its climate legislation, such as the Global Warming Solutions Act, is unusually vague for U.S. state or federal policy. It delegates numerous—and incredibly complex—policy design and implementation challenges to state agencies, which leaves considerable room for entrepreneurial license, and provides little direction. Other provisions, such as the renewable portfolio standard, have been given such ambitious targets that even the best-imaginable implementation plan may fall short of statutory requirements and result in elected officials' shifting blame to responsible departments. Thus, having demonstrated that a state's political institutions can unilaterally take bold climate policy action, the larger question of its capacity to implement those policies now comes into play.

The state has begun to come to terms with this issue and has committed to a governing framework that calls for the establishment of complex networks spanning various departments, agencies, and commissions. Many include links to formal advisory bodies, universities, and nonprofit entities. The next section outlines the lead governmental players and their varied relationships on particular parts of the California climate strategy. This discussion sets the stage for an early analysis of the prospects for successful implementation, based on initial experience in assembling this network and putting its pieces into operation.

California has begun to prepare for this challenge through external study and increased resource allocation. Delegations of state agency officials have toured other capitals, both state and national. Part of this activity reflects growing interest in formal collaboration between California and these jurisdictions, but a major motivating factor has been examining past failures "to make sure the mistakes are not repeated in California."[2] At the same time, the state's fiscal 2008 budget provided

2. Karen Breslau, "The Green Giant," *Newsweek,* April 16, 2007, pp. 51–59.

$32 million in new spending to assist in the process of implementing Assembly Bill 32. Much of this funding would be used to create an estimated 126 new positions in state government units, although portions of it would be used to secure research and technical support obtained through contracts.

California has been reluctant to tinker with department and agency structure and jurisdiction. In 2005 the state did seriously consider attempting to integrate the many units within California government that have some role in energy policy into one comprehensive Energy Department. Schwarzenegger initially backed such a cabinet-level entity to "consolidate the duplicative and overlapping energy functions that are the responsibility of multiple state agencies."[3] This would have brought together energy units in both the electricity and transportation sectors, with the emerging unit most likely taking a lead role in implementation of a good deal of the state's climate policy. Political opposition to this proposal was intense, most notably from the units most likely to be affected and their most loyal constituents. The governor and legislative supporters have since eschewed such far-reaching organizational redesign in favor of working with cross-institutional networks.

Part of the case against creation of an energy superdepartment stemmed from the fact that many of the programs that have contributed to California's enviably low rate of per capita greenhouse gas emissions were nurtured in one or more of the existing departments, agencies, or commissions. They consequently possessed unique expertise that could be tapped to meet the challenge of climate change. If path dependence can ease the development of a successful climate program, California may be uniquely positioned. Emissions trading, energy decoupling, incentives for expanded energy efficiency, and many other policy tools that may prove to be crucial elements in climate policy are largely unfamiliar in many state and national capitals but are old hat in various corners of the Sacramento bureaucracy. State officials also have considerable experience in attempting to implement policies that ultimately failed, such as the state's debacle in electricity deregulation (Brown 2001) and failure, after many years of effort, to win acceptance for select alternative transportation fuels such as methanol.

All of California's evolving climate policy is scheduled to move forward beneath the umbrella of the California Climate Action Team, a loose coalition of sixteen departments, agencies, and commissions with some role in climate policy implementation. The action team was created through executive order S-3-05, in 2005, which divided it into twelve subgroups, such as agriculture, energy, and forestry, and placed the California Environmental Protection Agency (CalEPA) in the lead role. CalEPA is the rough equivalent of the U.S. Environmental Protection Agency, with broad oversight over a range of environmental and pollution control

---

3. Office of the Governor, "Gov. Schwarzenegger Continues Push to Create New Cabinet-Level Energy Department, Details Energy Policy in Letter to Legislature," press release, August 23, 2005, p. 10.

programs. It also formally oversees the California Air Resources Board (CARB), which has substantial responsibility for the major California climate laws and a long-standing reputation for innovation. CARB retains some autonomy from CalEPA, with an influential oversight board and a large staff that is overseen by its director. The CalEPA secretary is responsible for convening the action team and issuing regular reports to the state on progress toward meeting all state greenhouse gas reduction targets. But CalEPA's formal powers to force coordination remain limited, and it oversees a diverse coalition that includes representatives from the Governor's Office, CARB, the California Energy Commission (CEC), the California Public Utilities Commission (CPUC), the California Department of Transportation, the California Resources Agency, the California Integrated Waste Management Board, and the California Department of Food and Agriculture. Other state government units, such as the Department of Forestry and Fire Protection or the Division of Oil and Gas Resources, are not formally part of the action team but can be integrated into activities where necessary.

Can a Network Approach to Climate Governance Work?

Abundant evidence from other policy arenas suggests that a network approach can be a successful mechanism for cutting across traditional boundaries and melding multiple units, areas, and disciplines to face new governing challenges. Network approaches entail new relationships between public sector entities and also between the public and private sector, with the goal of fostering new creativity and effectiveness. In theory, innumerable ways can be envisioned in which various forces might converge to implement Assembly Bill 32 or any of California's other climate policies. At the same time, network construction is not easy, and many pitfalls await networks assembled to tackle complex policy problems. "They must have the ability and the inclination to work across sectoral boundaries and the resourcefulness to overcome all the prickly challenges to governing by network," as Goldsmith and Eggers have noted (2004, p. 158).

California is attempting a network approach to climate governance, reflected in its decision to establish a Climate Action Team to play a coordinating role rather than an energy superdepartment. This builds on the established strengths of CARB, CEC, and other members of the action team, with the presumption that they can achieve needed integration across public units and work effectively with private sector constituents where appropriate. Many of the individual departments and agencies have commissioners or external advisory boards, which include some blend of representation from the private sector and nonprofit community. All of this suggests the presence of the necessary ingredients for a monumental experiment in climate network development.

In this case, the stakes appear unusually high. Alongside the saliency of the climate change issue, California's claim to national and global leadership in developing effective policy responses is drawing substantial attention to its efforts. European Union leaders, the federal governments of the United States and Canada, and other governments have already begun to turn to Sacramento as a possible model for their own evolving climate policy efforts. This is illustrated in Governor Schwarzenegger's official offers, to leaders in the U.S. Congress and around the globe, to offer "my administration's assistance and the benefit of our experience here in California" in developing climate policy and governing mechanisms. It is further reflected in the governor's decision to host a global climate change summit in Beverly Hills in November 2008, which drew a wide range of domestic and international leaders to California to sign a broad declaration of intent. All of this serves to raise the bar for those responsible for putting California's many ambitious policies into play. CalEPA secretary Linda Adams has noted, "If we do this right, we will be a model for other states, the nation, and other countries to follow" (Adams 2006, p. 14). On the downside, as one journalist has noted, "At the moment California is a beacon" to other governments. "If it fails, it will become an excuse for inaction."[4]

It is much too soon to tell how successful the California experience will prove, and there is no neat recipe to follow for constructive network development. Nonetheless, scholars have begun to outline some common design components in effective network experiments. These include such features as the ability to forge coordination and integration among multiple governing units and the development of reliable metrics for measuring and monitoring performance. Several of these features are reviewed below, with particular attention to early lessons out of California. Some of them raise sobering concerns, at least at this early stage. They highlight significant challenges to the attainment of the state's ambitious greenhouse gas reduction goals.

Fragmented Coordination

Fragmentation among governmental agencies and departments is a legendary problem that can have many adverse consequences. In environmental protection, the long-standing division of federal and state agencies into separate media of air, land, and water protection has precluded integrated approaches and created perverse incentives to shift environmental problems to other media instead of addressing them. In energy policy, divides by energy source are ubiquitous, often resulting in protection for favored sources and active discouragement of alternatives and open competition. Turf protection is a common response to efforts to coordinate across units and traditional boundaries. Clearly, an enormous challenge faces any effort to establish an effective network to address climate concerns, and it has proven a major stumbling block in a number of early climate policy efforts in U.S. states and abroad.

4. *The Economist*, "Arnie's Uphill Climb," June 23, 2007, p. 38.

In California, the Climate Action Team cannot compel horizontal cooperation across units, given the limited nature of its charge, and seemingly must rely on suasion and good will among various entities. Virtually every climate policy enacted thus far in Sacramento necessitates some form of networking among two or more key institutional players. In some instances, this may require coordination and cooperation between units that in many prior cases have been rivals, such as entities with jurisdiction over various areas of electricity generation or transportation. Early experience in California suggests that this dispersal of authority may be problematic in attempting to implement Assembly Bill 32 and related pieces of legislation, with each program calling for a differing set of integrative multilateral relationships.

For example, Assembly Bill 32 appears to give CARB a dominant role, reflected in the fact that it will receive the most funding from the new state allocation to climate change. Almost immediately, however, CARB has found itself working with other state government units, given the inherent complexities in assembling a comprehensive cap program and considering emissions trading provisions. Any engagement with the electricity sector invariably necessitates interaction between CARB and the CPUC, which regulates the investor-owned electric utility sector, and the CEC, which oversees a wide range of energy efficiency programs and regulates the publicly owned electric utility sector. About 70 percent of California's electricity is generated by the private sector, a share that could increase should California expand its imports of electricity from outside the state. One early illustration of potential tension across government units is reflected in the development of emission performance standards under SB 1398. Thus far, CPUC has insisted on a tougher standard for the privately held utilities it regulates than the CECs more relaxed standard for publicly held firms.[5] Private companies contend that this would create a double standard that would penalize them, and some have threatened litigation. CARB must somehow navigate these differences, although it has no real authority to encroach on the formal authority of either the CEC or the CPUC. Neither does CalEPA have any ability, from its role as chair of the Climate Action Team, to force cooperation. CEC and CPUC deliberations thus far resemble more a game of chicken than a serious exercise in policy coordination. The divide in electricity governance between these two entities is further revealed by the difficulties in developing consistent policies for renewable energy mandates between investor-owned and publicly owned utilities.

Coordination may also be problematic between policy tools that are potential rivals. A growing problem in all jurisdictions that have some version of a renewable portfolio standard and a carbon cap-and-trade program is to make sure these efforts work at common purpose. This includes needed coordination to avoid "double

---

5. One thousand and 1,100 tons of carbon dioxide per megawatt hour, respectively.

counting," whereby renewable energy credits granted for adding renewable supply to satisfy an RPS requirement are not also utilized for credit under an emissions trading regime. More generally, numerous other dimensions of these two programs require careful collaborative structuring to allow them both to achieve their goals, including developing methods for reporting and monitoring compliance. An early report from the Climate Action Team warns, "Any new program to limit GHG emissions from the electric power sector needs to be harmonized with other require-ments and programs. . . . Care is needed to ensure that the GHG emissions cap, the RPS, and ratepayer-funded energy-efficiency programs do not work at cross pur-poses" (Climate Action Team 2006, p. 24). In California thus far, RPS implemen-tation is almost exclusively under the aegis of the CPUC and CEC, whereas devel-opment of a cap-and-trade system belongs largely to CARB. The two programs appear to be moving along separate tracks, each unit being absorbed in immediate tasks instead of considering questions of fit and integration.

Goal Congruence and the Challenge of Competing Elected Officials

Policy implementation is difficult enough for a network when instructions it receives from elected officials are clear, through legislation or other channels. The U.S. system, which divides government by branches and often party control, opens the possibility that competing elected officials may demand different things from members of the implementing network. Conflicting demands may entail technical differences that can be easily resolved but that may also reflect funda-mental and philosophical differences suggesting a basic lack of congruence in the policy goals sought by respective branches. This problem can become more severe at the state level, where the executive branch includes multiple positions decided through partisan elections, leading to possible further proliferation of elected offi-cials and confusion for networks that must discern policy goals.

Failure to clarify a key policy goal in Assembly Bill 32 has confounded early efforts to interpret the legislation and begin to develop a regulatory framework to guide implementation. Although the California legislature and the governor con-curred with the idea of a statewide emissions cap for 2020 and 2050, they did not reach agreement in the statute as to what that entailed. Instead, they evaded the question of how to attain the emission reduction targets, whether through command-and-control regulation or through an emissions-trading program. The former approach would involve extensive development of uniform reduction requirements imposed on regulated parties and likely include mandates for across-the-board adoption of particular technologies to reduce emissions. The latter approach would add the terms "and trade" to the word "cap" and establish a fun-damentally different type of program. Such an approach would require the defini-tion and establishment of a market for the measurement and exchange of carbon credits, much like the emissions trading provisions created for sulfur dioxide in the 1990s or the EU Emissions Trading Scheme for carbon.

Unable to reconcile these differences but eager to claim credit for historic action, the Democratic legislature and Republican governor did not reconcile their differences before passing Assembly Bill 32 and laying claim to global climate leadership. The resulting legislation delegates to CARB and other units most of the key decisions over how to implement the cap. No sooner had the ink on Assembly Bill 32 dried than interbranch tensions surfaced over agency interpretation of the statute. The governor promptly concluded that cap-and-trade was the appropriate route and used his executive authority to require state officials to begin to assemble such a program. But the response from the legislature has been swift and intense, placing the entire future of the program under considerable uncertainty. Leaders in the California Senate have threatened CARB with steep funding cuts if they put too much effort into cap-and-trade instead of emphasizing a series of regulatory actions that could be implemented promptly. "The implementation of Assembly Bill 32 is getting bogged down in arcane discussions over intercontinental trading schemes, 'carbon markets,' and free 'credits,'" lamented Senate president Dan Perata in a comment representative of outrage from the legislative branch. "That may work for Wall Street traders and Enron economists, but it doesn't work for California."[6] Legislators in both chambers have become outspoken critics of any serious movement toward a trading system. They are expressing skepticism over its technical viability and concerns that it will generate "windfall profits" for firms that might find ways to manipulate the carbon trading mechanisms to their advantage. As Perata asserted in March 2008, the governor's embrace of cap-and-trade violates the "carefully negotiated" provisions of Assembly Bill 32 and "also has had the regrettable effect of engendering active political opposition from an unlikely cross-section of interests, from public owned energy utilities to environmental justice groups."[7] These types of concerns were registered repeatedly in Sacramento in 2007 and 2008, well before the national financial crisis served to intensify such debate in Congress's climate policy deliberations.

Thus far, CARB seems to be trying to walk a delicate line and somehow placate competing officials. It has continued to move, with caution, to outline the essentials for a possible cap-and-trade system. At the same time, it has rapidly accelerated its efforts to produce three dozen "early actions" intended to produce some degree of emissions reductions in relatively short order (California Air Resources Board 2007). All of this goes forward amid considerable uncertainty, compounded by the lack of successful models from other governments. "The uncertainties about how this system would be designed and implemented are

6. "Home Alone," *Carbon Control News*, February 22, 2007 (www.carboncontrolnews.com).

7. "California Democratic Leaders Blast State Energy Cap-and-Trade Plan," *Carbon Control News*, March 13, 2008 (www.carboncontrolnews.com).

almost infinite," says one observer, and the inherent complexity is only exacerbated by this fundamental struggle over core goals among competing officials.[8]

CARB's challenges have been compounded by interbranch battles over agency leadership, funding, and staffing. Amid all of the other controversies surrounding Assembly Bill 32's implementation, Schwarzenegger fired the CARB chief, Robert Sawyer, in June 2007, citing "disagreement over how to address global warming." Shortly thereafter, Sawyer's top associate, Executive Officer Catherine Witherspoon, resigned, alleging excessive micromanagement of CARB from the Governor's Office. This created an immediate leadership void and precipitated the decision in July by the California Assembly Resources Committee to hold special hearings on possible executive branch excesses in overseeing CARB. This in turn led Senate leaders to view confirmation hearings on prospective successors as an opportunity to revisit their concerns about cap-and-trade versus alternative approaches to Assembly Bill 32 implementation. Senate president Perata vowed to use the hearings to make sure that the nominee, former EPA assistant administrator Mary Nichols, "is both knowledgeable about the law—and the law's emphasis on strong regulation over market mechanisms—as well as independent, even if given a directive to take an action in conflict with AB 32." Even funding for new CARB staff positions was held hostage to radically divergent views on the part of the governor and legislature over the number of new hires who would be allowed to work on emissions trading provisions as opposed to other tasks. Interbranch battles have also continued over whether new positions at higher levels of various units should be exempt from legislative confirmation processes. Concerns over California's capacity to fund sufficient staff positions to implement its climate programs took a new direction in 2008, when the emergence of enormous state government deficits raised the possibility of significant reductions across multiple agencies and departments. Proposals from the governor to establish new fees on energy use to sustain staffing positions were derided as tax increases and faced considerable political opposition.

Governors and legislators are not the only elected principals in states such as California. Most state attorneys general reach office through the ballot and are constitutionally independent of other elected officials; many have used this latitude to explore multiple litigative venues to attempt to influence climate policy. The best-known example of this was the litigation brought in 2007 by the Massachusetts attorney general and joined by a dozen counterparts that was expected to force the federal government's hand to define carbon dioxide as an air pollutant. The U.S. Environmental Protection Agency's resistance to this designation in 2008 triggered continued litigation and has particular salience for the California program to reduce

8. This statement is drawn from an interview with a senior official in the state policymaking process—one of more than a dozen interviews that were conducted. Owing to the political sensitivity of these discussions, all interview participants were assured that there would be no direct attribution of their comments in any publication.

carbon emissions from vehicles. California's current attorney general (and former governor), Edmund Brown Jr., has joined the chorus of activist attorneys general with an ever-expanding series of legal challenges and threats to various industries, neighboring states, and even local California governments that he deems slow in responding to the challenge of climate change. In 2008 Brown frequently threatened to use his powers to attempt to increase reductions that would be imposed on particular sectors if certain policies intended for other sectors are not implemented. For example, Brown has vowed that continued reluctance by the federal government to deny California a waiver needed to implement its vehicle carbon emissions legislation will prompt him to take legal action to intensify reductions already envisioned for the electricity and industrial sectors under other laws. Consequently, all governmental units implementing Assembly Bill 32 and related policies may also need to prepare to adjust and impose additional reduction burdens in response to the evolving litigative strategy of the attorney general. These actions have garnered Brown enormous statewide and national media attention, fueling speculation that it is part of a strategy to restore him to his prior role of governor after term limits force Schwarzenegger to depart in 2011.

Oversight and the Demands of Hyperactive Officials

California elected officials may disagree on many key elements of what the state has legislated thus far or what state agencies should do in response. Nonetheless, they generally share the goal of continuing to push the emissions reduction bar as high as possible, thereby propelling California to the head of the pack of states and nations and securing its standing as a global climate leader. Such common cause on this very broad objective may, however, lead to an upward bidding war of sorts, setting such elevated expectations or setting so short a deadline for meeting those expectations that failure is almost foreordained. Many pieces of California's climate policy may fall prey to this phenomenon, but perhaps the most obvious example of how the hubris of elected officials can translate into an implementation impossibility is the state's renewable portfolio standard. In many respects, this program illustrates the risks of creating a "policy beyond capacity" of any reasonable agency effort to honor the demands of legislation (Jones 1975).

A number of states have been very successful in establishing RPSs and achieving consistent growth in their share of renewable energy. Texas, for example, is not only the largest state consumer of electricity in the nation, but its 1999 RPS has also generated an increase in the state's share of renewables from less than 1 percent at the time of enactment to approximately 4 percent in 2008. The state expanded its program in 2005 and projects continued growth in renewable capacity over the next decade, tapping primarily into the vast source of wind power in the western part of the state.

Other states have had similar experiences, though on a smaller scale, and none has yet demonstrated an ability to grow the share of renewables at an almost exponential rate. California's efforts to move along this path, compounded by the 2005 decision to accelerate its timetable for doubling its renewable capacity by seven years, have been unsuccessful. Some portion of this failure can be attributed to fragmented coordination between the CPUC and CEC, which has produced a cumbersome process for approving new renewable energy projects. Indeed, many initial contracts have been canceled as a result of regulatory complexities. Between 2002 and 2006, the state added only 240 megawatts of new renewable capacity, about a tenth of what Texas brought online during the same period.

Even Texas-like growth in California's renewable supply would only partially close the gap imposed by the 2010 target of 20 percent reductions. It is quietly acknowledged across the California state government that the RPS will not begin to approach that level, even if every conceivable renewable project moves forward very quickly in the next few years. Instead of planning for this looming failure, however, the governor and the legislature are racing to see who can elevate the state's target still higher. Indeed, both have expressed strong interest in making it 33 percent by 2020, which would enable California to hold the most ambitious RPS goal of any state. Senior agency staff fear a scenario in which elected officials impose ever-higher demands in the search for political credit but never come to grips with the current program's design flaws or attempt to match targets to the realities of current technologies. At some point, failure becomes evident, blame is affixed, and one or more units in the California climate network will likely be singled out by principals for their inability to complete a task that from the outset may have been unachievable.

Reliable Metrics and Analytical Integrity

A cornerstone of any credible form of network governance is an accurate and accessible flow of essential information. In many areas of environmental protection, significant strides have been made through mandatory emissions reporting programs, such as the Toxics Release Inventory. This program is widely thought to have had a significant impact, allowing for measurement of performance trends and creating very public incentives for polluting entities to reduce their emissions of hundreds of toxic substances released into air, land, and water (Hamilton 2005). The Toxics Release Inventory could be a plausible model for disclosure of carbon dioxide and other greenhouse gases. Wisconsin followed this strategy more than a decade ago and now possesses a longitudinal database on greenhouse gas releases from a vast array of in-state sources (Rabe 2004). Other states and the federal government have approached this matter with some trepidation.

Somewhat ironically, California has only begun to pursue this issue through its Assembly Bill 32 provision that calls upon CARB to develop a greenhouse gas emissions reporting mechanism alongside its other regulatory efforts. Previously, the state focused primarily on voluntary emissions reporting through an inventory that emitters may use to document releases and instances of emission reduction. Part of the allure of this approach has been the possible "credits" for entities that registered their emission reductions with the state in advance of any regulatory policies. In many respects, it has paralleled a long-standing U.S. Department of Energy program for reporting, known as 1605b, in that both have been purely voluntary and neither requires any third-party verification.

California has acknowledged that its program is limited and does not provide a reliable profile of emissions trends. Indeed, most of the existing data on state greenhouse gas emissions are derived from a combination of federal and state government estimates rather than any sort of database generated through actual emissions reporting. Consequently, there are enormous elements of imprecision to any current measurement of California emissions. Matters become even trickier when one tries to develop reliable metrics for other greenhouse gases such as methane or the impact of strategies such as sequestration through reforestation or subterranean storage of carbon dioxide.

The state has started to address this deficiency through early interpretation of the Assembly Bill 32 mandate as well as the creation of a multistate collaboration to develop a Climate Registry, which would measure, track, verify, and publicly report greenhouse gas emissions. As of late 2008, thirty-eight American states, nine Canadian provinces, and six Mexican states had joined with California in beginning to outline a common plan for such a registry. This effort could ultimately be folded into a national program, but initially it is intended to facilitate coordination of efforts that cross state and regional boundaries. At the same time it is still in early stages of development, and it is unclear how long it will take for California or its registry partners to develop a reliable body of greenhouse gas emissions data upon which to base policy and inform the citizenry. All of this adds to the complexity of developing an effective climate governance network.

Uncertainty over the reliability and integrity of core data underpinning the California climate effort is not confined to emissions reporting. As noted, a core element in California's advocacy for expanded policies such as Assembly Bill 32 has been the widespread argument that such steps would simultaneously foster environmental protection and economic development. This argument was bolstered through a trilogy of studies released in 2006, the most prominent one by the Climate Action Team. Utilizing an economic model developed at the University of California–Berkeley and used previously by CARB and CEC, the action team study concluded that "the overall impact of the climate change emission reduction strategies on California's economy" is "expected to be positive." In a widely quoted passage, the report also found that implementation of the state's strategies were "expected to result in a net increase of 83,000 jobs and $4 billion in income, above and beyond the substantial growth" projected in the state between 2006 and 2020 (California Climate Action Team 2006, xv).

The action team analysis has triggered considerable controversy, from both industry and a team of scholars who contend that the California economic analysis is fundamentally flawed. A group of prominent economists argue that the state has advanced a "too good to be true" outlook, based on a series of highly suspect assumptions. These scholars contend that the analysis was constructed to build political support for new policy proposals. They have concluded that "a careful examination of the California studies reveals that they underestimate the cost of meeting California's 2020 emissions target as a result of numerous flaws. . . . A few of the flaws individually lead to underestimation of annual costs that is on the order of billions of dollars. The California studies also overstate the emission reduction potential of the policies that they examine" (Stavins, Jaffe, and Schatzki 2007, p. 37). The debate underscores the uncertainty not only in measuring projected emissions reductions but also in attempting to apply a credible set of economic projections to various policy alternatives, thus placing a cloud of uncertainty over the entire California climate enterprise.

Jurisdictional Constraints

Even as engaged, populous, and influential a state as California faces constraints on its efforts to confront climate change. Excluding the issue of its standing on the global stage, California remains only one of fifty states in a federal system, though it commands enormous economic and political clout. In many respects, California is testing how far one state can move unilaterally, whether in attempting to secure what it wants from the federal government, impose its will on its neighbors, or build multistate networks to expand the scope of its policies. All of this intergovernmental activity represents yet another challenge for developing a viable climate network in the absence of national or international governance.

First, California is aggressively attempting to maximize its leverage with the federal government. This has included a political and litigative assault by the governor and his allies in other statehouses and in Congress to pressure the Environmental Protection Agency to reverse its denial of the state's request for a waiver that is necessary to allow it to go forward with the vehicular carbon emissions reduction program set forth in Assembly Bill 1493. At the same time, California leaders have stepped up their efforts to attempt to influence any future federal climate policy decisions, so as to thwart possible preemption of existing state policies. Instead, they are calling upon Washington to use the California model as a building block for any future federal action, granting individual states considerable latitude to sustain their own policies and also rewarding those that took early action. It is also increasingly evident that California intends to use its record of "early action" on climate change and relatively low rate of emissions growth to advance the case that it should be a beneficiary in any future federal cap-and-trade regime that would reallocate revenues back to states (Rabe 2008b).

Second, California is exploring ways of expanding the influence of its policies beyond its boundaries. Emissions performance standards are a prominent example, although other policies also will likely follow this path. This raises the inevitable issue of the Commerce Clause of the U.S. Constitution and the question of whether any California efforts to extend the reach of its climate regulation beyond its boundaries impede the movement of interstate commerce. Some industries and neighboring states have expressed this concern and threatened litigation depending on the outcome of the regulatory development process for performance standards. Vehicle manufacturers have made similar assertions against Assembly Bill 1493 and related regulatory provisions in the transportation sector. Even in the arena of RPSs, the evidence is growing that California and the other neighboring western states with some version of this policy have configured their programs so as to maximize the likelihood that any new renewable electricity sources established to meet the regulatory standards are created within that state. This has included an array of provisions that either give competitive advantage to intrastate sources or discriminate in some way against sources from outside the state. All of these issues elevate the prospect of an intergovernmental collision, perhaps to be resolved through the courts or new forms of federal legislation.

Third, California not only is trying to exert influence on its neighbors but also has been searching for ways to work cooperatively with them. The state has signed a flurry of bistate, tristate, regional, and cross-continental agreements on various aspects of climate change in recent years. It has even established formal partnerships with governments of European countries such as Sweden and the United Kingdom, Canadian provinces, and Mexican states, although these are confined largely to pledges of cooperation, information exchange, and common development of various technologies. Many of these partnerships appear to be mainly symbolic, but it is increasingly evident that California is exploring ways to develop a multijurisdictional network to establish common policies and thereby create larger regions and markets for implementation.

This may be most significant as the state attempts to move forward with carbon cap-and-trade through interpretation of Assembly Bill 32. In February 2007, Schwarzenegger and his gubernatorial counterparts in Arizona, New Mexico, Oregon, and Washington State created the Western Regional Climate Action Initiative.[9] It expressly calls for creation of a regional greenhouse gas emissions reduction goal and a cap-and-trade program to achieve a regional reduction target of 15 percent below 2005 levels by 2020, as well as development of a common carbon emis-

---

9. See the text of the February 26, 2007, governors agreement at www.westernclimateinitiative.org/ewebeditpro/items/O104F12775.pdf.

sions registry and tracking system. Montana and Utah and the Canadian provinces of British Columbia, Manitoba, Ontario, and Quebec have also joined the initiative. California has also taken the lead and continued negotiating with the northeastern states involved in the Regional Greenhouse Gas Initiative (RGGI) for a cooperative arrangement connecting these bi-coastal emissions trading systems in some manner. "I am happy to announce today that as we implement our new law we will form a greenhouse gas trading partnership with RGGI," declared Schwarzenegger in October 2006, after negotiations in Albany with George Pataki, the then governor of New York.[10] These multistate networks are being actively explored in other areas as well, such as the Climate Action Registry mentioned previously. At the same time, various multistate organizations are emerging to coordinate them, including the Governors' Climate Protection Leadership Council, established in March 2007. California is an active player and, in many of these efforts, the driving force.

Each of these three areas in which California has become linked with other governments is ripe with potential for innovative solutions and the possibility of creative intergovernmental network development. Enormous uncertainties surround all aspects of this venture, and the recent track record of state-and-federal relations in environmental protection is not one of collaboration or integrative problem solving (Rabe 2007). Much as is the case in Europe and other multilevel governance systems, stitching together the various policies that are emerging unilaterally presents both a huge challenge and an opportunity for devising effective policy for the near term as well as targets established for 2020 and 2050. Of course, these policy experiments also underscore the difficulty of devising policies that can work effectively over extended periods of time. As a 2008 CARB report notes, "And what will California look like in 2050? It is safe to say that no one can really predict how much technology and the state will have changed forty-two years from now. Looking back forty-two years to 1966, gasoline cost about a quarter a gallon, the state had fewer than 10 million residents, and few could conceive of personal computers, let alone the Internet" (California Air Resources Board 2008, p. 74).

Looking Ahead

The California odyssey into climate policy suggests that it is indeed possible to surmount political opposition and enact a wide range of policies to reduce greenhouse gases. As many states continue to enact their own policies and then link them together in some fashion, perhaps the politics of "doing something" on climate change is less formidable than once thought, even in the United States. This underscores the importance not only of taking some form of collective action but

10. Office of the Governor, "California, New York Agree to Explore Linking Greenhouse Gas Emission Credit Trading Markets; Gov. Schwarzenegger Tours Carbon Trading Floor," press release, Sacramento, October 16, 2006, p. 1.

also of developing policies that can be implemented reasonably effectively. The once-common presumptions that climate governance would be confined to vertical linkages between international regimes and member nations seem increasingly outmoded, raising the question of how best to weave together policies and networks across levels of government and traditional governmental boundaries.

California's experience to date gives considerable pause concerning the implementation prospects for a number of the key planks in its ambitious climate policy agenda. Few successful models are available for emulation, thereby placing the state in a unique position to begin to invent the wheel of climate governance. At the very time federal institutions such as Congress begin to give serious thought to various climate policy options it is evident that many of the issues challenging California will also confront any future federal policy. These problems may well be particularly profound at the federal level, because for a decade federal agencies have been precluded from taking on the kind of creative, entrepreneurial roles so many of their state counterparts have assumed. As a result, federal institutions may be poorly equipped for the inevitable challenges of climate governance, yet much congressional activity thus far presumes that any enactment will be followed by extensive collaboration across multiple federal units. State engagement provides a unique outlet for intergovernmental policy learning by Congress, including the possible development of a collaborative approach across governmental levels that might reflect the best features of a network approach. To date, Congress has devoted remarkably little attention to governance details, including careful scrutiny of existing state policies or experience from abroad. This suggests the sobering possibility of an intergovernmental collision rather than constructive collaboration.

References

Adams, Linda. 2006. "California Leading the Fight against Global Warming." *ECOStates*, Summer, pp. 14–16.

Bosso, Christopher J. 2005. *Environment, Inc.: From Grassroots to Beltway*. University Press of Kansas.

Brown, Matthew. 2001. *California's Power Crisis: What Happened? What Can We Learn?* Washington: National Conference of State Legislatures.

Brown, Susan. 2005. *Global Climate Change and California*. Sacramento: California Energy Commission.

California Air Resources Board. 2007. *Proposed Early Actions to Mitigate Climate Change in California*. Sacramento.

———. 2008. "Climate Change Draft Scoping Plan: June 2008 Discussion Draft." Sacramento.

California Climate Action Team. 2006. "Climate Action Team Report to Governor Schwarzenegger and the California Legislature." Sacramento.

Carpenter, Daniel. 2001. *The Forging of Bureaucratic Autonomy*. Harvard University Press.

Fiorino, Daniel. 2006. *The New Environmental Regulation*. MIT Press.

Goldsmith, Stephen, and William D. Eggers. 2004. *Governance by Network: The New Shape of the Public Sector*. Brookings.

Hamilton, James T. 2005. *Regulation through Revelation: The Origin, Politics, and Impacts of the Toxics Release Inventory Program.* Cambridge University Press.

Jones, Charles O. 1975. *Clean Air: The Policies and Politics of Pollution Control.* University of Pittsburgh Press.

Kettl, Donald F. 2007. *System under Stress: Homeland Security and American Politics.* Revised edition. Washington: CQ Press.

McCarthy, James. 2007. *California's Waiver Request to Control Greenhouse Gases under the Clean Air Act.* Washington: Congressional Research Service.

Montpetit, Eric. 2003. *Misplaced Distrust: Policy Networks and the Environment in France, the United States, and Canada.* University of British Columbia Press.

Orr, Shannon K. 2006. "Policy Subsystems and Regimes: Organized Interests and Climate Change Policy." *Policy Studies Journal* 34, no. 2 (2006): 147–69.

Petek, Sonja, and Mark Baldassare. 2007. *Public Opinion and Global Warming in California.* San Francisco: Public Policy Institute of California.

Rabe, Barry G. 2004. *Statehouse and Greenhouse: The Emerging Politics of American Climate Change Policy.* Brookings.

———. 2007. "Environmental Policy and the Bush Era: The Collision Between the Administrative Presidency and State Experimentation." *Publius: The Journal of Federalism* 37, no. 3 (Summer): 413–31.

———. 2008a. "Regionalism and Global Climate Change Policy: Revisiting Multistate Collaboration as an Intergovernmental Management Tool." In *Intergovernmental Management for the 21st Century,* edited by Timothy J. Conlan and Paul L. Posner, pp. 176–205. Brookings.

———. 2008b. "States on Steroids: The Intergovernmental Odyssey of American Climate Change Policy." *Review of Policy Research* 25, no. 2: 105–28.

State of California. 2005. *Energy Action Plan II: Implementation Roadmap for Energy Policies.* Sacramento: California Energy Commission and California Public Utilities Commission.

Stavins, Robert N., Judson Jaffe, and Todd Schatzki. 2007. *Too Good to Be True? An Examination of Three Economic Assessments of California Climate Change Policy.* Washington: American Enterprise Institute–Brookings Joint Center for Regulatory Studies.

Swope, Christopher. 2007. "Powering Down: Can Utilities Make Money on Energy Efficiency?" *Governing* (August): 24–30.

4

Networks in the Shadow of Government: The Chesapeake Bay Program

PAUL POSNER

The Chesapeake Bay is the largest estuary in North America, and with its watershed is home to more than 3,600 species and 16 million people. The watershed covers a land area of more than 64,000 square miles and includes portions of six states—Maryland, Virginia, Delaware, Pennsylvania, West Virginia and New York—and the District of Columbia. In recent decades, the Bay's ability to support fisheries and other forms of wildlife has been undermined by growing quantities of nutrients and other pollutants. More than 90 percent of the Bay is impaired, with low dissolved oxygen levels and poor water clarity, which undermines its ability to support diverse fisheries and serve the economic and recreational needs of the communities in its basin. Many of the sources of the pollution are diffuse, nonpoint sources—agriculture, urban runoff, septic fields, and air pollution—in addition to the more localized point sources of pollution, municipal and industrial wastewater.

With the many actors responsible for the problem and possible solutions, a network approach involving partnerships of governmental, nonprofit, and select private profit-making entities emerged to muster the necessary resources, authority, expertise, and political support to clean up the Bay. Since 1983, a network has become institutionalized in the Chesapeake Bay Program, a collaborative watershed management partnership of the surrounding states, the District of Columbia,

The author wishes to thank Jennifer Golub for her assistance in developing this chapter.

the Environmental Protection Administration and other federal agencies and non-profit advocacy groups, and local governments. The partnership has become a leading example of collaborative environmental governance; it was the inspiration for the creation of the National Estuary Program, which encompasses the governance of twenty-eight other major watersheds throughout the country. As a widely respected and long-lived collaboration, the Chesapeake Bay Program serves as a bellwether of both the promise and the pitfalls of network management in addressing complex, "wicked" problems such as the cleanup of major water basins throughout the country. In this chapter, the development of the network is chronicled, its management structure analyzed, some of its major accomplishments documented, and the challenges facing the network examined as it wrestles with the difficult prospects of restoring water quality to the Chesapeake Bay. This case study suggests some important lessons for the role that networks can play in addressing some of the most difficult policy problems facing the U.S. watershed system.

Frameworks for Conceptualizing Common-Pool Governance Issues

There have been several schools of thought about the politics of environmental sustainability for such "common pool" resources as the Chesapeake. One school of thought, associated with those such as Garrett Hardin who write about "the tragedy of the commons," suggest that problems of common-pool resources ("the commons") call for centralized regulatory approaches.[1] According to this thinking, voluntary cooperation will succumb to opportunistic shirking by many actors who will free-ride on the sacrifices of others and undermine collaboration in the process. Athough acknowledging that collaboration can prompt improved social relationships and dialog among stakeholders, some commentators suggest that collaborative institutions create the perception of progress while failing to bring about substantive change in behavior, which can be consistently produced only through regulatory approaches.[2]

Those in the school of Elinor Ostrom champion bottom-up collaboration that they argue can effectively govern common-pool resources through locally devised collective choice frameworks. In this tradition, sustainable environmental frameworks can best be arrived at not through central regulation but through grassroots efforts to organize coalitions and institutions that mitigate temptations to free-ride and opt out of such networks.[3] Potential shirking of collective responsibilities and other conflicts among responsible parties can be mitigated by collaborations that promote information sharing and goal congruence based on trust and reciprocity. Actors outside the ambit of traditional regulatory programs, such as farmers, can

1. Hardin (1982).
2. Kenney (2000).
3. Ostrom (1990).

be brought into these arrangements, providing them at least with the opportunity to bargain with the other actors in the network.[4] These collaborations promise to span boundaries and bring in the many actors whose cooperation is vital to solving environmental problems, providing opportunities to interact, share information, and pool resources. Networks enhance agreements by strengthening credibility of commitments that build trust and reciprocity.

For many years, federal environmental policy in general and water pollution control strategies in particular have focused primarily on a top-down regulatory approach, with an emphasis on point sources of pollution, such as sewage treatment plants, which are most directly amenable to measurement and control. The top-down model was prompted partly by the perception that state and local regulations of point sources were too weak or scattered to solve the nation's water pollution problems. Although some states and localities initiated strong programs, these were easily undermined by neighboring jurisdictions who exported their problems to others while encouraging the relocation of businesses tempted by low-cost regulations.[5] The top-down federal compliance approach was manifest in the EPA's approval of permits to individual public and private facilities regulating water pollution—important building blocks that are necessary but not sufficient to address the outcomes of clean water that all stakeholders desire for the nation's watersheds. Some observers, in fact, suggest that the point source permit programs have encouraged polluters to act independently rather than collaboratively, concerned only about their own permits and not the broader cumulative effect on water basin quality.[6]

Over the years, Congress recognized that controlling pollution from point sources would be insufficient to clean up the nation's waters and adopted several tools to address the threats to water quality posed by nonpoint sources. First, states were required to develop management plans to reduce nonpoint sources for "impaired waters" listed by the states. Although the EPA had to approve the states' plans, it could not mandate specific measures, reflecting congressional recognition of the politically sensitive land-use, zoning, and agricultural practices at the root of nonpoint source pollution. Second, for waters where EPA point source permits were not sufficient to enable a body of water to meet standards, a state must establish a Total Maximum Daily Load (TMDL) prescribing total limits for each pollutant from point and nonpoint sources and natural background levels. If the pollution level exceeds the standard, states may withhold new or renewed permits from point sources as a way to gain leverage over the total water quality equation. Although states are responsible for TMDL implementation, studies suggest that many have shied away from prescribing implementation plans for dealing with nonpoint pollution sources.[7]

4. Lubell (2004).
5. Donahue (1997).
6. Koontz and others (2004, p. 17).
7. National Academy of Public Administration (2007, p. 24).

Oversight of the TMDL process can come from several sources. The EPA can intervene by writing the TMDL if the state fails to do so. Although the federal government itself cannot plan or mandate implementation measures to actually meet the TMDL limits, it can use the lever of its review of point source permits to help meet TMDL load levels by ratcheting up standards for point sources such as sewage treatment plants. Environmental groups are watchful stewards of this process, filing lawsuits when it appears that governments are not cleaning up impaired waters.

The Emergence of the Environmental Collaboration Model

The traditional command-and-control regulatory approach suffers from limitations when applied to the problem of diffuse, nonpoint source pollution. As noted above, restoring impaired waters requires changes in local zoning, agricultural land management, and urban development programs that are often beyond the direct command of both federal and state governments. Moreover, traditional regulation was anchored in media-specific approaches that were insufficient to restore waters that were impaired as a result of complex interactions across media including air, water, and hazardous wastes.

Some twenty years after the founding of the EPA, many had come to realize that centralized federal efforts were insufficient to solve diffuse environmental problems.[8] Environmental collaborations arose as an alternative to traditional regulatory models to deal with the increasingly wicked problems epitomized by dirty water. Paul Sabatier and his colleagues have written that the "era of watershed collaboration" began in earnest in the mid-1980s.[9] Spurred partly by bottom-up regional, state, and local initiatives, the EPA promoted the collaborative model in the 1990s to engage the critical stakeholders in a broader, holistic approach to restore impaired waters. The agency's National Estuary Program, established in 1987, has developed comprehensive management plans for twenty-eight estuaries. In 1994 the EPA established the Watershed Academy, which offers training for the various actors involved in watershed management and produces manuals to help actors develop strategies for restoring impaired waters.[10]

Restoring impaired waters in watersheds spanning jurisdictional boundaries offers a "textbook" case for collaborative network governance. In the environmental arena, collaborations provided officials with the tools to steer clear of gridlock and lawsuits by engaging stakeholders in the policymaking process of setting watershed goals, thereby promoting more informed decisions, enhancing the legitimacy of decisions, and improving communities' capacity to govern their own affairs.

8. Dewitt (1994).
9. Sabatier, Focht, and Lubell (2005, chapter 1).
10. See the EPA's Watershed Academy website (www.epa.gov/owow/watershed/wacademy).

Collaborative approaches rest on voluntary cooperation as the principal strategy to mobilize collective action.[11] Unlike ad hoc coalitions, many watershed networks do not disband after tasks are completed but remain institutionalized to achieve multiple goals.[12] Robert Agranoff maintains that networks range in scale across four types: informational, developmental, outreach, and action. Action networks are the most ambitious in seeking to develop and implement policy objectives.[13] Each of these types of network can be found in the watershed arena.

Governance arrangements in watersheds vary as well, ranging from federally sponsored and managed networks to bottom-up committees of local actors to collaborative superagencies.[14] In a paper chronicling efforts to clean up the Great Lakes, Barry C. Rabe and Marc Gaden argue that neither the top-down regulatory nor bottom-up collaborative perspective alone suffices to encompass the range of activities that have led to demonstrable improvements in the sustainability of that basin's water quality. Rather, both approaches have been pivotal in the Great Lakes arena.[15] In fact, many collaborative environmental partnerships constitute a middle ground between grassroots and top-down regulation. Tomas Koontz and his colleagues note that governments play a wide range of roles in fostering and steering grassroots initiatives.[16] In some cases, government agencies serve the network as the hub and provide important information and motivation through scientific data and the threat of regulatory action. In other cases, government agencies adopt the outcomes of collaborative networks as public policy.

Despite the obvious advantages that can flow from a collaborative, networked approach to environmental governance, the approach itself has aroused controversy within environmental and academic communities. Collaboration is inherently fragile—bringing together people with both shared and different interests. Lynne Zucker writes that self-interest and a tendency toward disorganization conspire against it.[17] Michael McGuire suggests that these networks can be swamped by "collaborative inertia" as participants fail to agree on goals and fail to sustain trust, acting on their self-interest when it conflicts with that of the collaboration partners.[18]

In contrast with top-down regulatory models, collaborations require governments to bargain with diverse actors with conflicting interests, potentially com-

11. Altrer and Haige (1993).

12. McGuire (2006, p. 36).

13. Agranoff (2007).

14. Mark Lubell and others, "Conclusions and Recommendations," in Sabatier, Focht, and Lubell (2005, p. 262).

15. Barry G. Rabe and Marc Gaden, "Sustainability in a Regional Context: The Case of the Great Lakes Basin," unpublished paper, 2007.

16. Koontz and others (2004).

17. Zucker (1988).

18. McGuire (2006, p. 36).

promising or undermining important public values and interests.[19] Collaborative networks can also institutionalize advantages by placing certain actors in central roles and excluding others, a phenomenon called "closedness" in the network literature.[20] Political scientists such as Theodore Lowi and Grant McConnell raised these questions about federal collaboration with private interests more than forty years ago, in the 1960s. The danger was that public power might be handed to collectives of private interests, potentially undermining broader interests in the process.[21] It is unclear whether purely voluntary collaboration provides sufficient leverage to engage and overcome the resistance of actors that oppose network goals and interests. Pressed to govern by consensus, networks may squander their leverage over key actors in the interest of harmony and network maintenance. Finally, networks are administratively challenging to sustain. Relying on voluntary participation, these nonbureaucratic forms of collective action nonetheless require facilitation and information sharing.

Ironically, the same advantages that prompt the formation of collaborative networks in the U.S. federal system can also prove their undoing. The dispersion of power and complexity of interests provide strong impetus for adopting collaborative networks, but those very same factors can undermine the cohesion needed for the network to reach agreement on meaningful goals and to engage the commitment of key actors in implementing policy goals.[22]

The Chesapeake Bay as a Network Opportunity

In many respects, the Chesapeake Bay presented an ideal opportunity for collaborative governance. Many of the factors that network research posits as facilitating the formation of networks were present in the area during the inception of the Bay program in 1983.[23] In Ostrom's analysis, biophysical conditions, attributes of the community, and institutional arrangements together form the matrix that enables networks to grow.[24]

The biophysical condition of the Bay was perceived to be fast deteriorating, and the problems were too dispersed for any one government or program to deal with effectively. For instance, the contributors to the nutrient and sediment runoff that has impaired the Bay include a daunting array of actors: sod and row crop farms, lawn service companies, feedlots, nurseries, kennels, septic tanks, urban and suburban development, power plants and automobiles, wastewater treatment plants, and dairy, poultry, and beef farms. The agricultural sector is the largest source of

19. Ingram (1977).
20. L. Schaap and M. J. W. van Twist, "The Dynamics of Closedness in Networks," in Kickert, Klijn, and Koppenjan (1993, pp. 62–78).
21. McConnell (1961) and Lowi (1979).
22. Sabatier, Focht, and Lubell (2005).
23. For analysis of variables facilitating networks, see Thomson and Perry (2006).
24. Ostrom (1990).

nutrient pollution—both nitrogen and phosphorus—and sediment runoff. Water runoff picks up these nutrients, sediment, and concentrates from animal feeding operations and deposits them in streams and other tributaries to the Bay. Point sources such as wastewater treatment plants are the second largest contributor, followed by urban runoff from stormwater, commercial and residential development, and atmospheric pollution.[25] The number of actors possessing partial authority and resources necessary for effective restoration of the Bay is also daunting, including six states and the District of Columbia; 3,169 local governments; 678 watershed associations; two interstate river basin commissions; thirty-six tributary teams; 87,000 farm owners; 5 million to 6 million homeowners; hundreds of lawn-care companies and nurseries; land developers; construction companies; agribusiness and other companies; and large numbers of nonprofit organizations whose missions focused on the Bay.

Many of the attributes of the Bay community also lend themselves to supporting a broad-based network for the Bay's restoration. The presence of social capital and bonds of trust among actors throughout the Bay region has been one of the important assets supporting the network. Actors across the region have a history of working together on common problems for many years, and a common framework for defining and measuring the problems began to form some fifty years before the formal establishment of the Chesapeake Bay Program. As early as 1933, an Interstate Conference on the Bay was convened to address deteriorating water quality. The Army Corps of Engineers began a study in 1965 that culminated in a seven-volume report issued in 1973. A major environmental interest group, the Chesapeake Bay Foundation, was formed and started the "Save the Bay" campaign in 1966. Broad agreement had crystallized on the nature of the problem among both advocates and scientists, which many view as essential to legitimate and sustain a network.[26]

A strong sense of place is felt by many actors and publics surrounding the Bay. A former leader of the Chesapeake Bay Program said that "love for the Bay" is the most vital emotion that fueled the creation and sustenance of the Bay network.[27] The Bay serves a wide range of interests, ranging from those people like the watermen who depend on it for their livelihood to those who use it for recreation and still others who appreciate the ecological wonders it harbors. The overall sense of urgency about the nature of the problems facing the Bay has gained widespread acceptance across many interest groups, even if the solutions do not always garner comparable support.[28] The compelling nature of the problem has been reinforced by federal regulatory triggers that have added a sense of urgency to the

25. National Academy of Public Administration (2007, p. 24).
26. Haas (1992).
27. Rebecca Hanmer (EPA director, Chesapeake Bay Program), statement at a session of the National Academy of Public Administration, Washington, D.C., June 17, 2007.
28. Bryson, Crosby, and Stone (2006).

water quality problems besetting the Bay. As will be discussed further, the failure to restore the Bay could have significant regulatory consequences for all actors, with major consequences for regional development.[29] This pressure to meet regulatory goals can prompt actors to overcome the natural inertia among competing groups that prevents networks from forming or from taking decisive action to resolve problems.[30]

Finally, the institutional infrastructure facilitated the formation of the network for the Bay. Network formation and sustenance entails real transaction costs and risks to participants. Establishing information and scientific frames that all can agree on is a vital first step that requires expensive investments in science and informational capacities. Building accountability frameworks to assure network members that free riding will be controlled and dealt with is another vital task in building network governance institutions. The Chesapeake Bay Program had several advantages at the outset that enabled it to deal with the these potential obstacles. First, many of the key actors had a history of dealing with one another in other settings, which established the basic foundation for trust that is so important to building and maintaining collaboration among competing interests. Second, the network was centrally supported by the EPA, which provided a cadre of dedicated staff and also marshaled scientific resources to build models and metrics providing benchmarks to assess progress and assign accountability for restoration goals. Mark Lubell and colleagues found that external support and aid are significant factors in promoting the establishment and sustenance of watershed networks in other parts of the nation.[31]

Although the Chesapeake Bay embodies many elements that promote collaboration, other aspects can frustrate collaboration. Research suggests that small watersheds facilitate collaboration, because the number of stakeholders is smaller and stakeholders' contributions to creating watershed problems are clearer than in larger watersheds. But the Chesapeake Bay is one of the largest estuaries in the world, one surrounded by large land masses whose complex land-use patterns affect water quality to a much greater extent than in most watersheds. The Bay has the highest land-to-water ratio of any estuary in the world and is thus vitally affected by the many widely differing land-use policies and practices bordering its waters.

Such a complex watershed also multiplies the number of actors and blurs their relative contribution to problems. Apportioning responsibility for changes as well as monitoring and measuring the impact of network members' activities is a daunting task. Finally, the Bay actors are by no means homogeneous. The six states and the District of Columbia have differing political and policy priorities. The relative salience of Bay problems varies among states and communities; for example, Maryland and Virginia have a more immediate and direct connection than more distant

29. Heikkila and Gerlak (2005).
30. Zartman (1991).
31. Lubell and others (2002).

communities in Pennsylvania and New York, which are, however, also part of the watershed. The 3,000-plus local governments in the six states and the District may share a general commitment to clean up the Bay, but they also compete with each other for jobs and resources. Farming and agribusiness interests have a strong resistance to collective arrangements that regulate land-use practices, particularly when such rules are not accompanied by funding. Thus, although all agree on the overall objective of restoring the health of the Bay, the basis for cooperation can be undermined if certain actors think they bear a disproportionate responsibility for the cleanup, which puts them at a competitive disadvantage with other actors in the same market or region.

The Institutionalization of the Bay Network

Beginning in 1983, the network that emerged to support the cleanup of the Bay is among the longest-standing water basin partnerships in the nation. Centered in the Chesapeake Bay Program Office, managed by the EPA, the network began as a bottom-up initiative from local and regional citizens and environmental groups. Among the most prominent were the Chesapeake Bay Foundation and the Alliance for the Chesapeake Bay. The Bay Foundation started in 1967 with a group of Baltimore businessmen concerned about the future health of the Bay. Starting with a focus on public education through its "Save the Bay" program, the foundation established itself as a key lobbying and advocacy group, building to its current 170-person staff, $20 million budget, and more than 150,000 members. The Alliance for the Chesapeake Bay was established in 1971 to promote restoration not through lobbying but through collaboration and partnerships by funding seed money projects and convening groups of public and private officials to develop agreement on such issues as Bay-sensitive zoning codes. The Chesapeake Bay Trust was formed in Maryland in the 1980s to bring together financial contributions to support grants to civic groups and nonprofit organizations.

State and local governments also joined the coalition in support of Bay restoration. In the 1970s, the Chesapeake Bay Commission was established as a tri-state organization representing and advising the legislatures of Virginia, Maryland, and Pennsylvania. The commission has a small staff that identifies problems requiring interstate action and recommends actions to encourage effective restoration of the Bay to the states, the federal government, and other interested parties.

In the mid-1970s, these groups recognized that they needed broader support from the federal government in general and the EPA in particular to support an effective program to clean up the Bay. Building on studies by the Army Corps of Engineers that documented the decline of the Bay as a water resource, local and state officials approached their congressional delegations to gain support for an

EPA study of the Bay. The agency resisted, but Senator Charles "Mac" Mathias (R-Md.), through an earmark, provided the EPA with $26 million for the study. The study, produced in the early 1980s, established definitive problem statements and scientific baselines documenting the nature and extent of nutrient pollution and its effect on Bay waters. The complex watershed models initiated in this EPA study formed a critical component in legitimizing collective action to clean up the Bay by providing definitive and credible guidance in developing water quality standards and allocating pollution reduction goals.

The EPA study became the catalyst for the formation of the network. An interstate and intergovernmental Chesapeake Bay Program Office structure was established to give focus and support for what had already become an informal network. The Chesapeake Bay Program did not arise from formal federal statutes, as had many other watershed collaboratives.[32] The formal network began with a signed agreement among the governors of the three primary states (Maryland, Virginia, and Pennsylvania), the District of Columbia, the Environmental Protection Administration, and the Chesapeake Bay Commission acting on behalf of the three state legislatures. These formal partners were the original signatories of the 1983 Chesapeake Bay Agreement. The partnership was subsequently extended to the headwater states of Delaware, New York, and West Virginia.

The Design and Management of the Network

Sustaining networks and collaborations is not easy; it involves organizing and maintaining cooperation among actors with differing values, interests, and accountabilities. Public choice and game theory say that collective action problems mean that cooperation will be difficult and achieved only under duress.[33] However, a successful network is able to develop programs that convince network partners that the prospects for achieving their goals are better met through joint than separate actions. Although risks of self-dealing and shirking always haunt networks, successful networks help actors mitigate the risks of defection by institutionalizing rules that formalize commitments and forge bonds of trust and experience that in turn fortify cooperation.

The Bay network has dealt with each of the challenges that networks face in institutionalizing collaboration. The program's longevity is partly a reflection of its ability to meet these challenges. The following list highlights the key issues that faced Bay partners over the years in sustaining the partnership:[34]

32. Heikkila and Gerlak (2005).

33. W. J. M. Kickert and J. F. M. Koppenjan, "Public Management and Network Management: An Overview," in Kickert, Klijn, and Koppenjan (1993).

34. See Agranoff (2007) and Kickert and Koppenjan, "Public Management and Network Management."

—*Governance.* Developing rules to make joint decisions through agreement across members and enforce agreements through credible sanctions and incentives.

—*Framing.* Establishing a compelling rationale for collaboration to legitimize participation by key actors.

—*Knowledge sharing.* Agreeing on common information and theories to reinforce the legitimacy of problem framing and reduce information asymmetries and transaction costs.

—*Facilitation.* Fostering network consensus and management of network goals by setting and conducting meetings and monitoring performance and implementation to reduce transaction costs and promote effective network performance and accountability.

—*Social capital.* Building trusting relationships among partners to increase incentives to participate in network activities.

—*Membership.* Including all actors whose cooperation is essential for solving problems to achieving network goals and establishing network legitimacy.

Governance

Governance of the Bay network is accomplished by means of what Milward and Provan would call a managed network.[35] The Chesapeake Bay Program Office is a distinct hub, with a staff consisting of the EPA and several other federal and state agencies and a series of committees. This hub maintains central facilities, facilitates meetings, and prepares agendas and briefing papers for all committee meetings, including those of state-dominated oversight committees. The EPA, widely viewed by all actors in the network as the glue that holds the network together, is accorded broad respect and credibility by all network actors. The EPA has a staff of twenty-one and a budget of more than $20 million.

The Chesapeake Bay Program is structured to develop policy and implementation plans, directives, and assistance through a committee system (figure 4-1 shows the organization of the program). The program's governance is provided through the Chesapeake Executive Council, composed of the governors of the original signatory states of Maryland, Virginia, and Pennsylvania and the mayor of the District of Columbia, the EPA, and the chair of the Chesapeake Bay Commission representing state legislatures. The Bay Program was expanded to include the headwater states of New York, Delaware, and West Virginia. The council meets annually. Staff representatives of the principals, composed largely of cabinet-level secretaries and EPA regional administrators, meet more often; the meetings are open to the public.

The council's primary work is to set overall policy through explicit agreements and policy targets agreed to by all members, as is customary with most networks.

35. Milward and Provan (2006).

Figure 4-1. *Chesapeake Bay Program Organization Chart*

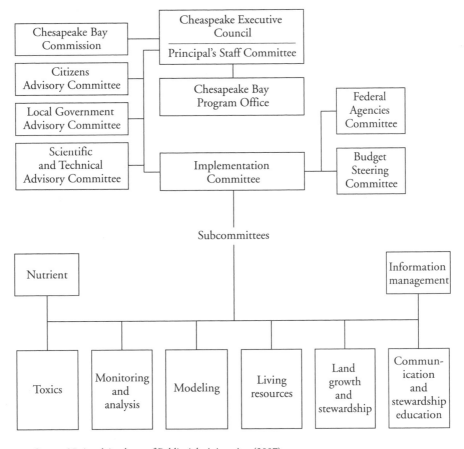

Source: National Academy of Public Administration (2007).

The agreements are key documents that provide an explicit framework and measurable goals for all network members to monitor compliance.

Among the most important committees is the Implementation Committee, which meets monthly to develop policy plans and coordinate restoration activities to support the overarching policy agreements of the principals. The committee membership is broader than the council membership, comprising representatives from the states, federal agencies, local governments, nonprofits, and academia. Other committees represent key stakeholder groups to the program, including local governments, citizen advocacy groups, federal agencies, and the scientific community. The program also maintains eight subcommittees to deal with specific types of pollution and restoration issues, including nutrients, toxics, and land use.

Framing and Knowledge Sharing

For any policy area, the definition of problems is inherently contestable, and those who can definitively frame what the debate is about have significant leverage in the policy process.[36] The problem definition for the Bay was anchored in scientific models developed by the EPA for the Chesapeake Bay Program Office. The $26 million received by the EPA in the late 1970s enabled it to conduct the definitive assessment of the problem. The resulting report established a measurable baseline that helped mobilize broader public support and provided the basis for allocating responsibility ("loads," in the environmental vernacular) across the actors for the cleanup effort.

Building on the scientific modeling of the problems, the specific goals and agreements reached among the partners for the restoration of the Bay both reflected and reinforced the collaboration. The partners adopted a series of agreements over the years establishing goals and targets for the Bay restoration. These overarching policy agreements were followed by a series of agreements, directives, plans, and technical guidance to further specify the goals. The initial 1983 agreement establishing the program was followed by agreements in 1987, 1992, and 2000. The 1987 agreement set a goal of achieving a 40 percent reduction in nutrients entering the Bay by 2000. Recognizing the critical role played by the thirty-six tributaries feeding into the Bay, the 1992 agreement called for strategies to clean up these rivers and streams to help meet the goal. The signatory states developed tributary strategies to reduce both nutrient and sediment flows to meet the overall 40 percent reduction target.

As was often the case, the setting of targets alone could not guarantee sufficient progress by the partners ultimately responsible for the cleanup. The states and the local tributary teams fell well short of the 40 percent reduction target by 2000, as the advances made in controlling pollution through policy changes were often undermined by continued growth and development throughout the watershed. With 170,000 new residents arriving annually, a recent EPA inspector general (IG) report concluded that development-associated pollution increases have overwhelmed the gains in controlling pollution from urban sources achieved through improvements in landscape design and stormwater controls.[37]

In 2000 the partners adopted a new set of targets to guide restoration through 2010. While partly motivated by continued frustrations in achieving earlier goals, Bay restoration acquired a new sense of urgency following a successful court suit in 1998 in Virginia that resulted in placing Virginia's waters on the EPA impaired waters list.[38] Although such an action normally triggers a regulatory TMDL for each of the Bay's tributaries, the states and the EPA agreed to a timetable requiring the Bay to be restored to standards by 2010 through network actions. If that

36. Rocherfort and Cobb (1994).
37. Chirigotis and others (2007).
38. *American Canoe Association* v. *EPA*, 54 F Supp 2nd 621 (E.D. 1999).

failed, the states or the EPA would be required to step in and establish a TMDL. Such a result would limit the flexibility of the states to pursue a broader range of regulatory strategies involving point and nonpoint sources of pollution. Federal and state regulators would have little choice but to ratchet up restrictions on point source pollution from wastewater treatment plants, potentially threatening to choke off new development in portions of the watershed.

The way that the court suit was resolved reflected the influence of the Chesapeake Bay Program network. Without such an institution, each state would have been on its own to deal with the legal obligations flowing from the suit and would in all likelihood have faced the consequences of a more traditional TMDL process. Instead, the institutionalization of the network enabled the states to respond to the court order together and to win time to develop new measures that reflected the broader set of tools available to the partnership for addressing both point and nonpoint source pollution.[39]

The 2000 agreement included more than a hundred commitments by the partners. A variety of measurable and unmeasurable targets were articulated to guide the restoration initiative, with the goal of removing the Bay from the impaired waters list by 2010. Specific targets included increasing the native oyster catch tenfold, restoring wetlands, achieving load reductions for nutrients for each Bay tributary, reducing the encroachment of development on forests and agricultural lands, and restoring brownfield sites. Once goals were articulated, the Bay Program worked with its partners and others to develop more detailed plans and implementation strategies to bring about the promised changes.

Following the 2000 agreement, several important steps were taken to facilitate the cleanup. First, in 2003 the EPA, in consultation with the network partners, developed new water quality criteria to better ensure that water quality goals would be reached. The standards were expanded from dissolved oxygen to include chlorophyll-a and clarity, two critical elements that have a direct bearing on the growth of underwater grasses and microscopic plants that form the food chain for Bay species. The new standards took advantage of recent advances in modeling to allocate load reductions for different portions of the Bay, based on the nature of its uses and underlying capacity. These standards are more attainable and more valid scientifically. Under the approach adopted by the network, a local water body is held to standards that are based not just on its own localized levels of pollutants but on its contribution to Bay-wide levels of pollutants. Accordingly, the network tributary loads are likely to be more stringent than those set in a traditional locality-based TMDL process.

Second, using the new criteria, annual caps were developed for nutrients and sediment to bring the Bay back to 1950s conditions. These caps were then translated into reduction goals allocated to the thirty-six tributary basins. Under the

---

39. National Academy of Public Administration (2007, p. 92).

2003 agreement, six states and Washington, D.C., accepted load limits and reductions of twice those that had been achieved for the past twenty years.[40] Under a traditional regulatory process of allocating loads under a TMDL, it would have taken a decade to reach this point. By engaging in cooperative effort, the Bay community accomplished the allocation in four years.

The point source permitting process also incorporated Bay-wide water quality goals under the network approach. Under the aegis of the Bay Program, the EPA and the seven jurisdictions, now part of the expanded Bay network, agreed to a common permitting approach to include nutrient limits in permits for wastewater treatment plans and other point sources. Notably, this Bay-wide permitting approach extends to states upstream from the Bay, an outcome resisted by up-watershed states in other regions.[41]

Facilitation and Social Capital

The program office, acting as the hub, manages the facilitation function. Simply making the hub work is itself an exercise in network management. The EPA leads the program office, but staff from other agencies are housed within the agency. State agency staff also work alongside their federal partners from time to time. In addition, other staff from federal agencies as diverse as the National Park Service, the Forest Service, and the Army Corps of Engineers have independent offices located in the same complex as the EPA Program Office. As one senior EPA manager put it, the Bay program is a case example of matrix management, where staff from many levels and agencies come together to work on common issues and projects.[42] The office not only fulfills the role of facilitating interaction across the many program committees but also provides assistance to state, local, and nonprofit organizations for various coordination, education, and monitoring programs promoting Bay-wide goals. The EPA budgets about $4 million for the office itself and allocates the remainder of its $20 million for grants and technical assistance to partners throughout the Bay region. Significantly, the allocation of this federal support by the EPA is generally based on the priorities established by the Bay network actors.[43]

The network has become institutionalized not only through the strength of the program office but also through the growth of trust and social capital among network partners. The network has promoted peer pressure and buy-in by the state partners to a set of policy goals as ambitious as they are politically demanding. The signatories have agreed to ambitious cleanup and regulatory actions that they might not have undertaken on their own. The peer pressure associated with net-

40. Environment Protection Agency (2003).

41. Michael Burke (associate director, Chesapeake Bay Program Office), testimony before the Little Hoover Commission, Sacramento, Calif., October 27, 2005.

42. Richard Batiuk, author interview, Chesapeake Bay Program Office, August 2007.

43. Hanmer statement.

works was largely responsible for gaining the buy-in of Pennsylvania, a state that must engage in significant changes in farm and urban land management practices even though most of its residents do not directly benefit from a cleaner Bay. Virginia's governor, Jim Gilmore, among the most conservative governors in the nation at the time, nonetheless agreed to the Bay agreements in 2000. The agreements articulated goals that would necessitate unprecedented regulatory changes in states' water quality standards, financial commitments to support the many enhancements of public and private infrastructure, and shifts in land use at the local level and in land practices by agricultural interests to address nonpoint source pollution and runoff from widely disparate elements throughout the Bay region. Commitment to goals was also fostered by a strong professional network among state environmental and natural resource agencies supporting the governors and Anthony A. Williams, mayor of Washington, D.C. These underlying professional relationships constituted an epistemic community that worked effectively together toward shared goals.

The states' buy-in was also reinforced by the consensus nature of the network decision rules, which in effect gave all core network actors a veto. Consensus rules ordinarily can be expected to produce buy-in, but at the cost of diluting decisions to the level of the lowest common denominator. However, the goals and standards adopted were viewed as overly ambitious and perhaps unrealistic by many. The fact that the network was not paralyzed by gridlock or inertia can be attributed in part to the important role played by federal regulatory policy in setting the agenda and in prompting anticipatory behavior to recapture control of the Bay before more stringent federal regulatory TMDLs were triggered. In the case of the Bay, the network and more direct regulatory models of collective action proved complementary.

Membership

The Chesapeake Bay Program was challenged to include in the network decisionmaking processes all significant actors with a role to play in restoring the Bay. Networks often face a tradeoff between the efficiency and inclusiveness of their decisionmaking processes. Other things being equal, a smaller number of actors will improve prospects for cohesion and conclusive decisionmaking; extending the range and types of actors threatens to complicate the decisionmaking process, as actors take advantage of consensus rules to limit or frustrate the ability of the network to take action on anything of importance. Yet the failure to involve key actors will undermine the ability of the network to achieve its goals over the longer run.

To assess the types of actors represented in the Bay network and their relative roles, the schematic in figure 4-2 was developed to depict the network. This schematic goes beyond the formal organizational structure presented earlier to illustrate the strength of the ties of various actors to the Bay Program and to each other. In the chart, the inner sector is designated by shaded boxes. These actors—

Figure 4-2. *Chesapeake Bay Network*

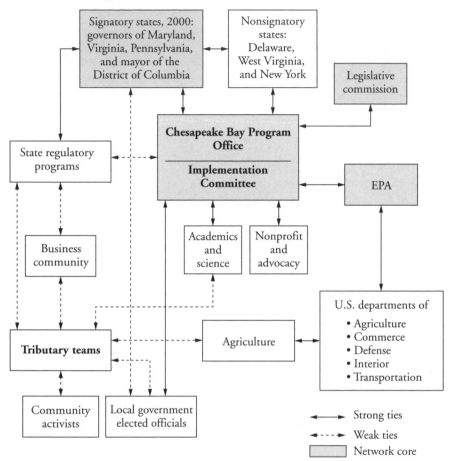

Source: Author.

the original signatory governors, the EPA, and the state legislatures—are the most central ones, as reflected by their standing as exclusive members of the executive council. The ability of this core set of actors to work together and reach agreement is reinforced by their history of collaboration, the commonality of their regulatory interests, and the support of professional staff. Other interests whose involvement and buy-in is vital to ensuring progress in the Bay restoration are not as centrally involved in decisionmaking. The three headwater states—New York, Delaware, and West Virginia—are not represented on the executive council, although their involvement and buy-in is critical to cleanup and restoration. Local governments and nonprofit organizations participate in various committees of the Chesapeake Bay Program, but the local government advisory committee reports that local governments do not have a central role in managing the network commensurate with their status as key implementers for Bay cleanup actions.[44] The advisory committee claims that local governments do not feel a sense of urgency about the 2010 deadline and do not understand the consequences of missing it.[45] The figure shows that business and agriculture are not directly tied to the network, except through their indirect ties to federal and state agencies and their participation on several subcommittees. Like local governments, the buy-in of these sectors is critical to the successful implementation of Bay-wide goals.

Figure 4-2 also shows the role played by tributary organizations, the substate entities established by the states in the Bay Program to carry forward the overarching goals at the watershed and community levels. In a sense, the tributary organizations constitute a separate network linked to the Bay Program through administrative decree and technical assistance. Although establishing the tributary teams was a crucial step in building a potential support network for achieving remediation measures, the figure shows only weak ties between these institutions and key actors, including local governments, agriculture, and business. Moreover, the figure shows no staff support offices for the tributary networks comparable to that of the Chesapeake Bay Program Office. (The implications of network participation processes for the achievement of Bay-wide restoration targets are examined in the section on network progress.)

The Federal Role

The prominent role played by federal agency officials in network management was clearly an important factor in the cohesion achieved over the years. Whereas network research has emphasized the capacity of actors at the service delivery level to achieve collaboration from the bottom up, the role of federal government agencies has not received significant attention by researchers. The EPA achieved its influence in two ways: by framing action setting through mandates and subsidies and through active engagement with subnational actors at state and local levels.[46] As O'Toole and his colleagues suggest, actors in networks can reach policy consensus through anticipatory reaction to the prospect of government regulation. The information and scientific modeling provided by the EPA also stimulated and supported network cohesion by providing problem definition and definitive information that all could support and use as the foundation for policy development and monitoring.[47] Underlying this role was the authority and

44. International City and County Management Association (2007).

45. Local Government Advisory Committee (2006).

46. L. J. O'Toole Jr., K. I. Hanf, and P. L. Hupe, "Managing Implementation Processes in Networks," in Kickert, Klijn, and Koppenjan (1993, p. 144).

47. Koontz and others (2004).

capacity enjoyed by EPA officials to engage with lateral networks in mutually supportive relationships. The agency recognized correctly that over the longer term, engagement with a network would enable more expeditious and effective realization of environmental goals for the Bay than traditional command-and-control approaches. Agranoff suggests that some agencies, which he calls "conductive organizations," more readily and easily can delegate to field structures and devolve their authority to collaborative partnerships.[48]

From the federal officials' standpoint, the network conferred significant benefits and advantages compared with traditional regulatory approaches. The network enabled collaboration to occur outside the normal constraints, such as the Federal Advisory Committee Act, that inhibit federal agencies from consulting informally with partners. The EPA also provided important input and support to the states as they developed their own regulations to implement Bay-wide goals. EPA staff testified in support of state agency proposals before the legislatures of states involved in the network. From the standpoint of one EPA official, the ability to work more informally with states provided better leverage with less conflict. By providing a venue for informal consensus building among federal and state officials, state standards received far more expeditious federal approval.[49]

This is not to deny the existence of tensions and conflicts among Bay network partners. The EPA itself was torn between its allegiance to the home agency and the network. EPA officials of the Bay Program experienced conflicts with other EPA officials over water quality regulations for the Bay that departed from conventional federal regulatory models. In effect, EPA staff had become intergovernmental officials responsive to a broader set of constituencies than their own nominal agency community. EPA Bay Program officials report having had to interact with a wide range of interests throughout the Bay literally day and night as they sought input and buy-in to network goals. This had consequences for accountability, as the tensions spilled over into the performance management arena. With pay partly driven by performance achieved during the year, EPA staff were encouraged to develop measures that specifically focused on what agency officials contributed to complex problems—what is known as output measures. In keeping with their network focus, EPA Bay Program officials departed from this model to measure themselves on the ultimate outcomes for the Bay, that is, whether the Bay itself met its broader restoration goals. As a result, when nutrient reduction goals for the Bay were not achieved, program officials appeared to fall short of their ambitious performance targets. Since employee pay was partly driven by the performance metrics at EPA, these tensions had both programmatic and personal consequences.[50]

48. Agranoff (2007, pp. 192–97).

49. Richard Batiuk, author interview, Chesapeake Bay Program Office, August 22, 2007.

50. Statements provided by former Chesapeake Bay Program officials at a meeting at the National Academy of Public Administration on June 19, 2007.

The EPA's leadership of the federal agencies was also limited by the failure of these agencies to buy in and support Bay priorities. Though leading a multi-agency federal agencies committee, the EPA was often unable to gain these agencies' buy-in in support of federal programs to meet the unique needs of the Bay cleanup. For example, the Agriculture Department was unable to significantly adapt its programs for farm conservation to the Bay's needs, resulting in funding shortfalls and coordination problems. Other agencies were unwilling to allow their employees to work at the Chesapeake Bay Program Office in Annapolis, Maryland, for fear of losing control of their staff to another agency. Collaboration was complicated by the inability of the EPA's Chesapeake Bay Program office, attached to the EPA regional office, to communicate directly with policymaking officials in headquarters offices of the other federal agencies.

Network Progress

The development of the standards and allocation of nutrient loads and reduction targets were important policymaking achievements. It took the first five years of the new millennium for states to develop implementation plans, standards, and loads for nutrients and sediments. The tributary load allocations were accomplished in 2003, and the common Bay-wide permitting strategy was completed in 2004. However, real progress would depend on the implementation of measures within each state to achieve real reductions in nutrients and sediments, entailing changes in behavior by the many widely distributed actors from local governments to farmers to homeowners.

The network has made some important advances. In 2006 the Bay Program reported that half of the pollution reduction measures necessary to achieve the 2010 nutrient reduction goals have been undertaken. Treatment plant discharges have been steeply reduced, with discharges of nitrogen at 72 percent and phosphorous at 87 percent of the reduction goals. Watershed land preservation efforts have protected 6.83 million acres, and the striped bass population has been restored.

The Government Accountability Office reports that eleven federal agencies, the three states, and the District of Columbia provided $3.7 billion from 1995 to 2004 to restore the Bay.[51] Of this total, federal agencies provided $972 million and the states and the District provided $2.7 billion for such projects as treatment plants, land acquisition, stormwater upgrades, and community education. As noted, the network approach itself has provided the impetus for progress in goal setting and consensus building between federal and state officials. The National Academy of Public Administration concludes that if leadership were left up to individual states, the restoration would not have come so far.[52]

51. U.S. Government Accountability Office (2005).
52. National Academy of Public Administration (2007, p. 102).

Despite this progress, the goals pledged for 2010 to head off EPA regulatory action are now in jeopardy. Specifically, less than a third of the water quality goals have been met. Dissolved oxygen is only 37 percent of the 2010 goal. In addition, 53 percent of tidal rivers had fish with chemical contaminants high enough to warrant advisories against eating them. The acreage of underwater grasses declined by 25 percent in 2006. Blue crab, oyster, and shad populations remained well below restoration goals, at 57 percent, 9 percent, and 3 percent, respectively, of goals. The EPA has stated that "it could take decades to reach target loads and even longer to reach ecological restoration goals."[53] The EPA inspector general found that it would take twenty-eight years to meet the nitrogen reduction targets and fifteen years to meet both the sediment and phosphorus targets.[54]

The progress achieved in policymaking has been undermined by the wicked nature of the underlying problems and the challenges of gaining the support of the numerous actors responsible for the problem and the solution. It is estimated that the pollution increases associated with population growth and land development (conversion of agriculture land to urban and suburban development) have overwhelmed the gains achieved from policy changes involving improved landscape design, stormwater management, and point source treatment.[55] Earlier agreements were undermined by the same forces, which is what prompted the revised agreement of 2000.

Some of the barriers are economic and environmental, but the key obstacles stem from the broadly distributed nature of the problem, the wide range of actors responsible, and the profound political ambivalence associated with the cleanup goals themselves. The network for policy development is actually quite different from the network for policy implementation. As the Bay network turns to policy implementation, an entirely new range of actors and tools comes into focus with its own challenges and barriers. Although a single network exists for developing policy agreements, the implementation of those initiatives is governed by a far more informal and less cohesive set of localized implementation networks, each with its own values and interests.[56] Many strategies lack sufficient funding and coordination to come to fruition. Further, some strategies and goals are widely viewed as infeasible—a tenfold increase in the oyster harvest is viewed as unlikely because of degraded habitats. The agency concluded that the lack of local actor buy-in to network goals and strategies was among the most important barriers to progress.[57] The disconnects between policy development and implementation are a well-known challenge for public administration and have been well docu-

53. Chesapeake Bay Program, News and Notes, March 31, 2006.
54. EPA Inspector General (2006).
55. Chirigotis and others (2007).
56. Hrern and Porter (1982).
57. U.S. Government Accountability Office (2005).

mented in the implementation literature.[58] The network literature has also recognized that separate networks can exist for different tasks.[59]

The daunting nature of the challenges can be illustrated by assessing the prospects for meeting the goals and reduction targets by several major sectors in Maryland.

Agriculture

The network and the states assigned agriculture the greatest share of cleanup responsibility because gains from reducing agricultural runoff will constitute 64 percent of the nutrient and sediment reductions while accounting for only 13 percent of total estimated cleanup costs. Maryland's strategy is based largely on voluntary implementation of best management practices by farmers through such actions as conservation tillage, soil conservation, crop cover planting, and manure transport initiatives. The only practice likely to meet its goals is nutrient and manure transport, aided by a state mandate requiring higher-income farmers to prepare nutrient management plans and by state assistance for the transport of manure from animal operations with excess waste.

Agricultural targets have proved elusive across the entire Bay watershed. A report by the EPA inspector general found that a significant percentage of the best management practices are not being implemented at all because farmers do not recognize them as cost-effective, technically feasible, or in their long-term interests. For example, alternative crops such as switch grass used for carbon sequestration currently have no market; planting cover crops entails seed and labor costs with uncertain prospects for marketing. The report concluded that the EPA does not enjoy the trust of the agricultural community and will need to establish relationships with the various agricultural organizations to promote the Bay Program's cleanup goals. Although most of the practices in the tributary strategy are to be implemented voluntarily, the agricultural community is concerned that the EPA as a regulatory agency may use information gained from their cooperation to take enforcement actions. Agriculture program officials stated that they did not want to jeopardize the trust that has developed over the decades with private landowners and the agricultural community by strengthening alignment with the EPA, which is focused more closely on the regulatory approach to corrective actions.[60]

Urban Sources

Growth and development are two escalating trends that undermine any progress already made toward reaching the Bay restoration goals. Growth is projected to

58. Hill and Hupe (2002).

59. Robert I. Agranoff, "Responding to Human Crises: Intergovernmental Policy Networks", in Gage and Mandell (1990).

60. EPA Inspector General (2006).

continue, so the important question is "Can state and local governments join together to adopt more environmentally sensitive growth strategies?" The Bay Program estimates that $18 billion will be needed for reducing loads from developed lands, much of it for stormwater management, septic tank upgrades, and initiating best management practices. For wastewater treatment, Maryland enacted a flush tax on users of sewage treatment plants, which goes into the Bay restoration fund for upgrading plants to reduce nutrients. However, other states have not adopted this measure.

The 2000 agreement commits to a 30 percent reduction in harmful sprawl, but definitions and indicators have yet to be developed. Maryland has a statewide plan to redirect development into priority funding areas, but the state does not have sufficient tools to enforce growth management approaches and has yet to gain the essential buy-in of county governments, which are responsible for land use and zoning. Several counties with strong environmental constituencies have risen to the challenge. For instance, Anne Arundel County has growth management on its agenda and has stopped several development projects. But other counties are deterred by economic development interests, and many local officials lack the expertise—and some also the will—to revise local codes and plans that are inconsistent with statewide growth targets.[61] The legislature of Virginia, a more conservative state, has rejected statewide growth management standards, leaving development largely in the hands of local officials.

Stormwater runoff plays an important role in the pollution of the Bay. Unlike the case with other sources of nonpoint source pollution, the federal government requires permits for larger urban area systems, enforced by participating states such as Maryland to control stormwater runoff, but these permits apply only to newly developed and redeveloped lands, not to existing development. Maryland pledges to require existing development to retrofit to meet more stringent standards, but the state has decided not to mandate these standards in favor of applying them only as funding becomes available. The National Academy of Public Administration concludes that funding will fall well short of meeting the goals.[62]

Septic systems are another area where additional funding will be necessary to meet restoration goals. One in five Maryland households has a septic system, and most of them use outmoded technology. The state provides funding for upgrades, but such subsidies are limited and the state has decided not to mandate new requirements.

Tributary Networks

To implement goals, all Bay partners adopted the critical strategy of engaging local actors by establishing thirty-six tributary networks organized around major

---

61. National Academy of Public Administration (2007, p. 60).
62. Ibid., p. 57.

watersheds flowing into the Bay. Most of the pollution originates in these watersheds. It was hoped that engaging the people responsible for implementing local problems and solutions would generate buy-in and support for the restoration throughout a diffuse intergovernmental system. Each tributary team was required to develop its own strategies for achieving the clean-up targets. Flexibility was emphasized, in order to provide for variation across and within states in capacity, ecology, and priorities.

The organization of tributary networks, the development of strategies, and the accountability systems were not prescribed by the Bay Program office but were left to each state to develop. Although state plans differed, most states relied heavily on the use of best-management practices and land conservation to mitigate nutrient pollution from nonpoint source local agricultural and urban sources. Reliance on nonregulatory tools was a common theme—funding subsidies, incentives, education, and technical assistance—to win the cooperation of farmers, local governments, businesses, and homeowners. Incentives do work, but the funding is often far too limited to satisfy the overall need for improvements in the near term. The Chesapeake Bay Watershed Blue Ribbon Finance Panel reported a shortfall of $28 billion in capital and $2.7 billion in annual costs.[63]

Maryland offers a good case study of tributary-based networks. Beginning in the mid-1990s, the state has done more than most to articulate a framework for tributary governance through the appointment of tributary councils consisting of officials from local governments, agriculture, business, environmental groups, and other important actors. Unlike the Bay Program network, however, none of the tributary networks has any staff or independent funding. The state's Department of Natural Resources assigns very limited state staff to perform network facilitation functions, including technical assistance and monitoring.

The cohesive network that has been instrumental in achieving policy agreements between and among states and federal agencies has so far not been evident at the tributary level. The tributary networks have turned out to be voluntary associations of unevenly committed partners that have comparatively little capacity to persuade the wide range of stakeholders to make the changes in land use, zoning, and economic development so important to controlling nutrient invasion of waterways. The fact that the officials on these teams are appointed by the governor rather than by local governments may inhibit the local ownership that may be essential to mobilize support. While the state has structured membership to be broadly representative of the stakeholders in water basins, the chair of a very active tributary organization on the southwest side of the Bay said that environmental activists are the mainstay at meetings, and agricultural, business, and other interests too often steer clear of active participation.[64] A recent survey of Maryland

63. Chesapeake Bay Watershed Blue Ribbon Finance Panel (2004).
64. Ginger Ellis (chair of Lower Eastern Shore Tributary Team), author interview, August 23, 2007.

tributary team members shows that many feel that locally elected officials, farmers, and developers have insufficient roles to play in these local networks. The lack of cohesion among local actors is reflected in a former state official's observation that many tributary teams' goals are watered down and mostly symbolic to appeal to the lowest common denominator of agreement among the partners.[65]

The networks have a low profile with little formal authority or financial capacity to encourage participation. The tributary networks do not take an official stand on development issues or proposed energy plants, nor do they wield regulatory oversight or financial assistance. Their state-assigned reduction targets under the 2000 agreement are viewed as voluntary by the state.

Unlike the federal-state Chesapeake Bay Program network, the tributary networks are oriented less toward action and more toward information and education, in Agranoff's taxonomy of network types.[66] Information and education networks achieve results by reframing problems and providing credible information to broaden the range of actors engaged in water policy debates. One participant in Agranoff's water network study remarked, "We are most useful when no one is scared of us."[67] One survey of tributary team members suggested that this softer form of leadership has value, because such groups' endorsements are often sought for policy announcements by local governments, business initiatives, and agricultural management innovations. One team member said, "The tributary team provides a great networking forum and a place to learn by osmosis. [But] I can't cite a specific change that has come about through the support of the team."[68] The problem is that networks without immediate impact can quickly become self-referential, failing to attract broader support. One state official said that the only audience at tributary organization meetings seems to be the tributary teams themselves.[69]

Soft power and public education can be persuasive, particularly when there is a consensus on shared values and perceptions of problems. Reframing of problems can be a powerful inducement to reaching newfound agreement and changes among participants who have not previously seen eye to eye. Indeed, the tributaries have achieved some notable successes in building alliances with businesses and other local interests through voluntary cooperation and the artful linkage of self-interest with broader public values. One major victory achieved by several tributary teams working together involved a plan to reduce the phosphorus content of lawn fertilizer. Though lacking regulatory or financial leverage over manufacturers, the teams gained the support of Scotts, a major national fertilizer com-

65. Former state official with the Maryland Department of Natural Resources), off-the-record interview, July 2007.

66. Agranoff (2007, p. 57).

67. Ibid.

68. Survey of tributary team members.

69. Former state official with the Maryland Department of Natural Resources, off-the-record interview.

pany, for producing a "greener" fertilizer for use by homeowners in the Bay region. Thus, if private firms can see a market for "green" products, they may support restoration goals. Local governments can become engaged in this agenda as well, particularly when cleanup goals are salient to local communities. Montgomery County, Maryland, for instance, has enacted fees to support stormwater retrofits, and other counties surrounding the Bay have formulated strict control on new development that undermines water quality.

All of the local actors—governments, farmers, business leaders—share a passion and concern about the Bay and want to see it restored to its former health, but as one local official commented, "Everyone wants to go to heaven, but no one wants to die."[70] Competition hampers the trust and joint sacrifice required, as local interests fear that their actions will be exploited by competing governments, farmers, or businesses. Often sacrifices are required when costs are borne locally to benefit other communities, such as in shifting land management practices and retrofitting storm sewers. Generally, externalities can be most effectively handled by regulation or by funding to realign actors' incentives with the scope of public problems, but few tributary organizations have access to these tools. Compounding the political economy dilemmas is a lack of capacity, information, and institutional support that has been so critical to the policy development and politics throughout the Bay.

Such rampant competition and deep conflicts are not necessarily fatal to the emergence of collaboration and networks, as attested to by the federal-state Bay network. However, the conditions for network formation are less fertile at the local level than they were at the regional level. The local actors have little history of trust among themselves and have conflicting incentives. Although some rivers bordering the Bay engender passion, the tributaries have regional boundaries that do not neatly correspond with conventional boundaries. Actors within a tributary organization often do not have a long track record of working together or have expectations of future interactions that provide incentives for cooperation.[71] The attempt to form local networks among farmers, developers, and local governments is often confounded and offset by the alliances each of these interests has with its own federal and state agencies and associations. These specialized networks provide assistance and signals that sometimes support and sometimes contradict local tributary team goals. For instance, the federal agriculture conservation programs provide piecemeal assistance to local farmers that is neither targeted nor informed by the relative priorities for cleaning up impaired waters in state or local plans.

Unlike the states, local tributaries do not typically have support from a strong network of like-minded professional public managers that transcends jurisdictional

---

70. Mayor of small Maryland town, off-the-record interview.
71. Axelrod (1984).

boundaries. The states in the Bay network did, however, have professional environmental managers who shared the same epistemic perspectives. Such common professional views have always been important in promoting intergovernmental cooperation, as specialists across governments often have greater cohesion with each other than with their nominal gubernatorial or legislative overseers in their home jurisdictions.[72]

The relative weakness of tributary teams and the problems of engaging local actors have inspired proposals for reform. Some observers have suggested that the Chesapeake Bay Program Office and the states need to abandon the voluntary approach in favor of a compulsory regulatory strategy to ensure that highly competitive local economic and governmental actors take their responsibilities seriously. Representative Wayne Gilchrest (R-Md.) from the Eastern Shore introduced legislation in 2005 to require tributary report cards and mandate goals for local governments to reduce pollution by treating tributary goals as TMDL allocations. In late October 2008 a coalition of environmentalists, fishermen, recreational sportsmen, and former political officials announced they would sue EPA to develop and enforce regulatory standards for the Bay, triggering a TMDL allocation process by federal officials.[73] If successful, this lawsuit would provide for EPA to impose sanctions on governments and businesses throughout the Bay.

Whereas the states and local tributary organizations have largely resisted using mandates to require changes in land management, the reliance on voluntary tools is characteristic of emergent networks where government managers and the numerous stakeholders involved have not yet developed strong ties to bind them to collective values and interests. At the outset of network relationships, government policymakers and managers must focus on persuading third parties to work toward a common agenda. As Ingram notes, participation is initially more critical to program survival than promoting compliance with goals, and it is hoped that goal congruence and compliance will emerge over time.[74]

Other observers suggest that the implementation challenges could be avoided by means of structural changes in the network itself. Many respected network members concluded that an overhaul of the governance structure and process for the Bay Program was necessary.[75] They recommended a new structure to more centrally include representatives of agriculture, local government, and business in network committees and governance processes. They also embraced strategies to strengthen staff support to local tributary organizations and improve transparency in accountability through performance metrics and report cards. These changes in network governance would establish a more inclusive—but potentially more conflictual and less cohesive—decisionmaking process. Broadening participation,

72. Wright (1988).

73. Pamela Wood, "EPA Hit with Bay Lawsuit," *The Capital*, October 29, 2008.

74. Ingram (1977).

75. Chesapeake Bay Program Implementation Committee (2007).

though complicating decisions and goal setting, may also broaden buy-in by the local implementers whose cooperation is critical to restoring the Bay.

Concluding Observations

The Bay network offers an important case study of the role that collaboration can play in dealing with complex public policy issues in decentralized environments. As a federal-state collaboration, the Bay network made much more progress in formulating ambitious goals and gaining the cooperation of a diverse range of actors than traditional governmental regulatory programs would have achieved. Although the problems are by no means solved and progress is slower than envisioned, the goals set may have been more audacious than any that individual states would have developed on their own. The network's progress in policy development is especially remarkable, considering the many barriers to collaboration, the high stakes involved, and the difficult trade-offs between competing values and interests.

Many factors were responsible for the cohesion of the Bay Program, including shared values, a history of trusting relationships, and well-accepted scientific models. In addition, the role played by the federal government, particularly the EPA, is among the most critical elements underpinning this network's maintenance and its ambitious goal setting. Network studies typically have a unit of analysis that starts at the bottom of the implementation chain, focusing on how partners come together to achieve mutual goals and interests. In the process, the "hidden hand" that government agencies often play in public service networks has frequently gone unheralded.

For solving major problems such as environmental restoration, networks do not eclipse government, but rather become a valued and essential adjunct and tool of governance.[76] Thus, for the Bay network, collaboration was institutionalized through the network, but in the shadow of hierarchy.[77] Grassroots collaboration was instrumental in prompting the Bay partnership in the first place—and the EPA itself was initially reluctant to engage in the scientific study that became the benchmark for collaboration. However, the network did need government to facilitate and manage relationships and to provide the essential framing of the problem and the motivation for collaboration through the regulatory backdrop.

The case of the Chesapeake Bay shows that just as networks need government to tackle difficult problems, so too does government need networks to engage actors in a decentralized federal system in working toward national goals. Even when government has regulatory authority as does the EPA, networks provide a sustainable and legitimate approach to gaining support, authority, and resources

76. Angranoff (2007).
77. Scharpf (1997).

from the widely disparate actors whose cooperation is essential to resolve such wicked problems as nonpoint source pollution. In the process, an iterative form of bargaining takes place as the goals of government and other network actors become moderated and mediated. Networks exert a decentralizing influence on government goals and priorities as the price for engagement with actors who do not necessarily share national goals and priorities, whereas government programs and policies exert a centralizing influence on local actors' values and priorities. All actors may gain from such a process, but the network relationship process elicits tension and disaffection among the many who might wish for unilateral control over their destinies, unburdened by the compromise and hard work required to fashion collaborative solutions from conflicting interests.

Participating in networks presents challenges to government managers. They must learn to use a new set of tools, including negotiation, communication, and collegial goal setting that is different from the regulatory mindset. Working to orchestrate the agreement of others empowered with roles and authority is different from operating in command-and-control environments. Gaining the buy-in of others to goals and strategies involves a trade-off. Agencies must juggle their accountability to Congress for achieving discrete national goals with the goals and priorities of network officials on whom they depend for achieving those national goals.

These same tensions affect other actors in networks, who must struggle to balance their allegiance to networks with their commitment to their home organizations and interests. Effective networks provide institutional structures that enable the collectivity to become more than the sum of its parts, whereas ineffective networks fail to overcome the particularistic tensions of their coalitions—a result that should not be surprising, given the deep-seated nature of many vested interests. One recent review of the experience with networks concluded that expectations for networks should be set very low—as a rule, successful collaboration should not be expected.[78] Imperial suggests that networks are best for win-win or win–no lose situations. As the stakes and conflict grow, networks will be less effective, as incipient conflicts among network members paralyze action or result in a lowering of goals to an ineffectual common denominator.[79] Ironically, the very advantages that prompt the formation of collaborative networks can also be their undoing. The presence of complex, decentralized organizations makes network approaches seem advantageous, even necessary, but this very same landscape undermines the ability of networks to realize success.

These tensions in network governance were reflected in the Bay. As effective as the federal-state partnership was in articulating ambitious goals, the decentralized tributary networks illustrated the problems networks face in gaining sufficient support from the decentralized actors in local systems who have few of the col-

78. Bryson, Crosby, and Stone (2006).
79. Imperial (2005).

laborative advantages and capacity of the federal-state network. Fundamentally, the commitment to environmental goals at this level proved more shallow than the allegiance to more compelling and immediate economic and social goals and interests. And the tributary networks have not been successful, for the most part, in changing this equation by providing a new basis for reframing the compelling interests and allegiances for local actors.

The sustainability of networks can be threatened by the tension between the relative effectiveness of policy agreement and the difficulties in implementation. The mismatch between cohesiveness at the top of the network and the lack of consensus at the local level guaranteed significant slippage between the policy formulation and the implementation process for the Bay. The bidding up of policy goals by relatively cohesive federal and state policy actors essentially submerged the incipient tensions and trade-offs that were bound to resurface during implementation. The failure to include agriculture, local governments, and businesses in the central policymaking structures of the Bay Program may have facilitated agreement at the outset, but at the price of exacerbated tensions and slippage during implementation. More generally, this trade-off between inclusiveness and cohesiveness appears in other settings as well. In one study of pension reform in European nations, Orenstein concludes that including more and various veto groups early in the decisionmaking process increased buy-in and compliance during implementation—but at the expense of faster and greater change.[80]

The challenges facing the Bay network epitomize those faced by other environmental networks to meet daunting goals. In one study of eight partnerships, when the democratic experience was not matched by empowerment or authority over implementation, trust in the partnership was undermined.[81] Pressures began to mount for overturning network arrangements by advocates disenchanted with the pace of change. Within the Bay network, advocates are beginning to advocate compulsory regulatory tools to effect local changes, and these pressures will continue as the 2010 deadline for federal TMDL imposition nears.[82] Congressional leaders are joining in, as members of the Maryland delegation have stepped up their oversight and advocacy of stronger tools. The lawsuit filed in late 2008 by environmental groups and fishermen, among others, reflects the frustration with the failure of the network for the Bay to actually achieve the ambitious goals it set for itself in earlier years.

As successful as the Bay network has been in setting policy goals collaboratively, it has reached a crossroads. As the deadlines approach, the actions necessary to head off stronger federal regulatory intervention call for more difficult and challenging actions and sacrifices by a wide range of local actors. It appears that the current tributary network approach will be insufficient to achieve the kinds of

80. Orenstein (2000).
81. Koontz and others (2004, p. 159).
82. Ernst (2003).

local changes that are necessary. When faced with goal slippage in the 1990s, the federal-state network was able to "borrow authority" from the EPA, thanks to the court suit that provided renewed impetus and commitment to embrace bolder steps to clean up the Bay.[83] Additional federal and state regulatory authority and financial resources will likely be necessary to further empower local networks in the states to become effective partners for change. Recognizing the deep-seated political conflicts surrounding the regulation of land use, agriculture, and development in most states, rethinking the balance between voluntary and regulatory approaches constitutes a major political watershed for the actors in the federal-state partnership.

The Bay Program illustrates the ironic and symbiotic relationship between networks and government regulation, as the foregoing indicates. Though voluntary organizations and government are commonly portrayed as mutually exclusive entities, voluntary forms of public action often depend on the presence of government in the background to overcome centrifugal forces that threaten to undermine voluntary networks' goals. Government officials are also beginning to realize that government regulation, similarly, relies on the presence of networks to promote its goals. In a society where power and resources are widely distributed, both central authority and voluntary forms of collective action may be essential. Undoubtedly, there are cases where these two forms of public action can conflict, but the public policy community needs to be alert to areas where government and networks must work together. The Chesapeake Bay Program illustrates both the advantages and limitations of such partnerships in achieving the goals of both government and network participants. As the unfinished business facing the Bay Program becomes more daunting, rethinking and renewing the balance between these complementary forms of public action is the new challenge for the program and for students of networks in public policy.

References

Agranoff, Robert. 2007. *Managing within Networks: Adding Value to Public Organizations.* Georgetown University Press.

Altrer, Catherine, and Jerald Haige. 1993. *Organizations Working Together.* Newbury Park, Calif.: Sage.

Axelrod, Robert. 1984. *The Evolution of Cooperation.* New York: Basic Books.

Bryson, John M., Barbara C. Crosby, and Melissa M. Stone. 2006. "The Design and Implementation of Cross-Sector Collaborations: Propositions from the Literature." *Public Administration Review* 66, no. 6 (supplement) (December): 46.

Chesapeake Bay Program Implementation Committee. 2007. *Reinventing the Chesapeake Bay Program.* Annapolis: Keith Campbell Foundation for the Environment, January.

Chesapeake Bay Watershed Blue Ribbon Finance Panel. 2004. *Saving a National Treasure: Financing the Cleanup of the Chesapeake Bay.* Annapolis, Md.

83. The concept of "borrowing authority" is borrowed from Manna (2006).

Chirigotis, Anthony, and others. 2007. *Development Growth Outpacing Progress in Watershed Efforts to Restore the Chesapeake Bay.* OIG Report 2007-P-00031. Washington: EPA, Office of the Inspector General, September 10.

Dewitt, John. 1994. *Civic Environmentalism.* Washington: CQ Press.

Donahue, John. 1997. *Disunited States: What's at Stake as Washington Fades and the States Take the Lead.* New York: Basic Books.

Environmental Protection Agency. 2003. *Ambient Water Quality Criteria for Dissolved Oxygen, Water Clarity and Chlorophyl-a for the Chesapeake Bay and Its Tidal Tributaries.* EPA publication 903-R-03-002. Washington.

EPA Inspector General. 2006. *Saving the Chesapeake Bay Watershed Requires Better Coordination of Environmental and Agricultural Resources.* Report 2007-P-00004. Washington: November 20.

Ernst, Howard. 2003. *Chesapeake Bay Blues: Science, Politics and the Struggle to Save the Bay.* New York: Rowman & Littlefield.

Gage, Robert W., and Myrna P. Mandell, eds. 1990. *Strategies for Managing Intergovernmental Policies and Networks.* New York: Praeger.

Haas, Peter. 1992. "Epistemic Communities and International Policy Coordination." *International Organization* 46, no. 1 (January): 1–36.

Hardin, Garrett. 1982. *Collective Action.* Johns Hopkins University Press for Resources for the Future.

Heikkila, Tanya, and Andrea K. Gerlak. 2005. "The Formation of Large-scale Collaborative Resource Management Institutions: Clarifying the Roles of Stakeholders, Science, and Institutions." *Policy Studies Journal* 33, no. 4 (November).

Hill, Michael, and Peter Hupe. 2002. *Implementing Public Policy.* New York: Sage.

Hrern, B., and D. O. Porter. 1982. "Implementation Structures: A New Unit for Administrative Analysis." *Organizational Studies* 3: 211–37.

Imperial, Mark T. 2005. "Using Collaboration as Governance Strategy: Lessons from Six Watershed Management Programs." *Administration and Society* 37, no. 3 (July): 281–320.

Ingram, Helen. 1977. "Policy Implementation through Bargaining: The Case of Federal Grants-in-Aid." *Public Policy* 25 (Fall): 499–526.

International City and County Management Association. 2007. *Chesapeake Local Government Action Plan.* Washington: July.

Kenney, D. S. 2000. *Assessing the Effectiveness of Watershed Initiatives: The Current State of Knowledge.* University of Colorado School of Law.

Kickert, Walter J. M., Erik-Hans Klijn, and Joop F. M. Koppenjan, eds. 1993. *Managing Complex Networks.* London: Sage.

Koontz, Tomas M., and others. 2004. *Collaborative Environmental Management: What Roles for Government?* Washington: Resources for the Future.

Local Government Advisory Committee. 2006. *Report to the Chesapeake Bay Executive Council.* Annapolis, Md.: September 22.

Lowi, Theodore. 1979. *The End of Liberalism.* 2nd ed. New York: Norton.

Lubell, Mark. 2004. "Collaborative Environmental Institutions: All Talk and No Action?" *Journal of Policy Analysis and Management* 23, no. 3: 549–73.

Lubell, Mark, and others. 2002. "Watershed Partnerships and the Emergence of Collective Action Institutions." *American Journal of Political Science* 46: 148–63.

Manna, Paul. 2006. *School's In.* Georgetown University Press.

McConnell, Grant. 1961. *Private Power and American Democracy.* New York: Knopf.

McGuire, Michael. 2006. "Collaborative Public Management: Assessing What We Know and How We Know It." *Public Administration Review* 66, no. 6 (Supplement) (December): 36.

Milward, H. Brinton, and Keith Provan. 2006. *A Manager's Guide to Choosing and Using Collaborative Networks*. Washington: IBM Center on the Business of Government.

National Academy of Public Administration. 2007. *Taking Environmental Protection to the Next Level: An Assessment of the U.S. Environmental Services Delivery System*. Washington: April.

Orenstein, Mitchell A. 2000. "How Politics and Institutions Affect Pension Reform in Three Post-Communist Countries." Report. Washington: World Bank Development Research Group, March.

Ostrom, Elinor. 1990. *Governing the Commons: The Evolution of Institutions for Collective Action*. Cambridge University Press.

Rocherfort, David A., and Roger W. Cobb. 1994. *The Politics of Problem Definition*. University Press of Kansas.

Sabatier, Paul A., Will Focht, and Mark Lubell. 2005. *Swimming Upstream: Collaborative Approaches to Watershed Management*. MIT Press.

Scharpf, Fritz. 1997. *Games Real Actors Play: Actor-Centered Institutionalism in Policy Research*. Boulder: Westview Press.

Thomson, Ann Marie, and James L. Perry. 2006. "Collaboration Processes: Inside the Black Box." *Public Administration Review* 66, no. 6 (Supplement) (December): 20–32.

U.S. Government Accountability Office. 2005. *Chesapeake Bay Program: Improved Strategies Are Needed to Better Assess, Report, and Manage Restoration Progress*. Publication GAO-06-96. Washington.

Wright, Deil. 1988. *Understanding Intergovernmental Relations*. New York: Harcourt.

Zartman, William L. 1991. "Conflict and Resolution: Contest, Cost and Change." *Annals of the American Academy of Political and Social Science* 518 (November): 11–12.

Zucker, Lynne. 1988. "Where Do Institutional Patterns Come From?" In *Institutional Patterns and Organizations: Culture and Environment*, edited by Lynne Zucker. Cambridge, Mass.: Ballinger.

5

Moving from Core Functions to Core Values: Lessons from State Eligibility Modernizations

STEPHEN GOLDSMITH AND TIM BURKE

For over forty years, millions of struggling households across all fifty states have relied on the same cumbersome system of county welfare offices to tap into the U.S. social safety net. With inconvenient hours, little customer service, and wasteful spending, many of these offices typify government bureaucracy at its worst. Simultaneously, the offices arguably represent American values at their best in their effort to help the most vulnerable. After a decade of adjusting to the 1996 welfare reforms, states are now reconciling this tension between the best and worst as it is reflected in their benefits eligibility systems.

In bringing access to Food Stamps, Medicaid, Temporary Assistance for Needy Families (TANF), and other federal- and state-funded benefits programs into the twenty-first century, diverse modernization strategies have arisen in public welfare or health and human service agencies across the states. All rely on replacing antiquated models with new, extensive networks of government, private business, and nonprofit organizations to perform the myriad functions involved, from calculating benefits to online support services to job placement to health care.

These eligibility modernizations come at an interesting point in the process of privatization of services and other networked governance models. After five years of relative dormancy, high-profile privatizations, mostly at the state and local levels, are grabbing the nation's attention. At the state level, several governors face the pressures of limited revenues and increasing demands, and are looking to new and private solutions to pernicious public service problems. Officials do so at significant political risk, but the potential for success and for breaking with age-old failures makes it seem worth the gamble. In 2004 Mayor Richard Daley secured a $1.8 billion deal to lease the operation of the 7.8-mile elevated toll road known as the Chicago Skyway to a private consortium for ninety-nine years. Two years later, Indiana made a similar deal with the same consortium, giving a seventy-five-year lease to operate the Indiana Toll Road in return for $3.8 billion. Other states have outsourced the operation of toll roads and bridges, and more are considering it. Several states are exploring privatizing their lotteries. One city—Sandy Springs, Georgia—essentially outsourced all of town hall with the exception of policy.[1]

Today's public-private partnerships differ significantly from those of the past two decades. Privatization initiatives, no longer limited to ownership of a public asset, are increasingly (1) ambitious, including not only mandates regarding service delivery but also requirements to achieve major policy goals; (2) complex, involving multiple parties and intricate relationships; and (3) technology-driven, relying on digital platforms, data warehouses, and strategic analytics.

No state or local effort in the first decade of the new century better represents these trends or the policy challenges of privatization than projects to modernize state welfare eligibility. These impressive statewide initiatives lie right at the intersection of the digital revolution, political ideology, and, for many people, basic survival. As such, they offer an almost unique opportunity to explore the changing nature of government and its evolution from provider of core functions to protector of core values.

This chapter compares the private sector's multiple roles in four such modernizations to the public sector's performance in similar roles, to show that any attempt to draw lines around which functions are core or inherently governmental is misleading and unhelpful. Results typically depend more on the goals, motivation, politics, and capacity of public officials than on any normative distinction.

What Is an "Inherently" Governmental Function?

The uncharted territory of this evolution—in some places revolution—in how government delivers services has left unanswered a number of serious questions. Can we say which tasks should be carried out by government entities and which not? Even if people agree on which governmental functions are core, or inherently governmental, functions that need to be walled off from contractors, what if government turns out not to be very good at carrying out these functions? What if the decision to contract out certain functions to private contractors were based on technology, quality management, and performance metrics rather than on a rigid and no longer helpful distinction between a core and a noncore government function?

1. See Porter (2006).

The Office of Management and Budget defines an inherently governmental function as follows:

> An *inherently governmental function* is a function which is so intimately related to the public interest as to mandate performance by Government employees. . . . These functions include those activities which require either the exercise of discretion in applying Government authority or the use of value judgment in making decisions.[2]

This definition, built on the concepts of public interest, discretion, and values, provides little meaningful guidance in a world where private companies guard prisoners, protect government office buildings, fight in overseas wars, hunt down wanted persons, and provide residential services for parolees, probationers, abused children, and the developmentally disabled—all under the authority of the state. These commonly outsourced functions are all intimately in the public interest, and all require high individual discretion at times. The reality today is that state officials do not rely on a definition to determine whether to use public employees or agents. They rely instead on the pragmatics of the situation.

In addition, government's definition of its core functions has slowly but substantially shrunk since the early 1990s. Seemingly intractable problems such as welfare to work responded well to new policies and outsourcing, causing many to "shrink" the concept of core down from the core activity to the core decision-making about that activity (a much smaller "protected area").

This shift has been facilitated by the explosion of businesses that now serve government in these formerly core (now niche) markets. In addition, in the context of the overall technology revolution, the private sector has substantially outpaced the public sector in its embrace of technology over the last two decades, making government systems increasingly less competitive at delivering even accepted core services. Finally, this trend has been further propelled by new contracting models, improved risk-sharing strategies, better tracking and monitoring technology, increased private sector specialization, better government contract managers, and increasing concern among public sector officials about meeting higher customer expectations.

The specific functions involved in large state eligibility-determination systems range from system-level operations to actions executed daily by individual employees at their own discretion. Yet they also involve policy decisions and performance accountability, control over both of which should reside firmly within state government. In other words, the component functions making up the whole fall both within and outside the traditional definition of "inherently governmental." Thus,

---

2. Office of Management and Budget, "Performance of Commercial Activities," circular A-76 (www.whitehouse.gov/omb/circulars/a076.pdf).

the test of whether or not to outsource should not be based on whether a function such as eligibility determination is inherently governmental (a point that could be debated over a lifetime) but on which arrangement would best ensure that the public purpose is met. If government's role is not distinguished from the role of private actors by definition, then are there any sharp lines that can configure the boundaries? This issue will be discussed in the last section.

Which Functions in the Network to Outsource?

Take, for example, the modernization in Indiana, where a million Hoosiers depend on the state's Family and Social Services Agency (FSSA) for disability payments, food assistance, medical care, and other services.[3] When Governor Mitch Daniels took office in 2005, he appointed Mitch Roob secretary of this important but ailing agency responsible for eligibility determination.[4]

Governor Daniels instructed Roob to reduce the growth of Medicaid by half, fix FSSA's operations, and transform its philosophy to one that encouraged self-sufficiency. Roob, a Notre Dame MBA who also served as president of Indianapolis's Health and Hospital Corporation and as the chief operating officer of the Indianapolis Water Company (privately owned at that time), took the charge seriously, stating:

> In way too many instances we are turning away people who probably do qualify for some of our services, and we are accepting people who don't qualify. That is just no way to run our business; our customers, the citizens of Indiana, deserve a system that addresses their needs for public assistance.[5]

Roob and his project manager, Zach Main, visited county offices across the state. They found "terrible customer service. Indiana's neediest citizens, the ones who have the least access to transportation, have to drag along children or leave a job in order to jump through a bunch of hoops to access the system."[6]

Analysts found that struggling citizens were forced to make more than 2 million unnecessary trips a year to a welfare or other government office.[7] A broken system, inadequately serving clients with little political or economic clout, had escaped public outcry for years.

---

3. Parts of the description of Indiana's modernization project were first presented in Stephen Goldsmith, "What's Left for Government to Do?" *The American,* January–February 2008.

4. Both officials advised Goldsmith while he was mayor of Indianapolis; Roob was the director of the city's Department of Transportation, and Daniels served as chair of the citizens' advisory group that helped the city accomplish several important competitive procurements.

5. Anita Risdon (FSSA), "FSSA Releases Audit Highlighting Agency's Past Failures," press release, June 15, 2005.

6. Zach Main, interview with Tim Burke, December 21, 2006.

7. Cyndi Cornelius, "Hoosier Coalition for Self-Sustainability, Response to State of Indiana's Request for Information 6-C," Executive Summary, 2006, p. 4.

Roob then took a critical step, but one often overlooked even by activist government officials. He deployed independent third parties to benchmark service quality and identified organizational risks. A review by a professional services firm, KPMG, exposed what Roob had anticipated: caseworkers did not apply eligibility rules in a uniform way. When county offices did exercise discretion to help someone, they did so without consistent processes to guide them or to verify accuracy. Main points out that FSSA "had 107 county offices and 107 different ways of doing business. More likely we had 2,200 caseworkers and probably 2,200 different ways of doing business."[8]

Further, Indiana's eligibility-determination system was plagued by waste, fraud, and abuse, leading to millions of additional dollars in benefits and administration costs. More important, the state was failing two fundamental purposes: ensuring equity and fairness and promoting self-sufficiency and independence. When Roob arrived at FSSA, Indiana was last among the fifty states in terms of caseload reductions since the 1996 welfare reforms.[9]

Simply put, Indiana's government was not very good at providing this governmental service. Unfortunately, governments that are not good at producing public goods are often not good at the contracting process either. As a result, in transforming complex business processes, the risk of failure is great. Indiana avoided this catch-22 by securing substantial outside consulting advice and relying on Roob's experience.

Having envisioned the transformation of FSSA, Roob and Main had to decide whether to produce the change internally or externally. They found ample reasons to look outside for a solution, including a lack of both management and financial capital and an abundance of constraints on internal change.

A transformation in the size and scope envisioned by Roob would likely require years of planning, development, and transition. Consistent commitment and direction from the highest echelons of the agency would be a necessity. Since its founding in 1991, twelve different secretaries had commanded FSSA, each with a new management strategy never fully implemented before the next secretary and next idea. Main felt that such discontinuity must be avoided; locking the agency into a long-term agreement with an outside partner, with agreed-upon performance metrics and penalties for nonperformance, would offer the necessary consistency.

Indiana faced a familiar obstacle to transformative change—the need for large capital investments in information technology (IT) that do not generally reach legislative budget priorities. Roob correctly determined that private partners should provide the sizable up-front capital investment, spreading the costs over the life of the contract. Roob also knew that another resource, proven technical expertise, was available only in the private sector.

8. Zach Main, interview with Tim Burke, January 18, 2007.
9. Erin Linville, "Eligibility Modernization: The Need for Change," Indiana Family and Social Services Administration, August 2006 (www.in.gov/fssa/2437.htm).

Roob understood that the state's systems, more than its employees, presented overwhelming obstacles to change. To effectively implement deep changes in the way 2,200 caseworkers and 107 county office directors had been doing business, some for thirty-plus years, would require flexibility in the state's merit-worker rules. As written, however, merit-worker rules made changing an employee's responsibilities extremely difficult. Will Oliver, a consultant to FSSA, observed, "Roob came into an organization with work rules that wouldn't allow him to change people's work responsibilities, that wouldn't allow him to do performance reviews or weed out the dead wood. He said he had to change but couldn't do it internally.[10]

Even if the "new" private hires came from among existing state caseworkers, Roob and Main believed that hiring a private firm would solve the challenge of working around the innovation-stifling rules that applied to state employees. The state would eventually take the added step of requiring comparable pay, benefits, and pensions to ease the transition and ensure fairness for FSSA employees.

Given the obstacles, an internal transformation would require a strong and experienced management team. Yet, as in most public organizations, many of FSSA's middle managers were individuals who performed well in field jobs and had worked their way up inside the broken system but were not experienced in managing a large bureaucracy. Others in the central office were political appointees who came and went with new administrations. The middle management required to successfully implement the vision simply did not exist.

Although FSSA may have lacked management experience in effecting organizational change, its new leadership team had ample experience in outsourcing. Both Governor Daniels, a leader and advocate in government outsourcing in Indianapolis and as director of the Office of Budget and Management under President George W. Bush, and Secretary Roob had relevant experience. Further, Indiana benefited from consultants and vendors, many of them experienced former public officials, who could see the challenges through the eyes of Roob and Main.

Despite all these convincing reasons to look to the private sector, Roob and Main had to consider three factors that favored an internal transformation, none of them related to the inherently governmental nature of the service. First, no state had ever successfully outsourced its eligibility-determination system for all major benefits programs. Florida and Texas were the only two states that had attempted anything similar, and their prognosis did not look good at the time.

Second, an internal modernization would avoid the inevitable political considerations typically involved in a major privatization initiative. Despite Roob's aspiration to dramatically improve a record of client service that had historically been among the worst in the country, political opposition to such change was inevitable. Legislative leaders and interest groups opposing the governor's efforts to privatize

10. Will Oliver, interview with Tim Burke, November 28, 2006.

the Indiana Toll Road could combine with client advocacy groups to create stumbling blocks for the transformation. Nevertheless, in the end Roob asked a simple but provocative question: Who could best organize and provide the most effective possible services to Hoosiers in need, public or private employees?

After looking at FSSA's available capacity and resources, Roob and Main decided to outsource the work. Indiana awarded a seven-year $1 billion contract (with an option to extend to ten years) to a group of private and nonprofit agents led by IBM and its subcontractor ACS. Indiana charged the IBM coalition with finding solutions to major problems within the state's social service system: inefficient and outdated business processes, out-of-control Medicaid expenses, poor customer service, and one of the nation's worst records in implementing federal welfare reforms. Any one of these problems would be a significant challenge for an agency or contractor to deal with.

The Demise of Core Government Functions

The fact that Indiana's broken eligibility-determination system is in the process of being transformed with an impressive network of private business, community-based, and government providers is a reminder that even functions considered inherently governmental might be better performed outside the public sector. It is also evidence that inside a complex service delivery network, the line between public and private is increasingly permeable. A state could use some combination of private technology, private management, and public employees or, depending on the circumstances, public management and private employees.

Dozens of other states are attempting to modernize their antiquated eligibility-determination systems. Among other actions they are taking is the basic step of making part of the application process available online. These state efforts include but are not limited to Louisiana's No Wrong Door, Utah Cares, Oregon Helps, ACCESS Wisconsin, West Virginia inROADS, and NJ Helps. In addition, efforts in three other states—Florida, Pennsylvania, and Texas—illustrate how motivation and leadership often determine the split between private and public work inside a successful network. In all three states some combination of private, nonprofit, and government actors participate in a network that delivers benefit eligibility services. It was leadership, pragmatism, and legislative relationships, more than a definition of fairness or the public interest, that determined roles inside the new networks and, ultimately, determined how well positioned the network was and is to succeed.

Officials in Florida, Pennsylvania, and Texas do not confront all the same issues as Indiana, which succeeded with a private sector–centric model of transformation. Just because the public sector is not always best positioned to remain in the center of these complicated networks doesn't mean that the private sector is "inherently" qualified. Florida and Pennsylvania have insourced their modernizations, improving eligibility and cutting costs with government at the center of a new net-work. Texas, meanwhile, started its privatized eligibility-determination modern-ization with quite problematic results, including accepting poor work by some of the vendors, changing too many system pieces at one time, and losing too many employees too quickly. How the many public and private pieces fit together, and who integrates rather than who owns the pieces, is the key to this puzzle. Whether a state can accomplish its objectives depends on the quality of the network, not on the sector.

Florida

In Florida, the agency analogous to Indiana's FSSA, the Department of Children and Families (DCF), had for years been the subject of sharp criticism. In 2004 new leadership took over a department that served more than 2 million Floridi-ans every year but was facing demands for change. Its mission is to "strengthen Florida's families through private, community, and interagency partnerships that promote economic self-sufficiency."[11] But the intake process had only just begun the transformation from a forty-year-old social service delivery model that looked almost the same in 2004 as it did in the 1960s.

Like Indiana's, Florida's eligibility-determination system was indifferent to cus-tomer service. For example, under the old model adult recipients took time off from work to make multiple unnecessary visits to county offices. For these working-poor Floridians, the very process of accessing Florida's self-sufficiency programs was creating additional barriers, and possibly actually jeopardizing clients' jobs.[12] Cus-tomer service deficiencies included unwelcoming and crowded lobbies, long waits, the need for multiple return visits, prohibitively long application forms, and incon-sistency in the application of eligibility rules and processes. Written communica-tions to clients complicated the process with jargon and legal terminology.[13]

Don Winstead, deputy secretary of the Florida Department of Children and Families, used a threat of privatization from the state legislature to produce internal reforms. The legislative mandate to save money would continue to affect the mod-ernization, but achieving early and substantial cost reductions helped Winstead avoid privatization. Florida's new system puts a premium on enabling its clients to take responsibility for their own applications, which it sees as a step in fulfilling another mandate to better focus on helping clients toward self-sufficiency.[14]

11. ACCESS, "Community Access Partnership Network," brochure (www.dcf.state.fl.us/ess/docs/brochure_partner.pdf [accessed May 2, 2008]).

12. Jennifer Lange, "ACCESS FLORIDA Presentation," Harvard University, Kennedy School of Gov-ernment, December 7, 2007.

13. Florida Department of Children and Families, "Long Range Program Plan: Fiscal Years 2005–6 through 2009–10," September 1, 2004 (www.dcf.state.fl.us/publications/plan/LRPP0506.pdf).

14. Don Winstead, testimony before the Subcommittee on Income Security and Family Support of the House Committee on Ways and Means, Tallahassee, Florida, April 5, 2006 (http://waysandmeans.house.gov/hearings.asp?formmode=printfriendly&id=4815); see also Innovations in American Govern-

The delivery network Florida put together, like Indiana's, relies heavily on an extensive network of community partners. The DCF describes its Community ACCESS (Automated Community Connection to Economic Self-Sufficiency) Network as "maximizing shared resources [to increase] customer access to services needed to strengthen families in the local community." Partners include community centers, county public health departments, domestic abuse centers, faith-based organizations, food banks, hospitals, libraries, public schools, and Work-force One Stops.[15] Primarily, the DCF relies on these partners to extend its reach, for example, to provide Internet access to their "mutual customers" (people who were customers of both the DCF and the partner agencies) who do not have computers or Internet access at home.[16] Community partners also help close the loop with data and pertinent feedback from the field.[17] The network has grown quickly, with 2,400 partners by March 2007 and another 700 in place and more than 135 in process a year later.[18]

Once the online applications process was implemented, ACCESS Florida experienced very high rates of online applications: by 2006, 77 percent of applications were coming in online; by 2007 the percentage reached 88 percent.[19] ACCESS Florida also continues to bring significant administrative savings.[20] The DCF reports that its 2006 eligibility-services budget was down $83 million (30 percent) from just three years earlier. ACCESS Florida also claims improved customer service. The average number of days to process a client dropped from 40 to 17, and more than 98 percent of applications were processed within federal time standards.[21] Feedback from customer surveys has been positive, and previously above-standard Food Stamp accuracy rates rose even higher, to 99 percent.[22]

---

ment Awards program, "Automated Community Connection to Economic Self-Sufficiency (ACCESS)," Government Innovators Network website (www.innovations.harvard.edu/awards.html?id=85371).

15. ACCESS, "Community Access Partnership Network."

16. See Government Innovators Network website, American Government Award program description (www.innovations.harvard.edu/awards.html?id=85371).

17. ACCESS, "Community Access Partnership Network."

18. Carolyn J. Heinrich, "Innovations in American Government Award Site Visit Report," report (Tallahassee: ACCESS Florida, March 2007); Florida Department of Children and Families, "DCF Quick Facts," March 26, 2008 (www.dcf.state.fl.us/publications/docs/quickfacts.pdf).

19. Florida Department of Children and Families, "DCF Quick Facts."

20. "Between 2001 and 2006 DCF reduced its annual inflation-adjusted operating costs by $100 million. Most of this reduction ($73 million) occurred between SFY2004 and SFY 2006" (Cody, Nogales, and Martin [2008]).

21. This is possible because the average staff person now processes 690 cases per year, as compared to 150 cases in the past (see Heinrich, "Innovations in American Government Award Site Visit Report").

22. Innovations in American Government Awards program, "Automated Community Connection to Economic Self-Sufficiency (ACCESS)"; "The federal standard for accuracy for the past fiscal year was 93 percent (GAA standard) and the state goal for that time period was 94 percent. For all dates between 10/01/03 and 2/29/04 (latest data available) the statewide error rate was 5.23 percent. The staff have been able to maintain a low error rate while changing operations and systems and with staff reductions imposed by state legislation" (Florida Department of Children and Families, "Long Range Program Plan: Fiscal Years 2005–6 through 2009–10."; Florida Department of Children and Families, "DCF Quick Facts."

Despite these improvements, the system is not perfect. Abandoned call rates—when people hang up while waiting for service—vary significantly between regional call centers, running as high as 25 percent in Jacksonville.[23]

Florida's $83 million in annual administrative savings under the new program came from reducing staff size and closing county offices. (This is in contrast to Indiana, which offered a contractual guarantee to all state workers of a job with the private vendor.)[24] The DCF's eligibility services workforce leveled off in 2006 at 4,100 employees, about 43 percent below its 2003 size of 7,200 full-time employees.[25] Florida eliminated the 2,900 caseworker, clerical, and managerial positions through a combination of attrition and merit-based layoffs, demotions, and transfers across state government.[26] Between 2003 and 2007, a third of its county office buildings closed in tandem with the workforce reduction, both as part of a plan to save money.

However, moderate budget increases might threaten these savings. The DCF budget approved for FY2008 included $214.5 million for eligibility determination and case management, up from $204 million in FY2006.[27]

Working with Program Director Jennifer Lange, Winstead produced rapid and definitive results by controlling the network themselves, forcing the downsizing of the bureaucracy, implementing an expansive network of community partners, and increasing access to benefits for Floridians.

Pennsylvania

Pennsylvania also chose to maintain control of the network as a government function, but its transformation is proceeding at a much more modest pace. Pennsylvania's Department of Public Welfare provides one in six Pennsylvanians with substance abuse treatment, food stamps, employment and training, adoption services, home heating subsidies, child protection, and medical assistance.[28] In FY2007 the department's Office of Income Maintenance (OIM)—responsible for administering TANF, Medicaid, and Food Stamps—spent $2.1 billion on both benefits and administration.[29] The OIM in 2008 had about 7,000 employees, 300 at the central office in Harrisburg and 6,700 spread throughout the ninety-seven county offices. About 85 percent of OIM employees outside Harrisburg are caseworkers.

23. In February 2008, for example, Tampa was 13.9 percent, Miami, 15.9 percent, and Jacksonville, 25.8 percent (see Florida Department of Children and Families, "DCF Quick Facts").

24. There is some irony in the fact that in the outsourced model former public employees were still employed afterward, albeit for the contractor. In Florida's internal model, many former public employees were without jobs.

25. Lange, "ACCESS FLORIDA Presentation"; Winstead, testimony.

26. Cody, Nogales, and Martin (2008).

27. Florida Department of Children and Families, "DCF Quick Facts."

28. Commonwealth of Pennsylvania, "Governor's Report on State Performance 2006–07" (Harrisburg), p. 46.

29. Ibid., p. 51.

By most measures, Pennsylvania's eligibility system was in better shape than Indiana's or Florida's. Medical Assistance, the state's Medicaid program, was distributing $10.1 billion worth of benefits to 1.83 million recipients by FY2007, and experienced a moderate annual growth rate.[30] Its TANF (Temporary Assistance to Needy Families) caseload was at its lowest since 1961 after making significant progress in implementing the 1996 welfare reforms, and the program was spending about half as much (in inflation-adjusted dollars) on cash assistance in 2006 as in 1996.[31] Pennsylvania's administration of the Food Stamps program, often measured by accuracy rates, had also seen significant improvements.[32]

But like Florida's and Indiana's systems, Pennsylvania's lacked measurable client outcomes or any focus on customer service or operational efficiency. Among the work-eligible Pennsylvanians receiving TANF benefits, Deputy Secretary of Income Maintenance Linda Blanchette notes that the state's "work participation rate was really bad, really, really bad, probably less than 10 percent."[33] In Pennsylvania, too, a paperwork- and labor-intensive system meant that clients often needed to make multiple visits and stand in long lines during regular business hours—even though most of its recipients were now working.[34] Written client notices suffered from opaque language that was believed to cause confusion and the need for further information seeking or verification.[35]

Owing to a long tradition of strong county government, Pennsylvania's application processes varied significantly across the County Assistance Offices and even from worker to worker in the same office.[36] Certainly, there were benefits of decentralization—including better relationships with local service providers and a culture of innovation within individual county offices—but the commonwealth struggled with standardization and accountability.[37]

30. Pennsylvania Budget and Policy Center, "Understanding Welfare Spending in Pennsylvania," report, June 2007 (www.pennbpc.org/pdf/PBPCUnderStdWelfare.pdf).

31. For total recipients and total job placements, see Commonwealth of Pennsylvania, "Governor's Report on State Performance 2006–07," p. 52; Lisa Sprague and Randy Desonia, "TANF and Work Support Services: On the Job in Greater Philadelphia," National Health Policy Forum Site Visit Report, April 18–20, 2001 (www.nhpf.org/pdfs_sv/SV_phila01.pdf); Pennsylvania Budget and Policy Center, "Understanding Welfare Spending in Pennsylvania."

32. Pennsylvania Budget and Policy Center, "Understanding Welfare Spending in Pennsylvania," and Commonwealth of Pennsylvania, "Governor's Report on State Performance 2006–07" (www.state.pa.us/papower/lib/papower/attachments/2006_07_govperformancerept_web.pdf).

33. Linda Blanchette, interview with Tim Burke, April 18, 2008. As a proxy illustration, in FY2005 job placements by TANF-funded contractors totaled 6,175 out of 280,000 recipients. The trend has been upward—in FY2007 placements climbed to 16,300 while the total caseload dropped over 50,000 recipients—but not enough to meet federal requirements (see Commonwealth of Pennsylvania, "Governor's Report on State Performance 2006–07," p. 52).

34. Will Oliver, interview with Tim Burke, March 24, 2008; Sprague and Desonia, "TANF and Work Support Services."

35. Oliver interview, March 24, 2008.

36. Blanchette interview.

37. Sprague and Desonia, "TANF and Work Support Services"; Lucas Group, "Office of Income Maintenance, State of Pennsylvania: Final Report," PowerPoint presentation; Blanchette interview.

Processing a typical application involved 100 steps, only a third of them computer-automated, with one hand-off and one decision for every two steps.[38] A survey of caseworkers' call activity revealed that they spent an average twenty-five minutes per hour on the phone, mostly answering simple questions from clients.[39] Staff members were often confused as to the exact nature of their roles: "Am I an IRS agent or social worker?"[40] Despite the emphasis on work and job seeking in the 1996 welfare reform, caseloads were so large, and processes so inefficient, that caseworkers complained about not having the time to really help clients.[41]

To address these inefficiencies, the OIM initiated its Model Office (later Modern Office) project. According to Blanchette there were multiple change drivers—policy changes made by both commonwealth and federal regulatory agencies, increasing case complexity, and a need to better integrate policy, technology, and operations.[42] But there were two specific events that triggered Pennsylvania's modernization effort. First, even as its workload increased in size and complexity, the OIM experienced significant staff reductions—about 800 positions were lost in one year—at the hands of state legislators and through retirement.[43] Then, a client-organized grassroots campaign forced the state to address poor customer service, unresponsiveness, and a laborious application process.

OIM technology systems were already in the middle of a significant overhaul; an updated system was scheduled to come online in approximately two years, unlike Indiana, which had neither the system nor the money for such improvements.[44] Even so, Pennsylvania also had reason to consider outside help. Blanchette lists her agency's liabilities as a lack of institutional agility, weak communications infrastructure, and lack of confidence in the ability of both staff and clients to adapt to change.[45] Furthermore, the OIM's county offices lacked any culture, history, or mechanisms of performance measurement or process improvement.[46] One consultant noted, "Pennsylvania's 'well fare' department has less focus on

---

38. Lucas Group, "Office of Income Maintenance, State of Pennsylvania: Final Report."

39. Oliver interview, March 24, 2008.

40. Ibid.

41. Sprague and Desonia, "TANF and Work Support Services"; Lucas Group, "Office of Income Maintenance, State of Pennsylvania: Final Report."

42. Linda Blanchette, personal communication (e-mail), April 21, 2008.

43. Blanchette interview.

44. Blanchette e-mail; Oliver interview, March 24, 2008.

45. Blanchette e-mail.

46. Sprague and Desonia, TANF and Work Support Services"; Oliver interview, March 24, 2008. Blanchette (e-mail) believes that the anticipated benefits are now the primary driver of the Modern Office effort, including improved client satisfaction; improved and enhanced staff morale; improved operational efficiency; decreased number of office visits; and decreased cycle times. Lucas Group consultants observed that OIM currently measures inputs or internal processes rather than client outcomes, such as "time to complete a determination or redetermination (expectation is to meet federal timeline); errors rates (as federally defined); and individual employees' caseloads (promotes client-to-caseworker culture) (see Lucas Group, "Office of Income Maintenance, State of Pennsylvania: Final Report"). The language of increased

customer service than a bank or airline."[47] The OIM had few tools for bench-marking its performance, other than customers' complaints regarding the slow application processing times and lost paperwork.[48]

In addition, introducing change in Pennsylvania also included dealing with the two unions—the Pennsylvania Social Service Union, representing caseworkers, and the American Federation of State, County, and Municipal Employees (AFSCME), representing clerical workers—and required a cooperative labor-management approach. Blanchette pointed out that "the union contract, while restricting us to some degree, is clear that management controls the work and can make changes to business processes and work assignments if it is in the best interest of the taxpayers and the consumers."[49] Accordingly, she created a planning team to work on defining specialized eligibility-determination functions that brought together all stake-holders—union representatives, county office managers, and chiefs of the different OIM bureaus (for policy, technology, and so on). They incorporated into the planning process the concerns of clients and studied experiences of other states, including Maryland, New York, and Florida. Blanchette describes the new vision for Modern Office as "a whole set of improvements: improved technology, improved business practices, policy simplifications, communication, and staff training."

Pennsylvania's planning process resulted in a pilot of Modern Office in the York County office in 2006. The first step was to break the application process down into different tasks, but the OIM soon recognized that specialization would work only if it replaced the paper trail with an online system. The state put the York County pilot on hold and redirected its attention to developing a "Workload Dashboard" to help caseworkers organize the selection of services specific clients needed. The Workload Dashboard also allows the OIM to distribute workloads between caseworkers and, eventually, between offices.

Pennsylvania's modernization is taking longer than the other states', both because it is internal and requires more time for employee buy-in and because it relies on an existing state technology project. Adoption rates of Pennsylvania's online application system, COMPASS (Commonwealth of Pennsylvania Access to Social Services), were low, only about 18 percent of all applications, so the OIM is making efforts to encourage more clients to go online or call its Change Center for information, reporting, and other simple tasks.

Pennsylvania's internal reform depends on some nongovernmental players in its network. Welfare-to-work services are provided by county governments, nonprofits, and for-profit organizations.[50] Other partners in the Modern Office network

---

self-sufficiency, household economic security, access to health services, and more food and nutrition did not come up in talks with Blanchette.

47. Oliver interview, March 24, 2008.

48. Blanchette interview. The following two paragraphs draw on this interview.

49. Ibid.

50. Sprague and Desonia, "TANF and Work Support Services."

include advocates from the legal community, local universities, and consultants. The OIM also wants to expand the number of community partners that help its clients apply for benefits. In another model OIM is piloting, hospitals help patients to set up a Medicaid claim by entering the appropriate data into COMPASS.[51]

Pennsylvania is not as far along in its modernization as Florida or Indiana. Yet according to Blanchette, accuracy and efficiency measures have already improved: "We are probably now at about 98 percent accuracy, 97 percent timeliness."[52] Operational success depends much more on Blanchette personally than on Indiana's Roob, who in effect outsourced cultural change. Blanchette needs to work through existing state systems, employees, and unions to accomplish the necessary culture shift, which she correctly claims as an integral part of the reform effort:

> You can't just change technology; you can't just change the process. It really is about a culture change and an understanding that the work is important. It is important from the [stand]point of accountability to the taxpayers, it is important [from the standpoint] of customer service to people who need the benefits, it is important from the [stand]point of making sure that workers are well trained and recognized for their work. You have to wrap around the technical aspects of improving the eligibility process. You have to wrap around the management, cultural change, and leadership effort to make it all happen.[53]

By March 2006, Pennsylvania officials had already identified useful lessons on creating transformative change from the inside from its COMPASS update—although it is far from complete: "Share the common goal of serving citizens; start on a small scale; build upon early successes; involve community organizations; seek input from advocate groups; and develop supportive collateral materials."[54]

Texas

Texas decided in 2005 to outsource transformative change in its eligibility system, encouraged by an estimated 50 percent additional savings over a comparable internal modernization.[55] But Albert Hawkins, the well-respected Texas Health and Human Services executive commissioner, soon ran into a problem similar to the one discovered by Indiana and many others: agencies that are not very good at supplying a service are not very good at procuring it either.

51. Oliver interview, March 24, 2008.
52. Blanchette interview.
53. Ibid.
54. George L. Hoover and Jerry Koerner, "Improving Access to Work Supports," PowerPoint presentation, National Governors Association Center, March 31, 2006, pp. 9–10 (www.nga.org/Files/pdf/0603 WORKSUPPORTSCOMPASS.PDF).
55. Texas Health and Human Services, "HHSC Estimates $646 Million in Savings from Call Centers," press release, June 30, 2005 (www.hhs.state.tx.us/news/release/063005_CallCenters.shtml).

Like the other states, Texas described its system as one created forty years ago and showing its age. An internal audit found vast inefficiencies affecting staff and clients alike: a paper- and labor-intensive process, applicants shunted from three to four employees each visit, three out of four cases requiring multiple visits, business hours during the normal work day causing inconvenience for clients, and prohibitively lengthy paper communications.[56]

In 2003 the Texas state legislature mandated a massive reorganization of the state's entire human services system, which comprises twelve agencies, spends $19.5 billion annually for administration; runs 200 programs; employs 50,000 state workers; and maintains 1,000 different offices.[57] The legislature also cut the Health and Human Services Commission (HHSC) eligibility staff by 900 employees while at the same time giving it responsibility for integrating eligibility determination for the newly streamlined service structure in Texas.[58]

Led by Hawkins, HHSC envisioned a new system with multiple access points, including new online interfaces and automated call centers. By 2005 the state had signed a five-year, $900 million contract with Accenture, a consulting and outsourcing services company, to modernize its eligibility-determination system. HHSC originally projected net savings of at least $400 million over five years.[59]

Like Indiana's, Texas' new system would offer more convenient access, a streamlined recertification process, and a single application for multiple benefits programs.[60] It would also retain a minimum number of state caseworkers, cutting almost 3,000 full-time employees from HHSC's eligibility-services budget and closing down 100 of its 380 county offices.[61] In Indiana, the number of retained state workers reflected a federal requirement (one driven more by politics than by efficiency) that a state merit employee sign off on every decision, regardless of

56. Texas Health and Human Services Commission, "Integrated Eligibility Determination Discovery Report" (Austin, February 2004) (www.hhs.state.tx.us/consolidation/IE/IE_DiscoveryRpt.shtml).

57. Hogg Foundation for Mental Health and others, "Legislative Update: A Citizen's Guide to the Mental Health-Related Actions of the 78th Texas Legislature" (Austin, 2004) (www.hogg.utexas.edu/PDF/LegUpdate.pdf).

58. Albert Hawkins, "Integrated Eligibility and Enrollment Contract," presentation to the House Subcommittee on Integrated Eligibility and TIERS Implementation, April 4, 2007 (www.hhsc.state.tx.us/reports/040407_TIERS_Subcommittee.pdf [accessed May 9, 2007]); Texas Health and Human Services Commission, "Integrated Eligibility Determination Discovery Report."

59. Hawkins, "Integrated Eligibility and Enrollment Contract"; Carole Keeton Strayhorn, Texas comptroller of public accounts, letter to Senator Eliot Shapleigh, Chairman Carlos I. Uresti, and Representative Carter Casteel, October 25, 2006, p. 3 (www.window.state.tx.us/comptrol/letters/accenture/accenture_letter.pdf); Reason Foundation, "Privatizing Welfare Eligibility," Annual Privatization Report 2004, pp. 76–77 (www.reason.org/apr2004/welfare.pdf).

60. Texas Health and Human Services Commission, "Streamlined System Will Expand Access to Services, Save Money," May 2004 (www.hhsc.state.tx.us/Consolidation/Projects/IE/060804_FactSheet.html [accessed May 2007]).

61. Albert Hawkins, "Integrated Eligibility and Enrollment Contract"; Strayhorn, letter to Shapleigh, Uresti, and Casteel.

vendor accuracy or accountability. Anne Heiligenstein, deputy executive commissioner of HHSC, notes that Texas did not exactly match its number of retained caseworkers to the minimum required by federal regulation: "The state had always envisioned a menu of ways that consumers could apply for services—in person, by phone and over the Internet."[62] But for both states a set of illogical federal rules did make designing their models, in particular estimating the rate of conversion and speed of transition, significantly more difficult.

Almost immediately, the new system was plagued by customer service and insurance coverage problems. Within the first three months, policy changes that included a shorter enrollment period led to 21,000 children losing coverage under the State Children's Health Insurance Program and almost 80,000 people being cut from the Medicaid rolls.[63]

Texas terminated its relationship with the general contractor in March 2007 to a chorus that suggested the problem was the outsourcing itself. A more accurate conclusion, however, is that creating the right network, implementing performance metrics, and initiating transformative change in a forty-year-old system serving millions of clients pose enormous challenges. Heiligenstein describes the Texas modernization effort by comparing it to remodeling "a forty-year-old house that has four million people living in it."[64]

In its second attempt, Texas downsized the project and concentrated first on deriving the highest value through consolidated call centers similar to Florida's and Indiana's. The revised contract that Texas signed in May 2007 was rigorously vetted to ensure that it protected the state's interests and that there was a smooth transition of services. Some of the resulting provisions were that the state would hold the contractor accountable if services did not meet its standards and would pay only for work delivered. Officials from the Food and Nutrition Service and the Centers for Medicare and Medicaid Services reviewed and approved the state's emergency actions so as to not disrupt services to Texans.

As of September 2008, four call centers in Austin, San Antonio, Midland, and Athens had created an infrastructure to support a more modern system. Since the initial rollout began in January 2006, the centers had answered over 13 million calls from Texans, including more than 1 million after five p.m. from people taking advantage of extended call-center hours.[65] The contractor also supports a new website first tested in early 2006 that by September 2008 had allowed more than 175,000 Texans to complete an online screening to see if they qualify for state services. More than 50,000 people had submitted online applications.[66]

62. Heiligenstein, e-mail to Goldsmith, October 8, 2008.
63. Ibid.; Strayhorn, letter to Shapleigh, Uresti, and Casteel.
64. Heiligenstein, e-mail to Goldsmith, September 23, 2008.
65. Ibid.
66. Ibid.

Both phases of the Texas experience provide valuable insights. The first attempt presented the state with increased potential benefits and much increased risk. Commissioner Hawkins explained the debacle by saying that administrators didn't "draw the line between state and vendor in the right place." Additionally, Texas coupled its outsourcing effort with major systemic and policy changes that resulted in too many large moving parts. Texas unexpectedly received a high volume of calls from applicants across the state to its two pilot regional call centers, which quickly overwhelmed the centers and resulted in frequent dropped calls after long wait times.[67]

An ironical twist was that problems arose because of an IT system change that resulted in a too rigorous application of rules. Before the system change, caseworkers had compensated for technical glitches by making exceptions while processing applications; the new system's efficient operations refused coverage to many. This tightening, coupled with system errors and a concurrent cut in benefits to children, produced an insurmountable backlash from the public.

Further, Texas's community partner network was not as strong as those in other states. In its 2006 comprehensive study on the Texas modernization initiative, the Austin-based Center for Public Policy Priorities found that while HHSC would provide person-to-person access for clients by maintaining its staff in over 200 hospitals across the state, in the final plan the system limited the role of community partners more than in the state's original plan.[68]

That Texas caught the troubles in its pilot sites and suspended rollout after just six weeks might speak to effective oversight and management of the contract, but the HHSC inspector general subsequently found that the "absence of effective management of project and contract oversight" was a major contributing factor and recommended bringing in outside experts to put the process back on track.[69] Indiana, meanwhile, invested heavily in contract monitoring and brought in significant outside expertise. Equally important, Indiana's decision to force its contractor to hire former state employees proved an important differentiating factor between the approach in Indiana and in Texas, where new hires were undertrained and underinformed.

In its sequel, Texas laid the foundation for a new and improved eligibility system for its clients. Instead of one large network of providers controlled by a single general contractor, as before, Texas broke off the complicated task of

---

67. Heiligenstein, e-mail to Goldsmith, October 8, 2008.

68. Center for Public Policy Priorities, "Updating and Outsourcing Enrollment in Public Benefits: The Texas Experience," November 2006, p. 29 (www.cppp.org/files/3/CPPP_PrivReport_(FS).pdf); Reason Foundation, "Privatizing Welfare Eligibility," Annual Privatization Report 2004, pp. 76–77 (www.reason. org/apr 2004/welfare.pdf).

69. Texas HHSC, Office of Inspector General, "TIERS/IEES Review," April 18, 2007 (www.oig. hhsc.tx.us [no longer posted, accessed June 4, 2008]).

updating the state's data system and continues to upgrade its technology more deliberately.

The second contract corrected some mistakes and resulted in increasingly smoother service transitions, but left Texas with a largely outdated IT system. By September 2008 a new Internet-based interface was helping in the processing of benefits each month for 633,000 clients,[70] but most of the local offices still use a computer system built on a programming language that colleges no longer teach; moreover, the system costs 1 million dollars a month to maintain and is plagued with regularly recurring downtime.

Lessons from the Four States

The contrasts among these states' new eligibility-determination networks are illustrative. Their differences stem not from different definitions of "inherently governmental" but instead from a series of pragmatic factors.

Lesson 1. Role of Politics versus Practicality

In Indiana, leadership came from the top of the administrative hierarchy: the governor and cabinet secretary were the two key advocates of modernization. They laid out their vision and priorities at the start, then proceeded methodically, resisting accommodations that might have compromised their goals.

In Florida and Texas, in contrast, direction to launch initiatives came from state legislators. In 2003 legislative leaders in Florida sought to "mandate the Department of Children and Families to achieve administrative efficiencies" and considered private contractor participation.[71] In 2004 they forced a change dynamic by cutting the DCF's $287 million eligibility-services budget almost 5 percent and its 7,200 staff by 750 full-time-equivalent positions.[72] In effect the legislature forced DCF employees to compete with the market to maintain operations. The DCF responded with a detailed study in 2004 showing both internal and outsourced modernization options; the latter would have been Florida's largest privatization effort to date.[73] Later, just as the request for proposals (RFP) process for private sector competition approached readiness, leading DCF officials were caught up in an ethics probe, and other high-profile privatization initiatives in the state hit rocky times. Governor Jeb Bush eventually opted for an internal system and stipulated that the new system must incorporate major staff

---

70. That portion may have represented only 12.5 percent of the caseload in Texas, but it exceeded the total Medicaid caseloads of a dozen states (Heiligenstein e-mail to Goldsmith, September 23, 2008).

71. Health and Human Services Appropriations Committee and Senator Bernie Saunders, "Senate Staff Analysis and Economic Impact Statement," March 23, 2005 (www.leg.state.fl.us/data/session/2005/Senate/bills/analysis/pdf/2005s0408.ha.pdf).

72. Lange, "ACCESS FLORIDA Presentation."

73. Winstead, testimony; Reason Foundation, "Privatizing Welfare Eligibility."

reductions, improved customer service, stream-lined workflows, policy simplifications, community partnerships, and a "refocusing [of] operations to the work-first philosophy."[74]

In Pennsylvania, the leadership for change emanated from the senior levels of the bureaucracy itself, with support from the Office of the Governor. This produced a more incremental internal approach. Pennsylvania began with a well-trained state bureaucracy that enjoyed the confidence of its top leadership.[75] Blanchette had more trust in her middle management capacity than Roob or Main had in Indiana. After meeting twenty or thirty middle managers, the consultant Will Oliver agreed with Blanchette, stating that the OIM "has some pretty solid middle managers—for the most part willing to innovate, willing to take some risks."[76] Experienced consultants characterized staff as dedicated and "passionate about the mission of helping those in need."[77] Still, by ruling out any competitive outsourcing of much of the delivery system, Pennsylvania will make it more difficult for managers of the County Assistance Offices to convince their 6,700 personnel to implement reform throughout the state's 97 offices.

Lesson 2. A Decentralized Network Is More Difficult to Manage— and Reform

Indiana and Florida took different approaches to reform—one inside and one outside government. Both, however, resulted from very strong unitary leadership at the top of a troubled state organization. In both situations, the directors had the complete confidence of the governor.

Pennsylvania officials confronted dual challenges: managing their own horizontal network of providers and the decentralized network of the state's county offices, where the tradition of independence was strong. This precluded Blanchette from rolling out a "cookie cutter approach"; instead, she introduced a rough template that included digitization, client self-service, and other best practices. Relative local autonomy will make adoption of new practices an ongoing challenge and will make it significantly more difficult to sustain improvements over time. Change will require leadership and commitment on the part of county office directors. Blanchette notes, "Any change is met with resistance and concern and a certain amount of fear and even complaining, but at the same time they are performing. . . . You have your few sour apples, but for the most

74. Florida Department of Children and Families, "Supplementary Application," December 5, 2006, Harvard University, Kennedy School of Government, Innovations in American Government Awards program; Florida Department of Children and Families, "Long Range Program Plan: Fiscal Years 2005–06 through 2009–10."

75. Blanchette e-mail.

76. Oliver interview, March 24, 2008.

77. Lucas Group, "Office of Income Maintenance, State of Pennsylvania: Final Report."

part I think there is a recognition that change is needed and they are onboard with helping us do it."[78]

Blanchette maintains the sense of urgency among her leadership team by keeping the goals of the reform and modernization on the table at all times: improving customer service, improving efficiency and accountability, and using resources wisely.

Lesson 3. Outsourcing: Rapid but Riskier Change

All four states committed themselves to reforming their systems and improving client interactions, three through new centralized systems. One of them, Indiana, by outsourcing, created the dynamic for change and is now ahead of the others. Pennsylvania's internally managed, decentralized approach started from a higher base level of performance but will likely take longer to accomplish, and change will be harder to sustain over time.

Florida's internally led network depended on persuasion, courtesy of the legislature—and a boost from the hurricane seasons of 2004 and 2005. The emergency responses forced centralization of service delivery and provided a business reason to eliminate a highly fragmented and inefficient county-by-county system predicated on multiple visits by both caseworker and client. In particular, the 2004 season triggered a new Web-based system for Florida's Disaster Food Stamps program and the distribution throughout the state of the processing of emergency benefits for more than 1 million Floridians.[79] The 2005 season tested existing elements of the new system and contributed to the development of backroom processing, document imaging, preregistration, and electronic linkages.[80]

Because of significant external pressures, including the very real threat of outsourcing, Florida's transformation, though internal, likely unfolded more rapidly than it otherwise might have done. But externally driven transformation involves risk. Legislative pressures mandated Texas to drive change with an external integrator of services, but the speed of the change exceeded the capacity of the network to absorb it.

The first part of the Texas story shows that public officials who really stretch for bold changes subject themselves to larger risks. For example, the HHSC inspector general's report points to a particular risk of big change: that it can easily be second-guessed and measured against a standard of perfection by a third party, whether from within government or outside. The state's second attempt shows that if the network involves multiple antiquated systems such as, in this case, front office and back office, separating them out reduces risks but slows transformation. In continuing to push for improvement and finally, now, making

78. Blanchette interview.
79. Winstead, testimony.
80. Lange, "ACCESS FLORIDA Presentation."

gains, Commissioner Hawkins and Deputy Executive Commissioner Heiligenstein also demonstrated the value of resiliency in effecting change, despite operational and political setbacks.

Lesson 4. Skills, Not Sectors, Drive Sourcing Decisions

The debate about privatization tends to be framed in all-or-nothing terms: privatize all eligibility-determination processes, or none. Yet these states' efforts are a reminder that complicated systems are made up of multiple components. In this study, the components of eligibility services—only one part of the larger social welfare system—comprise network management and integration, management, IT, back-office processing and call centers, training, contract and performance management, financial wherewithal, and more. Yet government's role is, first, to ensure a focus on public value, not solely on the cost of providing each specific function or service. Second, it must hold parties accountable by requiring outcomes based on the desired public purpose, whatever it may be. In Indiana, accuracy at first and eventually self-sufficiency were written into the original contract and then monitored effectively via performance metrics.

The private sector is often, but not always, better suited than government to provide training, management expertise, new technology, and financial capital. Private sector business platforms often greatly exceed those of governments in their technical sophistication. In Indiana's case, digital platforms will help consolidate important data sources and make them more accessible. Using the capital and expertise of a large corporation such as IBM and its major subcontractor ACS, Indiana will replace its paper-based system with online capabilities, document-processing centers, call centers, and new information system interfaces.

Another benefit of private sector partners is that they, as network integrators, can transcend government funding silos to meet the multiple needs of individual clients in ways that government itself either cannot or will not do. Instead of hiring dozens of private and nonprofit agencies to do the work of the state's 2,000-plus caseworkers, support staff, and contractors, the state is contracting with IBM to serve as the integrator of the entire network. In particular, the vast network of community partners—who offer credibility, outreach, peer influence, and opportunities for civic and volunteer participation—requires management and coordination.

Indiana's experienced administrative talent recognized that IBM could integrate the diverse pieces of its network better than the agency itself could—yet these same officials played a very significant role in establishing the rules of the network. They knew that they had to concentrate on the availability of the requisite skills and technologies, not on the source sector. In the end, states can combine private and public elements (management, employees, and technology) in a way that best suits their situation. If any sector can be the locus of almost any function, it naturally follows that few if any functions are inherently governmental.

Controlling Public Value Is Inherently Governmental

Indiana's bill for both the ten-year IBM contract and Indiana's retained costs will total roughly $1.5 billion—$300 million less than the projected ten-year cost of the "as is" system and $500 million less than the projected ten-year cost of modernizing the system internally. The state also expects to reduce benefits expenditures by closing the front door to ineligible applicants and holding vendors responsible for any errors in determining eligibility. IBM will share responsibility for meeting work participation requirements mandated by Congress under the TANF program. According to the governor, total savings from administration, penalty avoidance, new third-party revenue recruitment, and the reduction of waste, fraud, and abuse will equal $1 billion over ten years.

In Indiana, the transformation of public service was as important as the savings realized. The improved processes will eliminate up to 2 million unnecessary visits a year by working mothers to apply for Food Stamps and other benefits. After the vendor took over, and without any significant change in the Indiana economy, the value of the Food Stamps benefits distributed rose significantly, from $54.5 million in December 2005 to $55.8 million in December 2006 to $61.7 million in December 2007. A large increase in Food Stamps applications suggests just how many people were discouraged by the old system's inconvenience and inefficiency. These early improvements raise fundamental questions about what happens when the private sector is materially better than government at functions generally considered core governmental functions.

Disconnecting the deep-seated link between caseworker and client in county welfare offices was once unthinkable. Yet in Indiana as in the other three cases, breaking this link was essential to transforming operations, improving customer service, and reducing fraud. The same can be said for the deep-seated link between supposedly inherently governmental functions and employees in merit-based personnel systems. A break in this thinking is fundamental to a public official's ability to marshal the requisite capacities and resources to transform service delivery and, more broadly, to achieve the public purpose.

Yet Congress continues to attempt to draw lines based on the "inherently governmental" definition. In June 2007 the American Federation of State, County, and Municipal Employees expressed its support of a congressional effort to limit outsourcings like Indiana's. AFSCME explained:

The inherently governmental function of the eligibility-determination process, including taking applications, determining the facts of the individual's situation, conducting the interview, resolving disputes, and conducting the hearing process, would remain in public agencies with employees in merit-based personnel systems. They are inherently governmental activities because they require the exercise of discretion in applying governmental authority.[81]

It has been seen that the process of collecting a piece of paper and asking questions about eligibility can in some cases be done dramatically better by a private contractor. The AFSCME argument may prohibit outsourced activities and in the process may penalize welfare recipients through politics, but it does not further the analysis for public officials sincerely looking for guidance. Using this definition to conclude that Indiana turned over control of too many important public activities to the private sector would be easy—and wrong. Instead, Indiana's nuanced approach helps answer the question, "What should government actually do in a post–core functions world?"

Indiana's focus on increasing value over cutting costs allowed it to start in the right place. In their quest to repair the dilapidated FSSA, Governor Daniels and Secretary Roob refocused the agency's goals and established a strategic direction for the agency that emphasized big-picture issues: supporting work rather than paying benefits, and enhancing health rather than funding Medicaid bills. They realigned the agency with a new mission centered on improving clients' lives while acknowledging caseworkers and taxpayers as important stakeholders.

Indiana's leaders amplified public values by asserting tighter and more focused policy control than when the state spent its time caught up in the details of an inferior operation. The leadership retained tight control over the rules and policies around eligibility and modified some in their determination to make it easier for deserving Hoosiers to receive benefits. Indiana also maintained responsibility for determining service levels, such as application processing time, which they will require IBM to maintain above the state's historic benchmarks. In fact, one key value of Indiana's modernization project—one that other states might do well to follow—is never to let the quality or volume of service decrease during the transition. Roob insisted that the state accomplish its new strategic goals in a system that worked better for clients, caseworkers, and taxpayers.

AFSCME also argued that clients are somehow worse off in Indiana's outsourced model. Roob was determined to rally state employees around his aspiration that caseworkers spend more time supporting people's efforts to achieve self-sufficiency instead of wasting countless hours on paperwork. Unfortunately, AFSCME's definition of core governmental functions traps employees behind their desks, processing paper instead of working diligently as caseworkers. Furthermore, Indiana preserved its employees' jobs while Florida's insourced modernization forced hundreds

81. American Federation of State, County, and Municipal Employees, "Privatization of the Food Stamp Program: Chairman Baca's Proposal," June 2007 (www.chn.org/pdf/2007/foodstampprivatization.pdf).

of state employees out of their jobs. According to the contract, IBM must initially hire all caseworkers not retained by the state. Roob understood that his commitment to the state employees would drive up costs and reduce taxpayer savings, but the FSSA's caseworkers knew the system and its rules. Also, says Roob, "We intentionally bought ourselves an insurance policy in case IBM failed."[82]

Indiana's focus on value allowed the FSSA next to identify its limitations and then supplement its capacity. Roob well knew that troubled government agencies often lack the capacity to negotiate with large, sophisticated vendors. He attacked this problem by adding to his team, hiring consultants and lawyers proficient at managing RFP processes, and by establishing appropriate contract-monitoring techniques. Although the system integrator and main vendor could serve as a single point of contact for the state, a contract of that size, scope, and complexity would magnify FSSA exposure to liabilities ranging from abuse to poor performance. In recognition of this risk as well as the FSSA's poor contract-management and -monitoring capacity, the state also set aside $3 million annually to hire an outside oversight and verification vendor to monitor the contract. Rounding out the new network, IBM recruited 1,000 local social service providers and other agencies into its Voluntary Community Assistance Network to help the state reach more households.[83]

Indiana's bold move attracted special attention as the governor headed into a reelection campaign where the IBM contract became an issue. Although customer service improved, this occurred in fits and starts and there were some complaints, such as call center wait times that were longer than promised. Before the outsourcing, Indiana's record in helping poor working mothers and abused children was among the worst in the nation, but there was little public outcry. Yet change produces critics regardless of outcomes. Despite dramatic improvements from Indiana's eligibility modernization, Governor Daniels's upcoming election created a target for critics of privatization. The ongoing battles Indiana faces over its bold move illustrate the political nature of the opposition that reformers always face. Indeed, in these situations, the perfect is truly the enemy of the good.

Conclusion

What, then, is government's core function? First, to ensure public purpose. In the case of eligibility modernizations, the public purpose is to ensure family and

---

82. E. Mitchel Roob, personal communication to Stephen Goldsmith, February 2, 2007.

83. IBM Coalition and Family and Social Services Administration, "V-CAN Overview: Working Together to Improve Services to Indiana Families," May 2007 (www.in.gov/fssa/files/vcanoverview 0507.pdf [accessed February 5, 2008]); Family and Social Services Agency, Quarterly Report, January 2008 (www.in.gov/fssa/files/January_2008_QFR.pdf).

household self-sufficiency. Indiana realigned the FSSA mission in accordance with this purpose. Second, to provide funding pursuant to certain rules. Officials use a number of mechanisms to ensure the good stewardship of taxpayer dollars spent on public goods. Finally, the government ensures the democratic values of fairness and equity. It ensures the application of rules in a fair and consistent way and makes an appellate process available for people who feel wronged.

Public officials should care strongly about ensuring the values that are most important to the public. Through effective contract management, including the use of performance metrics and interfaces such as "dashboard" tools, government can ensure accountability in benefits programs. Effective social safety nets reflect the American values of solidarity and generosity. The eligibility-determination process, as the gateway to these benefits programs, is uniquely placed to ensure additional values such as equity and fairness. The primary mission of most of these agencies responsible for eligibility determination is neither to develop technological interfaces nor to set up and staff call centers but rather to ensure household or family self-sufficiency. As a public purpose, one that almost everyone would agree on, this mission helps answer the question "What is core to government?" By tying the application process directly into work and training programs, state officials express support for the values of independence and self-sufficiency. And by making the system an efficient operation overall, state agencies responsible for health and human services, public welfare, or children and families remain good stewards of taxpayer dollars.

Smartly, Indiana put four issues front and center early on:

1. *Strategic direction.* Does the government just want to be cheaper or also better and faster? It is easy to find a provider that delivers an obsolete, ineffective service efficiently. Roob sought a higher goal: a system that works better for clients, caseworkers, *and* taxpayers.

2. *Policy development.* Well-planned transformations emphasize policy goals and address big-picture issues. Roob wanted to address the state's workforce support efforts and Medicaid's outreach to people who need coverage.

3. *Contract management.* Proficient contract management is a government necessity. Yet public employees routinely lack the necessary experience, training, and tools to meet this challenge. Roob strengthened his team's capabilities for contract negotiations, contract monitoring, and more.

4. *Personnel management.* What happens to employees and their institutional knowledge? Roob believed that caseworkers should spend less time moving paper and more time using their knowledge to counsel and support people in need.

By setting these four priorities, Indiana was able to concentrate on what is truly "inherently governmental": expressing democratic values through strategy and policy while ensuring the equitable implementation of policies. Shuffling pieces of paper or creating digital images is not inherently governmental, even when these actions support critical governmental functions. Determining the range of financial benefits and services necessary to promote self-sufficiency among struggling citizens is inherently governmental.

References

Cody, Scott, Renée Nogales, and Emily Sama Martin. 2008. "Modernization of the Food Stamp Program in Florida: Final Report." Princeton: Mathematica Policy Research, Inc., February (www.mathematica-mpr.com/publications/pdfs/FSP_Florida.pdf).

Porter, Oliver W. 2006. *Creating the New City of Sandy Springs—The 21st Century Paradigm: Private Industry*. Bloomington, Ind.: AuthorHouse.

6

"Integration and Innovation" in the Intelligence Community: The Role of a Netcentric Environment, Managed Networks, and Social Networks

G. EDWARD DESEVE

The United States is challenged by many different and evolving threats, including enemies with many faces and no borders—terrorism, weapons of mass destruction, proliferation, infectious diseases, cyber attacks, and illegal trafficking. The intelligence community (IC) is adjusting to meet this new complex threat environment and adapt to the new strategic context in which it now operates. To do so, the IC must have people, process and technology that provide seamless integration and cross-agency collaboration. *The 500 Day Plan for Integration and Collaboration* continues to build the foundation to enable the IC to work as a single, integrated enterprise so we can collaborate across critical missions, enhance our support to a wide range of customers and partners, contribute to our national security priorities, and reduce the risks that the nation faces today and in the future.

—J. M. McConnell, director of National Intelligence, October 10, 2007

The potential for "collaboration and integration" in the intelligence community (IC), particularly for combating terrorism, is the focus of this chapter.[1] The problems identified after 9/11 and in intelligence gathering on weapons of mass destruction are the backdrop for the analysis.[2] Also explored are responses to

1. The intelligence community is defined as "a federation of executive branch agencies and organizations that work separately and together to conduct intelligence activities necessary for the conduct of foreign relations and the protection of the national security of the United States." A list of these agencies can be found at www.intelligence.gov/1-definition.shtml.
2. Kean and others (2004) and Silberman and others (2005).

these problems such as creation of new organizational structures, increases in staffing, implementation of technology, understanding the importance of social networks, and creation of interorganizational mechanisms. Finally, the continuing need to recognize that future solutions may lie in implementing "netcentric" strategies externally, within the community, and within each agency is discussed. The implications of these strategies for leadership development in the IC are of particular concern.

9/11 and Subsequent Developments in the Intelligence Community

The attacks of September 11, 2001, shocked the intelligence community into reexamining its place in a changed and changing world. The cold war was over, but the capabilities of many of the U.S. and international intelligence community agencies were still trained on Russia and Europe, particularly on the potential for armed conflict there. The growing threat of non-state-sponsored terrorism was apparent, but IC agencies were not equipped to deal with it. They had not built robust international alliances for close situational monitoring and had cut their own ranks by more than 40 percent from the cold war high.

Even after 9/11, the pace of change was less rapid than many observers had hoped. Not until November 2002 did President Bush announce the creation of the 9/11 Commission—he had been reluctant to empanel such a group.[3] The commission issued its report on September 22, 2004.[4] Among the commission's major findings regarding the intelligence community were that information needed to be shared and duties needed to be more clearly assigned. The commission found that outmoded structures and bureaucratic rivalries hindered the work of the IC in anticipating and responding to terrorist threats.

Two important organizational changes in the intelligence community's structure were recommended. The first was the creation of the Office of the Director of National Intelligence (ODNI); the second was the creation of the National Counter Terrorism Center (NCTC). Both recommendations were enacted in the Intelligence Reform and Terrorism Prevention Act of December 7, 2004. Even as the ODNI and NCTC were being created in the spring of 2005, a second commission, looking into the intelligence failures surrounding the absence of weapons of mass destruction (WMD) in Iraq, was issuing its report.[5]

Not surprisingly, the WMD Report found that "the intelligence community is . . . fragmented, loosely managed, and poorly coordinated; the 15 intelligence organizations are a 'community' in name only and rarely act with a unity of pur-

---

3. See, for example, www.cbsnews.com/stories/2002/05/15/attack/main509096.shtml.
4. Kean and others (2004).
5. Silberman and others (2005).

pose."[6] Further, the report observed that the community had "too little innovation and too little integration to succeed in the 21st century."[7]

This criticism struck a cord with the newly confirmed director of national intelligence (DNI), John Negroponte. His foreword to the "National Intelligence Strategy" report of October 2005 recognized the need for change:

> A strategy is a statement of fundamental values, highest priorities, and orientation toward the future, but it is an action document as well. For U.S. national intelligence, the time for change is now. There are no easy answers to the risks contemplated here, or the risks that might emerge. This strategy therefore accepts risk as intelligence's natural and permanent field of action and is based on the proposition that to preserve our society in a dangerous century, vigilance is not enough. U.S. national intelligence must do more.[8]

Key to the achievement of the National Intelligence Strategy was the role of the National Counter Terrorism Center. Central to the NCTC's ability to execute its dual missions of "integrating and analyzing *all* intelligence" and "conduct[ing] strategic operational planning by integrating *all* instruments of national power" is its role as a "multiagency organization" (emphasis added).[9] Personnel are detailed to the NCTC from every agency in the intelligence community, and from other governmental agencies where appropriate. Though clearly identified with their agencies, these individuals are detailed to and under the jurisdiction of the NCTC director. This concept of joint operations is controversial, as will be seen later, but it is crucial to information exchange and coordinated action.

The concept of jointness has been highly successful in the military. The Goldwater-Nichols Department of Defense Reorganization Act of 1986 was a major milestone in defense reorganization. The act centralized operational authority in the chairman of the Joint Chiefs of Staff as opposed to the service chiefs. The chairman was the principal military adviser to the president, the National Security Council, and the secretary of defense, and the act streamlined the operational chain of command from the president to the secretary of defense to the unified commanders.

The effect of Goldwater-Nichols can be seen in U.S. and allied operations in the Gulf War, Bosnia, and now in Iraq and Afghanistan. The doctrinal aspects of the act are currently being implemented in Joint Vision 2020 (2000), which stipulates that to be most effective, the force must be fully joint: intellectually, operationally, organizationally, doctrinally, and technically. "The joint force, because

6. Ibid., p. 6.
7. Ibid., p. 17.
8. Office of the Director of National Intelligence (2005, p. 4).
9. National Counter Terrorism Center, "About the National Counterterrorism Center" (www.nctc. gov/about_us/about_nctc.html),

of its flexibility and responsiveness, will remain the key to operational success in the future."[10]

One of the "Core Initiatives" of the DNI 500-day plan is to "implement Civilian IC Joint Duty Program."[11] The desired impact of this program is to "make Joint Duty a reality." The Joint Duty program provides rotational opportunities for civilian IC professionals and is a prerequisite for senior rank. As part of this initiative, a companion Joint Leadership Development Program (JLDP) is designed and developed and begins to deliver and reinforce joint duty experiences. It also ensures that senior leaders gain a community-wide focus.[12]

These actions will implement Intelligence Community Directive 601, "Human Capital Joint Intelligence Duty Assignments," effective May 16, 2006. This directive implements the director of national intelligence's responsibilities under the National Security Act of 1947, as amended, to establish personnel policies, in consultation with the elements of the intelligence community, that

> . . . encourage and facilitate assignments and details to national intelligence centers and between elements of the intelligence community [and] . . . make service in more than one element of the intelligence community a condition of promotion to such positions within the intelligence community as the Director shall specify.[13]

This directive has the effect of requiring joint duty in a way that was previously not in place and mirrors military service requirements that individuals have a joint duty assignment before they are eligible for promotion to general or admiral.

Assessing Success and Approaching the Future

Three documents from within the IC provide a perspective on how well the DNI and NCTC are doing.[14] These documents, available to the public, focus primarily on how the IC has responded to the challenges of terrorism and how it should respond in the future.

The NCTC progress report clearly recognizes the complexity of its assigned task: "Information sharing in support of the nation's counterterrorism objectives isn't about 'flipping a switch'; it involves a diverse landscape of players and technologies, and myriad cultural, security, and policy barriers."[15]

---

10. National Defense University, "Goldwater Nichols Department of Defense Reorganization Act of 1986" (www.ndu.edu/library/goldnich/goldnich.html).

11. Office of the Director of National Intelligence (2007c, p. 3).

12. Ibid, p. 5.

13. Office of the Director of National Intelligence (2006b, p. 9).

14. National Counter Terrorism Center (2006); Office of the Director of National Intelligence (2007b); Office of the Director of National Intelligence (2007c).

15. National Counter Terrorism Center (2006, p. 4).

To answer questions about access to information and to allow efficient and secure collection and dissemination of information, a "role-based" philosophy has been adopted to protect sources and methods of information collection and allay fears that inappropriate parties will have inappropriate access to information. This philosophy is similar to the one used by the Centers for Disease Control and Prevention (CDC) in sharing information about potential public health crises.[16] Each individual in the CDC Public Health Information network has a role with particular abilities to contribute information, use information, edit information, and so on. These roles prevent an individual from accessing or changing information and enhance the security of the data.

The CDC has created an information-sharing backbone. This backbone receives information from multiple sources according to their individual ability to gather and rapidly share information. The CDC then has a responsibility to provide this information to individuals and agencies that have a "need to know" it. Not all individuals or agencies have access to all information. The role of the individual or agency is crucial in dissemination.

Beyond information access, the NCTC prides itself on improving situational awareness with secure video conference calls several times a day to allow all authorized personnel within the community to have up-to-the-minute information about what is and what is not going on. The NCTC also maintains information on terrorists in its online service that is available to both IC and non-IC members that need real-time information on individual terrorists. More than 6,000 people in more than sixty agencies use these data.[17] The NCTC is proud of its role in coordinating production, analysis, and dissemination of information across the community and with foreign partners. There are formal interagency processes as well as less formal ad hoc conferences with foreign parties that have a need to know.

Despite these advances, the NCTC indicates that some issues remain to be resolved, including privacy, access, sources and methods, liaison information, source credibility, information technology, data acquisition, and access to state, local, tribal, and private sectors. The NCTC realizes that "resolving these issues will require managing an extremely complicated balance between technical, legal, policy, and security issues."[18] A clear illustration of this balance in terms of policymaking was the controversial Information Awareness Office established by the Defense Advanced Research Projects Agency (DARPA) and the Defense Department in 2002. The privacy and legal issues created by this program led to intensive media

---

16. Gerberding (2004). Although the CDC is not a member of the intelligence community we cited it as an example of best practice in the collaborative use of information.

17. An example of this is the Terrorist Internet Datamart Environment (TIDE). This product alone contains the identities and information about more than 300,000 individuals worldwide.

18. National Counter Terrorism Center (2006, p. 11).

scrutiny and eventually congressional action to terminate funding for the office, although a number of its programs continue in other institutional settings.

The DNI takes these observations further in its "100 Day Plan." Its assessment of the current situation is as follows:

> Significant progress has been made in enhancing the effectiveness of the intelligence community. Much more, however, must be accomplished to counter today's threats effectively. To [better] serve . . . the nation and our principal customers—from the President, the Congress, and the warfighter to state and local authorities—the IC must become more agile and effective by enhancing integration and collaboration.[19]

A primary aspect of IC integration and collaboration is the necessity of dealing with disparate cultures. For example, although the NCTC is seen as a multi-agency organization, the concept of jointness is foreign to the culture of much of the IC. Citing the success of the military under Goldwater-Nichols in promoting joint activity, the DNI calls for promoting jointness "through recruitment, training exercises, education, retention assignments, and career and leadership development."[20]

Information sharing and dissemination is the name of the game at the NCTC, but the DNI realizes that without a change in collection and analysis, simple information sharing is not enough:

> We need to foster collection and analytic transformation by strengthening integration, collaboration, and tradecraft. This focus area emphasizes the radical transformation of analysis through integration of analytic workspaces, analytic products, analytic tools, and the analytic direction of intelligence collection."[21]

Still, the DNI is not totally satisfied with information sharing. A new approach is needed:

> We need to move from a "need to know" model to a "responsibility to provide" collaborative environment by developing an implementation plan for an IC-wide identity structure with attribute-based access, such as clearance level, project affiliation, or other such attributes.[22]

This imperative is also cultural in nature. The concept of "need to know" drove data sharing for more than fifty years, after the end of World War II, especially when it came to protecting sources and methods of collection. The shift to

---

19. Office of the Director of National Intelligence (2007b, p. 2).
20. Ibid., p. 3.
21. Ibid., p. 4.
22. Ibid., p. 9.

"responsibility to provide" will involve a major change in the way individual agencies do business and collaborate.

Transformation and the Workforce

One cannot read the 100-day plan, the 500-day plan, and the progress report without thinking of the massive changes taking place in the jobs of people in the intelligence community and the changes in the environment in which they work. These changes come at a time when the workforce itself is changing dramatically.

The importance of the IC workforce was recognized in the October 2005 National Intelligence Strategy: "A high-performing intelligence workforce that is results-focused, collaborative, bold, future oriented, self-evaluating, [and] innovative" is central to the community's ultimate integration and its ultimate success."[23]

The current workforce has some unusual characteristics, however: a disproportionate number of new hires since 9/11 and individuals nearing requirement. Draw-downs of personnel and hiring freezes after the end of the cold war have left relatively few persons in the middle. In other words, "The IC literally skipped a generation of new hires with serious ramifications for our overall capacity and leadership succession."[24] This fact has significant cultural implications for the IC as Internet-socialized generation X and Y types work side by side with need-to-know veterans of the cold war who are nearing retirement.

The goal of jointness is also under pressure. The *Washington Times* reported in April 2007 that Defense Intelligence Agency (DIA) representatives had been withdrawn from the NCTC operations center in November 2006. Commenting on the situation, Senator Carl Levin (D-Mich.), chair of the Senate Armed Services Committee, said at a committee hearing on March 8, 2007, that the officials had been withdrawn "because Northcom and the Defense Intelligence Agency found that it was just too hard to get information and cooperation from the NCTC."[25] This withdrawal caused the *Washington Times* to observe,

> The vision of a seamless network of networks has bumped up against the reality of complex and overlapping rules and regulations governing the ways different agencies can acquire and use information, especially about Americans.[26]

The writer could have added an observation about the clash of cultures and social networks as well.

23. Office of the Director of National Intelligence (2005).
24. Office of the Director of National Intelligence (2006a, p. 4).
25. "Military Observers Absent from Center for counterterrorism," *Washington Times,* April 1, 2007 (http://washingtontimes.com/national/20070401-120127-1566r.htm).
26. Ibid.

The DNI recognizes that more needs to be done. As noted in the 500-day plan, it is important to make joint duty a reality. The joint duty program provides rotational opportunities for civilian IC professionals as a prerequisite for achieving senior rank. As part of this initiative, a companion Joint Leadership Development Program (JLDP) is being designed and developed, and is beginning to deliver and reinforce joint duty experiences. It also ensures that senior leaders gain a community-wide focus.

An example of the recent changes in joint duty can be seen at the NCTC, where individuals were previously assigned by their agencies. Now they are formally detailed to the NCTC and are under the jurisdiction of the NCTC director. Personnel evaluations are performed by NCTC managers and sent to the home agency.

Transformation, Leadership, and "Netcentricity"

The two examples just outlined—the problems of a workforce divided into two opposite age clusters and the absence of jointness between agencies—combined with a "war for talent" between agencies and other potential employers described in the National Security Strategy have led to a focus on leadership development at every level of the IC. This focus starts with the need to reinforce an ethos among all members of the IC, but particularly among leaders at every level:

> The most powerful way to strengthen and unify our community is to foster a common *ethos* amongst all who serve in it. That *ethos* embodies the "code" of shared values that guides the way an individual (and an organization) behaves, and it defines an institution's culture.[27]

This ethos incorporates the values of *commitment* to selfless service in support of the mission, *courage*—moral, intellectual, and physical—and *collaboration* as colleagues, working together as members of a single team.[28]

These values are seen as the "binding glue" of the IC culture. The DNI realizes that "an attempt to create and sustain a common institutional culture across the IC, especially where none really exists today, may be [its] most difficult human capital objective."[29] In the 500-day plan, the first focus area is "creating a culture of collaboration." The recognition that culture plays a vital part in the transformation is a key factor in initiating the needed changes.

There are indications that these changes are under way, but improvement is still needed. In a survey of IC employees, completed in 2007, 84 percent agreed with the statement "Our mission depends on IC agencies and components shar-

27. Office of the Director of National Intelligence (2006a, p. 28).
28. J. M. McConnell, Memorandum to All Intelligence Community Employees, August 7, 2007.
29. Ibid., p. 27.

ing knowledge and collaborating."[30] This was an increase of 9 percent from the previous survey. Still, less than 50 percent believed that it was easy to work outside their agency at another IC organization.

The articulation and inculcation of an ethos and values can be reinforced by the human capital plan objectives of providing joint training and leadership development programs across the IC, establishing and validating leadership competencies, and creating a National Intelligence Service that takes in the whole intelligence community. In all these efforts, the human capital plan recognizes fundamental differences in the way work is organized in today's connected global environment as compared to how it was organized before the spread of the Internet. The human capital plan refers to a "netcentric" world "where rigid hierarchies and formal chains of command may not have the necessary agility to deal with the threats we face"; in this environment, "every member of the IC must be prepared to step up to the leadership challenge when it comes."[31] This concept provides the backdrop for the balance of this chapter.

A construct is created in the next section linking the concept of netcentricity, as defined by the Department of Defense (DOD), with the broader idea of *managed networks*. previously defined by this author.[32] Various types of managed networks can be invoked separately or in combination to deal with specific problems or provide a long-term means of exchanging information or coordinating action.[33] Managed networks are organizational constructs that go well beyond any simple orientation toward technology and encompass the entire range of organizational structures that the DNI envisions in the 500-day plan.

Each type of managed network requires that key elements be included in its design if it is to work. The success of a netcentric environment and a managed network is also often affected by the presence or absence of social networks. A social network can be used to support the work of the managed network or can be hostile to it and create unexpected difficulties. If no social network exists, it may be necessary to create one to implement the managed network. In any case, social networks must be taken into account as change is implemented. Additional tasks of managing networks and managing in networks will be presented to highlight the work that is necessary to continue the proper functioning of managed networks.[34]

---

30. Office of the Director of National Intelligence, "IC Employment Climate Survey," March 2008.

31. Ibid, p. 30.

32. For a definition and discussion of this term, see DeSeve (2007, p. 47).

33. I have coined this use of the word "invoke" to give the reader the sense that no one person runs the network but that many can use it for their own purposes. They "invoke" it on behalf of the mission of the group or the mission of the organization that is using it. For example, the Centers for Disease Control and Prevention invoke the public health information network to send and receive information on epidemics. The New York City Department of Public Health also invokes the network to see how cities around the globe respond to public health emergencies.

34. Milward and Provan (2006).

Netcentric Environments, Managed Networks, and Social Networks

The primary function of a netcentric environment is to create an orientation and capabilities that enable the creation, invocation, and operation of *managed networks* that exist within a framework of preexisting *social networks*. Let's define these terms.

—A netcentric environment is "a framework for full human and technical connectivity and interoperability that allows all DOD users and mission partners to share the information they need, when they need it, in a form they can understand and act on with confidence, and protects information from those who should not have it."[35]

—A managed network is "an integrated system of relationships that is managed across formal and informal organizational boundaries with recognized organizational principles and a clear definition of success."[36]

—A social network is "the personal or professional set of relationships between individuals. Social networks represent both a collection of ties between people and the strength of those ties. Often used as a measure of social 'connectedness,' recognizing social networks assists in determining how information moves throughout groups, and how trust can be established and fostered."[37]

In the sections that follow I analyze how the netcentric environment enables managed networks in the context of the social networks existing within the intelligence community.

Netcentric Environment

The late admiral Arthur Cebrowski was the originator of the term "netcentricity." He used it to describe two fundamental network concepts. First, netcentricity is an environment based largely on technical capacity. Second, the technical capacity is necessary but not sufficient for implementing netcentric operations in response to more complex missions. Admiral Cebrowski stated:

> Net-centric capabilities and attributes can be viewed through a model consisting of two areas: the Knowledge Area and the Technical Area. The Knowledge Area comprises the cognitive and social interaction capabilities and attributes required to effectively function in the Net-Centric Environment. The Technical Area is composed of the physical aspects (infrastructure, network connectivity, and environment) and the information environment where information is created, manipulated, and shared.[38]

---

35. Department of Defense, "Net-Centric Environment Joint Functional Concept, Version 1.0, 7 April 2005" (www.dtic.mil/futurejointwarfare/concepts/netcentric_jfc.pdf), p. v.

36. DeSeve (2007).

37. Government of Australia (2007).

38. William Eggers, "Interview with Vice Admiral (Ret.) Arthur Cebrowski," Government Technology's Public CIO, November 2004.

This view of netcentricity encompasses a broader definition than the one provided earlier. Still, it focuses on the central role of information in support of a mission, not in organizing the approach to the mission itself. In one "vignette" described in a DOD publication the distinction between the use of information in support of the mission and the organization of the mission itself is blurred.[39] (A vignette is a simulation designed to create a view of the future based on the employment of new technology.) Although the availability of information plays a key role in the exercise, other elements, including structure, governance, and trust, are central to its success.

The vignette, called "Network Respond," was designed to simulate a response to an earthquake, which also had important geopolitical implications. The vignette described numerous connected networks, strategically placed sensors, and databases to provide area data and information. The network uses a number of redundant systems and dispersed data storage mechanisms to protect against the effects of another catastrophic earthquake.

The vignette concluded that success in the simulated exercise lay not in the power of the technology but instead was achieved because of the U.S. Joint Forces' ability to operate seamlessly at the tactical level in dynamic communities of interest that included other governmental entities, allied forces, and nongovernmental organizations. This gave them access to numerous coordinated resources. The agile unified effort could rapidly combine capabilities from different services and partners at the appropriate levels to accomplish efficiently an increased range of missions. This ability to achieve constructive interdependence should be the norm, not the exception.

While Joint Functional Concept 1.0 (see note 35) focuses on "Knowledge and Technical" areas, a more inclusive concept would be "Organization, People, Processes, and Technology," which would parallel the observation of Admiral Cebrowski.

Types of Managed Networks

What kinds of managed networks exist and what elements must be present when they are created and invoked? At all levels of government, most departments and programs were established to deal with specific problems with defined boundaries. This has had the effect of creating "silos" within and across governments. There has been relatively little incentive in government to work across boundaries and even less training in the knowledge, skills, and abilities required to do this. In fact, some people are concerned that public managers who involve parties outside government in achieving a governmental mission violate a public trust.

---

39. See Department of Defense, "Net-Centric Environment Joint Functional Concept."

External forces (including the increasing complexity of problems facing governments), the interconnectedness of public and private activities, and the need to respond to opportunities and threats globally are at work to upset the siloed form of organization. In an agency such the NCTC these forces have created more complex challenges whose solutions often depend on interaction beyond these silos and involve a broad set of government and private or international allies. Despite the need for new organizational and systems design concepts, constructs such as those at the NCTC are still "platform-centric" in that information is centrally located and cannot easily be shared with other mission partners.

In government as a whole there are few models and rules of engagement for managing the process of multiparty program delivery or outcome improvement. The netcentric environment contains elements of a solution, but it is important to generalize beyond this concept to that of a managed network.[40]

Technicians have no trouble defining what constitutes a managed computer network: the result of linking hardware and software to accomplish a particular purpose, such as communication or computation. It is more difficult to define managed networks that are scale-free and do not have manager-imposed boundaries.[41] The Internet is a classic example of a managed network that is open and continually growing. Still, some elemental rules and protocols bring order to the seeming chaos. The need for these is clearly recognized in the vignette discussed earlier.

When the concept of a managed network is extended outside the realm of pure technology, many different types of networks are evident. Steven Goldsmith and William Eggers describe the diversity of networks in government management:

> Public-private networks come in many forms, from ad hoc networks that are activated only intermittently—often in response to a disaster—to channel partnerships in which governments use private firms and nonprofits to serve as distribution channels for public services and transactions.[42]

Here I discuss three important factors in invoking and using managed networks. First, there are various types of networks—one size does not fit all purposes. Different types of managed networks can be used to accomplish different tasks and can be linked together to attack complex interrelated problems. In the initial stages of designing a network, it is important to study various types of networks similar to the one being established and to explore their successes and failures. Second, although there are many types of managed networks, just a few common elements should be included in the conceptual design of a network. The elements provide the designer with a checklist of all the steps necessary to make a managed network work. Making sure that all those elements are present is a big step toward ensuring the network's successful operation. Third, the con-

---

40. Milward and Provan (2006).
41. For an explanation of the term "scale-free," see chapter 8, note 9.
42. Eggers and Goldsmith (2004).

tinuing ongoing management of networks themselves and managers' work in the networks is the final step in using managed networks as tools to solve complicated problems.

There are many types of managed networks. A typology of networks was previously developed and used as the basis for research.[43] Although not all types of managed networks are germane to the IC, it is important to recognize that multiple types are capable of multiple uses.

First among network types is the *community* of *shared-mission*. This is defined as a networked collection of actors from the public, private, nonprofit, or civic sectors working to achieve a common purpose. (The importance of mission in driving the work of networks is discussed further in a later section.) A second type of managed network is communities of shared practice. These consist of groups of individuals organized around common interests or expertise. Often these networks perform valuable functions such as information exchange or setting of standards and can be used in combination with other network types.

Managed networks like those used at the CDC to respond to a specific emergency such as the SARS virus or anthrax attacks are called *issue-response networks*. For example, the CDC's laboratory response unit organizes reactions to chemical or biological terrorism and emerging infectious diseases and coordinates reactions to other public health threats and emergencies.

Another type of managed network is the *strategic alliance*. This type of network can be loosely or hastily formed and designed to work at the operational (program delivery) level, to function at the advocacy (public relations) level, or to conduct a major research program that requires the resources, information, and expertise of more than one group. A hallmark of such networks is often their focus on a single issue or event where melding each partner entity's unique resources provides an advantage to all parties. The response to the Year 2000 computer crises is an example of such alliances. The federal government helped bring relevant parties together, and industry-based groups worked in an alliance to share information and take action in a way that would not have been possible in the normal course of business. Once the crisis passed, the effort was disbanded and many of the alliances were terminated.

Joined Up Government is a service provision network that seeks to create "one-stop shopping" for consumers of multiple governmental services. The British government under Prime Minister Tony Blair advocated this approach. Blair stated that he wanted to ensure that services were better coordinated (joined up) by putting many governmental facilities in a single location. This approach was often used to coordinate access to and distribution of benefits and housing services.

Robert Agranoff has identified service integration as a type of managed network and suggests that its function is to "promote coordinated responses to persons

43. Morse, Buss, and Kinghorn (2007).

most at risk."[44] Recent U.S. examples include the integration of welfare and work-force services at the state and county levels following welfare reform. This approach led to positive results in states such as Wisconsin, where beneficiaries could receive a combination of services focused on the outcome of helping the individual find and keep a job.

Supply chains are managed networks of vendors, distributors, and end users connected to ensure the availability of material wherever and whenever it is needed. For example, during the Hurricane Katrina response, the Defense Supply Center of Philadelphia arranged for shipment of 1.8 million cases of Meals Ready to Eat to the disaster victims from multiple points around the United States. The network was managed from Philadelphia.

Intra-organizational networks involve the use of managed networks to connect disparate parts of an organization. The Baltimore CitiStat program is an excellent example of a data-driven managed network that connects agencies and the central administration to improve program performance. It also provides an element of data transparency that improves the quality of outcomes.

Dispute-resolution networks, which conduct negotiated rule making, have been an effective way of resolving disputes about regulatory activity in several federal departments. They bring together representatives of various interest groups and a federal or state agency to negotiate a proposed rule or regulation. The goal of a negotiated rule-making proceeding is for the group to achieve consensus on the text of a proposed rule so that the entity authorized to promulgate it can do so. Use of this type of network speeds the process of issuing the regulation and ensures faster and more complete compliance with these issuances than is conventionally the case.

Combinations of network types may occur in all kinds of everyday situations. For example, the authors of the DOD's Net-Centric Environment Joint Functional Concept (see note 35) used an example based on an issue-response network but connected it to communities of shared practice.[45] This connection was critical to create the depth and breadth of a solution necessary to respond effectively across multiple mission areas. "Exclusivity" in the types of networks invoked is not necessary. Mission-oriented networks can work smoothly with supply-chain networks to respond to an issue. This orderly interconnection of interdependent managed networks provides the highest-quality response to a mission or an issue.

The concept of network typology is particularly important in planning for and creating networks. Network designers can learn much from the successes and failures of similar types of networks. Some examples of networks in the area of computer security include the Computer Emergency Response Team (CERT) and the Systems Administrators and Network Security Institute (SANS), which combine information dissemination and training (in their role as coordinators of

44. Agranoff (2007).
45. These may also be called communities of interest.

a shared-practice community) with assistance with issue response. Using the knowledge gained from running this type of network can help the IC to design its own structures.

Critical Elements for Managed Network Development

For any type of managed network to succeed, certain common elements must be present, and network designers must consciously include each one. The relative importance of each element varies with the type of network being created.[46]

Networked structure and technology. This is often the starting point for designers and planners creating managed networks. Nodes and links are joined together to represent the physical and technical elements of the managed network, which also includes the system components supporting this structure. Technology by itself, however, is not enough.

Commitment to a common purpose or mission. This commitment is the reason for the managed network's existence and identifies commitment to achieving positive results.

Trust. Central to gaining agreement on the common purpose and working together to achieve it is trust among the participants, the glue of organizations and networks. Building on a foundation of formal or informal professional or social relationships, the participants believe they can count on the information or effort of others in the network to achieve the common purpose. The more complex the task, the more "trust" needs to be formalized in protocols and procedures agreed to and understood by the participants.

Governance. Trust is typically expressed explicitly or implicitly in a governance structure. Several aspects of governance for managed networks need to be taken into account: *boundary* and *exclusivity* involve some definition of who is and who is not a member and a delineation of members' entitlement to information on the basis of their membership and role; rules for members' behavior and sanctions for misbehavior; and self-determination, embodied in individual components' right to participate in network operational and membership decisions.

Network management. Managed networks need to have a mechanism for internal dispute resolution, resource allocation, quality control, organizational maintenance, and other administrative issues agreed necessary for smooth network functioning. The network manager may be designated formally or informally. In the intelligence community, the National Counter Terrorism Center plays the role of network manager, especially in deciding who has access to critical information.

Access to authority. Access to authority is critical for managed networks that seek to achieve particular missions, promulgate binding standards, or see formal

---

46. The critical elements discussed here may not be present to the same degree in social or other types of networks as they are in managed networks.

regulations put in place. This access makes available to network members a set of definitive, broadly accepted standard-setting procedures, meaning that the network should be able to enlist authority when necessary to achieve its mission, and not that the network must be based on or subject to any particular authority. An example of this in the federal government was the creation of the "Capital Programming Guide" in 1996 by a network of seventy-odd volunteers from various agencies. At the request of the group, the guide was made part of the Office of Management and Budget (OMB) Circular A-11. This publication gives agencies guidance on the form and content of the president's budget, and the inclusion of the guide in A-11 gave the network group access to presidential authority.

Leadership. Individuals or groups must be willing to serve as network advocates, or leaders, to propel its work toward the desired results. People often have to be shown that time spent providing network leadership is time well spent. Here, the network's mission or interests and those of the organization or individual providing leadership must be aligned, and a "force multiplier" effect must be demonstrated. The ability of public health professionals around the world to follow the CDC's leadership in using the Public Health Information Network to mobilize action on public health threats constitutes a "force multiplier" for these professionals.

Distributive accountability and responsibility. Shared governance and decision-making among members of a managed network confers upon them both incentives and responsibility for achieving the desired results. This sort of collective action may seem cumbersome in the beginning, but with appropriate governance structures it should improve outcomes in the long run.

Information sharing. The rules for information sharing mirror those of the intelligence community. They boil down to giving members easy access to information, protecting their privacy, ensuring data quality, and restricting nonmembers' access to privileged information. The "responsibility to provide information" should be coupled with the classic concept of need to know. This can be done in a roles-based environment such as the one used by the CDC in their Public Health Information Network.

Access to resources. The network manager must continually ensure the availability of financial, technical, human, and other resources that the managed network requires to sustain operations and fulfill its objectives.

Using these elements of managed networks within the construct of a netcentric environment can create the kind of "shared awareness," "constructive interdependence," and "dynamic communities of interest" described in the DOD's "Net-Centric Environment Joint Functional Concept, Version 1.0" (see note 35).

Management of and in Networks

H. Brinton Milward and Keith Provan have supplied an excellent framework for looking at a manager's tasks when he or she is moving from the conceptualization and design phase to operation of a managed network. They are divided into two groups, tasks for management *of* networks and tasks for management *in* networks. This distinction is a valuable reference point for managers and an analytic tool for researchers.

Milward and Provan also describe five basic management tasks— accountability, legitimacy, conflict, design, and commitment—and discuss how they are carried out by a network manager.[47]

Management of Accountability

In the management of a network with a clear mission and goals, accountability consists of identifying who is responsible for which outcomes, rewarding and reinforcing achievements, and responding to free riders. Accountability means making sure the organization is participating in accordance with its mission and getting the resources it needs for its work and the credit it deserves for the outcomes. Viewing accountability from the intelligence community's point of view, the DNI must be a seamless goal setter. The component agencies must be seen as even-handed network managers or as organizations that take seriously their "responsibility to provide."

Management of Legitimacy

The idea of a managed network has to be sold constantly, both internally and externally. This is done by continually reinforcing the value of the network to participants and reinforcing the value of network participation to outsiders. In focusing on leadership training, the ODNI Chief Human Capital Office has emphasized the need for emerging leaders to use networks to lead across the community and to develop skills that are agency interoperable.

Management of Commitment

Management of commitment involves motivating participants and giving them guidance regarding their role. Motivation often consists of showing an organization the benefits of participation. Different organizations will have different reasons for participating. For example, the National Reconnaissance Organization may participate in an NCTC-sponsored network to improve the design and deployment of its own resources by learning how other agencies use them. Commitment in networks is also about conviction and utility. If organizations find that working for network goals helps them achieve their own organizational goals, they are more likely to participate enthusiastically than if they see no gain for their organizations. In the earlier example from the CDC, far-flung health departments are more likely to provide quality data about the presence of communicable diseases in their areas if they can get similar data about how the spread of these diseases in other areas might affect them.

---

47. Milward and Provan (2006).

The Role of Social Networks

Social networks play a critical role in the creation of a netcentric environment to promote managed networks and the use of managed networks to achieve individual organizational and network common goals. The netcentric environment is defined by both its technological structure and the social context of interactions between and among the individuals and organizations within it. The quality of relationships and the existence of trust and cooperation are not determined simply by information technology and processes designed to create the managed network. Social networks are the summation of relationships between individuals across organizational and social boundaries. The strength, frequency, and form of the connections that define these relationships are also the definition of the social network. An important related concept, social capital represents "social networks, norms of reciprocity, mutual assistance, and trustworthiness," as the term is used most famously by theorists such as Robert Putnam.[48]

These behavioral aspects of reciprocity, assistance, and trust are additional parameters in the definition of social networks. Putnam has argued that social capital can act both as a force for group bonding and as a bridging mechanism between groups and organizations. Creating this bridge can, however, present a challenge for leaders seeking to create a netcentric environment between organizations, such as components of the intelligence community, with their strong internal cultures and histories of dispute and division. In short, the dynamics of social capital, as defined by social networks, can work against effective partnerships by promoting exclusivity, secrecy, and distrust of outsiders. For a netcentric environment to be effective with multiple organizations, some effort must be made to balance the bonding social capital of a strong organizational culture with the bridging social capital that informal relationships between network partners can develop.

Social networks heavily influence managed networks. For the intelligence community to successfully invoke managed networks, it will need to consciously take into account the existing and evolving social networks within it. Enhancing understanding and promoting social networks within the netcentric environment will enhance the application of innovative processes and technologies that define the managed network. The DNI recognizes this reality in the 500-day plan (although the term "social network" is not used):

> These initiatives are designed to help build a collaborative culture for the IC—a culture that develops a diverse workforce with a common understanding of collaboration, and one that sustains and promotes incentives for collaboration across boundaries.[49]

48. Putnam and Feldstein (2003, p. 3).
49. Office of the Director of National Intelligence (2007b, p. 4).

Social networks may not be immediately visible, and some may think that the concept of the social network is a metaphorical construction. Yet communication patterns and relationships between individuals can be analyzed to discern the existence and structure of a social network. Social network analysis is collation of data points about social relationships into standardized models of social interaction. The data points can be anything from self-reported relationships via survey data to records of telephone and e-mail activity. The analysis can be based on simple relations between individuals, but advanced analysis can also examine the strength of relationships, based on the frequency and scope of the interactions that define a social relationship. Social network analysis is one method for promoting the creation of positive social capital in networks. Such an analysis can also help illuminate the structure of the social networks that underpin managed networks.

Rob Cross and Andrew Parker suggest that there are multiple benefits from social networks and social network analysis: "Getting an accurate view of a network helps with managerial decision making and informs targeted efforts to promote effective collaboration."[50] They suggest that many applications for well-constructed social network analysis can benefit the intelligence community, supporting partnerships and alliances by highlighting the effectiveness of information flow and knowledge transfer in decisionmaking. Strategy execution is also enhanced by determining whether cross-functional collaborations support overall network goals. Social network analysis can improve decisionmaking by providing managers at every level with valuable diagnostic information. This analysis also encourages innovation within a community of practice and enables better implementation of large-scale change. Social network analysis provides network managers and designers with opportunities for understanding the organizational dynamics defining the conditions in which their netcentric environment will operate and could reveal a dysfunctional social network. Considering how common distrust is between intelligence services, a parallel informal social network might exist, one built on distrust and competition for resources and detracting from the ideal realization of a netcentric environment.

Social network analysis should be complemented by efforts to understand the dynamics within and between organizations that define social capital within the netcentric environment. Organizational culture can be understood in terms of the interplay between the historical commitments and resources and the alignment of tasks between the organizations involved in the netcentric environment.[51] The extent to which these elements of culture are compatible or competitive will provide indications of the strength of the social capital between organizations. Understanding, and addressing proactively, the weaknesses in social capital and

50. Cross and Parker (2004, p. 7).
51. Khademian (2002, p. 44).

networks that stem from organizational culture will be a powerful insurance policy for a burgeoning managed network.

In moving to a netcentric environment and the creation of managed networks, the intra- and interorganizational social networks have to be analyzed to see how they can be enlisted to support the new effort. Any social networks within organizations that are resistant to change need to be identified, and cultural changes need to be undertaken. Similarly, if social networks do not exist across agencies, they need to be created. Stories of disaster response efforts are replete with references to the importance of social networks, or the lack thereof, in the success of rapid response to natural and man-made disasters. Trust is an important element in the creation of managed networks, and it is indispensable if social networks are to support managed networks' efforts, particularly in a netcentric environment.

Leadership Development Implications for the IC and Its Managed Networks

The intelligence community may harbor, rooted in its social network culture, a cultural bias against a netcentric environment. This bias may inhibit transformational efforts at collaboration and integration.

The Challenge

The challenge of overcoming this bias is evident in a report submitted in April 2007 to the Chief Human Capital Office of the DNI:

> IC leaders did not use the term "transformation" lightly as they discussed leadership challenges—they acknowledged that the move to an adaptive and flexible community would be a cultural shift of tectonic proportions. More than one leader noted with some degree of irony that many IC entities were created under a paradigm that placed the highest value on secrecy, exclusivity, and the protection of one's tradecraft. Sharing was anathema to these organizational cultures.[52]

The further challenge for leadership development was stated as follows:

> If the IC intends to evolve into a more network-centric structure, it must develop, retain, and reward leadership talent that can thrive in this environment. . . . The IC leader of the future will require a markedly different set of skills than those required today. In particular, the IC needs to place increased emphasis on behaviors related to boundaryless communication, information sharing, empowered decision making, and rapid adaptation. These behaviors are incorporated into the IC focus competencies of Enterprise

---

52. Ibid., p. 23.

Focus and Collaboration and Integration and the leadership competency of Leading Change that are incorporated into the Integrated Model."[53]

Leaders can be grown or recruited. Whichever technique is employed, there must be a cohesive, comprehensive, consistent strategy and implementation plan for leadership development. To implement this approach, the 500-day plan calls for the creation of a joint leadership development program.

Official Recognition of Need for Leadership Development

To address these leadership and training issues, the Office of the Director of National Intelligence convened the "Netcentric Leadership Event" on June 4, 2007.[54] The forum brought together participants from agencies and bureaus throughout the IC. The purpose of the forum was to identify the pertinent components of netcentric leadership for the IC; recommend the best ways of integrating them into the IC leadership competency model and indicating the relationship among these components and the model; recommend the most important learning activities for training netcentric leadership; and suggest research and innovative experiments that would expand the DNI knowledge about developing skillful leaders and managers for a netcentric environment.

As described in the report, many participants said that despite the recognized need, their respective agencies were ineffective at growing leadership talent and that there is no deliberate process for leadership development within the IC. Some people thought the organization hires technically skilled people and moves them into leadership roles, often without much preparation. The theme that emerged was that the leadership development processes within the IC were inadequate to meet future leadership requirements. A summary of other main findings of the report follows.[55]

"INTEGRATION OF VISION." Although the National Intelligence Strategy is clear in its vision for the intelligence community, the IC must become a unified enterprise of innovative intelligence professionals with the common purpose of defending American lives, interests, and values. Jointness and collaboration are equally important in advancing this integration. The IC will have to recognize important new competencies at every level—from analysts, collectors, and support personnel to senior community leaders—for their effective functioning in networked organizations.

SHIFT TO VALUE-CENTERED LEADERSHIP. Senior IC leaders must broaden their perspectives to create new ways to enhance public value and see beyond traditional organizational boundaries. Instead of focusing solely on allocation of

53. Ibid.
54. Office of the Director of National Intelligence (2007a). The views of the participants are reported and summarized here.
55. Ibid.

strategic resources, senior leaders must become adept at managing organizational culture.

DECENTRALIZED DECISIONMAKING. A focus on strategic leadership means that senior leaders must delegate some of their operational responsibilities to project and mission managers and other personnel. Delegation gains in importance as challenges from netcentric enemies grow. Dealing with networked threats requires intelligence professionals to give and take authority as necessary.

BUILDING NEW COMPETENCIES. New competencies within a collaborative IC workforce should include flexibility, exceptional communications skills, and relationship management. These skills should be integrated into the IC leadership competency model. To satisfy the model's focus on collaboration and integration, leaders should emphasize attracting new hires and better utilizing current employees in the work of furthering community goals of jointness and netcentricity.

PROFESSIONAL STANDARDS OF EXCELLENCE. To achieve the collaboration and enterprise goals of the model, leaders should be encouraged to promote a common standard of practice across all areas of the intelligence community. One step toward standardization would be the creation of a community of intelligence professionals. Right now each agency trains its own members without regard for common, cross-community competencies or standards.

HORIZONTAL LEADERSHIP AND MANAGEMENT SKILLS. As intelligence work becomes more netcentric and collaborative, the development of all employees' ability to lead horizontally gains importance even in situations where they lack formal authority. This competency requires individuals with strong relationship and project management skills to lead collaborative projects effectively.

COMPLETE INTEGRATION OF NETCENTRIC BEHAVIOR. The IC should integrate netcentric behavior and leadership into every aspect of training so that collaboration becomes a daily work mindset. Classes should be designed in a way that allows participants to engage instructors and experts to encourage knowledge sharing and networking.

INTERAGENCY SCENARIO-BASED TRAINING. The forum participants expressed a near-universal concern that a crisis would expose serious deficiencies in both interagency cooperation and collaboration with agencies and organizations outside the IC. One popular idea to emerge was to create scenarios in which agencies and individuals could gain real experience working together.

ORGANIZATIONAL LEARNING. Organizational learning is just as important as training individuals and leaders for making strategic progress. Therefore, the intelligence community should emphasize new and innovative ways of enhancing self-awareness and organizational learning. Using social network analysis to enhance its understanding of its actual processes and workflows could enhance the IC's self-awareness and fill an important information gap.

MEASURING PERFORMANCE. Most forum participants agreed that a netcentric organization needs effective means of measuring performance and that performance elements had to be altered to reflect the community's collaboration and netcentric priorities. A suggestion was also made to promote formal and informal social networking across agencies.

Summary

The transformational changes occurring in the intelligence community are rapid, comprehensive, and dramatic. This chapter had to be updated while it was being written so as to include new material arising from ongoing events.[56] Members of the intelligence community voice a clear commitment to change. To be fully effective, this change must recognize the need to develop a netcentric approach to implementing managed networks and the importance of existing and to-be-created social networks in this effort. The IC leadership is committed to meeting the challenges of integration and innovation using network principles.

References

Agranoff, Robert. 2007. *Managing within Networks: Adding Value to Public Organizations.* Georgetown University Press, 2007.

Cross, Rob, and Andrew Parker. 2004. *The Hidden Power of Social Networks: How Work Really Gets Done in Organizations.* Harvard Business School Press.

DeSeve, G. Edward. 2007. *Creating Managed Networks as a Response to Societal Challenges.* Washington: IBM Center for the Business of Government.

Eggers, William D., and Stephen Goldsmith. 2004. *Governing by Network: The New Shape of Government.* Brookings.

Gerberding, Julie. 2004. "Protecting the Public's Health with Small World Connections." James E. Webb Lecture, National Academy of Public Administration, Washington, D.C., November 18 (www.napawash.org/Pubs/gerberding.pdf).

Government of Australia, Scrutiny of Acts and Regulations Committee. 2007. "Victorian Electronic Democracy: Final Report." East Melbourne: 2007, glossary (www.parliament.vic.gov.au/sarc/E-Democracy/Final_Report/Glossary.htm).

Khademian, A. 2002. *Working with Culture: The Way the Job Gets Done in Public Programs.* Washington: CQ Press.

Kean, Thomas H., and others. 2004. *The 9/11 Commission Report: Final Report of the National Commission on Terrorist Attacks upon the United States.* New York: Norton.

Milward, H. Brinton, and Keith G. Provan. 2006. *A Manager's Guide to Choosing and Using Collaborative Networks.* Washington: IBM Center for the Business of Government.

Morse, Ricardo S., Terry F. Buss, and C. Morgan Kinghorn, eds. 2007. *Transforming Public Leadership for the 21st Century.* Armonk, N.Y.: M. E. Sharpe.

---

56. An example of such a material event is the issuance on July 30, 2008, of President George W. Bush's revision to executive order 12333, which aligned DNI authorities and strengthened its ability to lead the intelligence community.

National Counter Terrorism Center. 2006. "NCTC and Information Sharing—Five Years since 9/11: A Progress Report." Washington: September.

Office of the Director of National Intelligence. 2005. "The National Intelligence Strategy of the United States of America: Transformation through Integration and Innovation." Washington.

———. 2006a. *DNI Human Capital Strategic Plan*. Washington.

———. 2006b. "Human Capital Joint Intelligence Duty Assignments." Intelligence Community Directive 601. Washington.

———. 2007a. "Netcentric Leadership Event, Final Report." Washington.

———. 2007b. "United States Intelligence Community (IC) 100 Day Plan for Integration and Collaboration." Washington.

———. 2007c. *United States Intelligence Community 500 Day Plan for Integration and Collaboration*. Washington.

———. 2007d. "Technical Report Development of an Integrated Competency Model for Senior Leaders within the U.S. Intelligence." Washington: April 23.

Putnam, R. D., and M. L. Feldstein. 2003. *Better Together: Restoring the American Community*. New York: Simon & Schuster.

Silberman, Laurence H., and others. 2005. *Report to the President of the United States*. Washington: Commission on the Intelligence Capabilities of the United States Regarding Weapons of Mass Destruction.

7

The United States Coast Guard and a Port Security Network of Shared Responsibility

ANNE M. KHADEMIAN AND WILLIAM G. BERBERICH

The U.S. economy and economies around the globe depend upon safe, secure, and just-in-time maritime trade. A third of the world economy and more than a quarter of the U.S. economy are dependent upon international trade, and more than 95 percent of non–North American trade enters the United States by ship, through our ports. There are 361 ports along coastal and inland waterways throughout the United States, each distinctive in its combination of governance, location, and the dominant form of cargo it handles. These trading hubs are the destination and departure points for cruise ships and ferries, tankers and barges loaded with crude oil, liquid natural gas, dry bulk, and automobiles, and for ships loaded with standardized containers—the innovation that revolutionized the speed and safety of maritime trade. More than 100 million containers move through the maritime transport system each year (7.5 million containers enter the United States each year) on more than 8,000 internationally flagged ships making approximately 51,000 ports of call (Walsh 2002; Harrald, Stephens, and vanDorp 2004). Some ports are dominated by one commodity, such as oil, that arrives in the United States exclusively by ship, and many ports are the location of vital physical

Captain Suzanne Englebert was the featured speaker at the first Network Performance Project Forum at the Fels Institute of Government at the University of Pennsylvania in Philadelphia on March 23, 2007. Material for this chapter is drawn in part from the material presented and discussed at this forum, as well as from other interviews with Captain Englebert and other members of the Coast Guard involved in port security.

infrastructure such as power plants, refineries, and factories that make use of incoming cargo as soon as it arrives in port. Each port provides a unique hub in the fast-paced, sweeping maritime trade system.

So vital are many of the ports in the United States and across the globe for the just-in-time functioning of the economy that an attack on one port would send not ripples but gale force waves through the U.S. economy (Loy and Ross 2002; Public Policy Institute of California 2006).[1] The expression "There is no security unless everyone is secure" illustrates the interconnectedness of ports across the United States and the globe. Disruptions and damages to individual ports and the surrounding communities and environment could come in many forms—from a nuclear weapon smuggled within a cargo container to an attack on a liquid natural gas vessel in a port to the explosion of a dirty bomb to a sunken, crude oil–laden tanker in a harbor—any one of which would trigger a closure and suspension of activities in one port that would ripple throughout the U.S. economy and other ports in the international system (Parformak and Fritelli 2007). The ports of Los Angeles and Long Beach on the West Coast and New York and New Jersey's Hoboken on the East Coast are among the largest and most active ports in the world. A suspension of activities stemming from an act of terror in either set of ports would be devastating for the entire U.S. economy. Estimates range from $65 million to $150 million in losses a day (Public Policy Institute of California 2006; Gerencser, Weinberg, and Vincent 2003; Congressional Budget Office 2006). Then customs commissioner Robert Bonner (2002) noted:

> One can only imagine the devastation of a small nuclear explosion at one of our seaports. As horrific as the immediate damage would be, one must also consider what would become of the global shipping industry and global trade if a sea container were used to smuggle and then detonate a nuclear device. Simply put, the shipping of sea containers would stop. The American people, for one, would not likely permit one more sea container to enter the United States until there was a significantly greater assurance—such as 100 percent inspections—that no additional terrorist weapons would be smuggled into the country. Governments in other major industrial countries would no doubt adopt a similar policy, thus bringing the global economy to its knees.

1. Among the largest ports in the world by container volume (the total number of TEUs imported and exported each year, measured in twenty-foot-equivalent units, or TEUs) are Singapore, Shanghai, Hong Kong, Shenzjen, China; Busan, South Korea; Kaohsiung, Taiwan; Los Angeles; Rotterdam; Hamburg; and Antwerp, Belgium (Dibenedetto 2008; Lim Fang Jau 2002). In the United States, the top ten ports, measured by number of TEUs imported and exported each year, are Los Angeles, Long Beach, California; New York; Charleston, South Carolina; Savannah; Norfolk, Virginia; Oakland, California; Houston; Tacoma, Seattle, Washington. From year to year the import and export volume of these ports varies. See statistics by the U.S. Maritime Administistration, U.S. Department of Transportation, "U.S. Waterborne Foreign Container Trade by U.S. Custom Ports" (www.marad.dot.gov/library_landing_page/data_and_statistics/ Data_and_Statistics.htm).

Since passage of the Espionage Act of 1917, the United States Coast Guard has played the lead role in port security.[2] The act was passed in response to the 1916 detonation by U.S.-based German saboteurs of 2 million pounds of explosives bound for Great Britain and stored in New York Harbor. The explosion resulted in the total destruction of Black Tom Island along with several warehouses, barges, and a large ship, and severe damage to the Statue of Liberty—an act of terror that parallels the scenarios driving port security today (Allen 2006). The Espionage Act provided the basis for the captain of the port (COTP) authority, which today places thirty-five Coast Guard captains in Coast Guard sectors to oversee safety and security of port areas, waterways, and coastal areas.[3] As the articulation of COTP responsibilities has expanded and deepened over the decades in response to wartime demands, oil spills, drug interdiction, and now homeland security, the understanding of "port security" has expanded to include the practices within the broader maritime domain including activities in and between international ports. In short, "port security" rests with the activities of a vast network focused on anticipating, preventing, and responding to disruptions in the maritime trading system with core operators among U.S. government agencies at the state, local, and federal levels of government, public and private sector commercial interests across the globe, governments and government agencies in the international arena, and international organizations such as the International Maritime Organization (IMO).

This chapter examines an evolving network aimed at reducing the threats posed to ports in the United States by adopting a broader focus on maritime security. The lead agency in this effort is the United States Coast Guard, which is working to build and sustain a network founded on three premises:

—Shared responsibility for security across the public and private sectors in the maritime world by adhering to collective commitments and balancing authority with participation

—Risk reduction as a network goal and benefit and flexibility in how risk is reduced

—Leveraging of established strategies and practices

Implementation of this strategy has required a management approach that is inclusive to evoke deliberation and information sharing, and experimental to adapt the regulatory effort to the vagaries of the maritime trading environment. These practices are exemplified by the efforts of Captain Suzanne Englebert of the United States Coast Guard; we draw on her participation as featured speaker in the first network forum of this project to illustrate our points. We also refer in this

2. The Coast Guard also derives authority for port security from the Ports and Waterways Safety Act of 1972 (Public Law 92-340).

3. The 2005 reorganization of the Coast Guard created sectors that integrate operations and marine safety field units. Organized under the activities of prevention and response, each sector is led by a sector commander who serves as both COTP and federal maritime security coordinator (Greene 2005).

chapter to interviews with other members of the Coast Guard involved in port security and extensive documentation of the port security effort. We take a "funnel" approach: First we examine the vast and complex context within which port security practices must be conducted. Then we explore the challenges of building a network to accomplish port security. Finally we explore the strategy used by the Coast Guard for network building and maintenance across the maritime domain.

The Complexities of the Maritime Security Environment

> If you think about trade as a process of integrated pieces, then the port should be considered the point of last—not first—resort in our war on trade terrorism. . . . So, focusing on stopping a weaponized cargo at the U.S. port is too little, too late.
>
> —Robert Quartel (2002)

If, as this statement by the maritime trade specialist Robert Quartel suggests, port security begins with overseas manufacturers, transportation companies, and foreign ports, security efforts must span the maritime domain. But such efforts must also focus on U.S. ports—pushing back the boundary to the broader maritime domain does not eliminate the need to make ports in America safe. Port security efforts that sweep the maritime domain must also be cognizant of the ability of the global supply chain to function with amazing efficiency to deliver goods on a just-in-time basis. The speed of this system depends heavily upon the flexibility of the participants, yet the flexible points in the system are often unsecured portions of the supply chain and can become points vulnerable to tampering and terrorism (Lim Fang Jau 2002).

These twin tensions—the need for security that is vast in its reach yet attentive to each port and efforts that enhance security without compromising flexibility—begin to define the complexities of the maritime security environment. In this section we examine three additional dimensions of the environment: the multiple participants involved in maritime trade; the complex systems that constitute ports across the globe and the threats different cargos pose to ports; and the multiple security missions and mandates that reach across the maritime domain.

Multiple Participants

The most obvious complexity in the maritime security environment is the number of participants with a role in maritime commerce, and hence with an ability to influence maritime security. Within the U.S. government, two agencies in the Department of Homeland Security play prominent roles in port security, the Coast Guard and Customs and Border Protection (CBP). Their authority and organizational efforts intersect at many points, and both have authority beyond the roles they play in port security. The fundamental distinction between the two regarding port security, however, rests with ships and ports versus cargo: the Coast Guard is the lead federal agency responsible for port security that focuses on the ships and the infrastructure and traffic of the ports, while the CBP is responsible for regulating the cargo coming across the ocean and entering the ports, with a primary focus on preventing weapons and terrorists from entering the country through ports (U.S. Department of Justice, Office of the Inspector General 2006; Government Accountability Office 2005).

Many other federal agencies also have slices of the port security challenge. The Federal Bureau of Investigation (FBI), through the attorney general, has lead investigative authority over terrorist crimes including violations within the maritime domain, and the agency plays a lead role in counterterrorism efforts that may extend beyond national boundaries to the maritime domain (U.S. Department of Justice, Office of Inspector General 2006). The Transportation Security Administration (TSA) is responsible for the security of all major surface modes of transportation and plays a role in screening and regulating people working on ships or in the ports, and in developing passenger screening programs for ferries and cruise terminals. TSA also works with the Coast Guard to implement Port STEP (Port Security Training Exercises Program) an annual exercise in which select ports respond to a variety of terrorist scenarios and test the Area Maritime Security Plans developed by committees composed of stakeholders from each port (Parformak and Fritelli 2007). The Department of Energy's National Nuclear Security Administration oversees the Megaport initiative, providing a growing number of major international seaports around the globe with radiological detection equipment to screen containers for nuclear material and the training needed to implement the screening program.

Other U.S. government participants include the U.S. Navy and its Visit Board Search and Seizure teams, which board flagged vessels identified as weapons or nuclear threats. The Federal Maritime Commission regulates the practices of port terminal operators and oversees the rate-setting processes. Finally, the Department of State plays a key role through its overseas embassies in coordinating port security efforts among other nations, particularly in the Caribbean, and the department's Bureau of International Narcotics and Law Enforcement Affairs also plays a role.

Individual ports are complex systems of governance with multiple public and private stakeholders. Major U.S. ports are owned by port authorities that are public or quasi-public organizations established by a city, county, regional, or state government. Port authorities administer the property, terminals, and other facilities in a port complex, but they are nested within city, county, or state jurisdictions that also play a role in law enforcement, security actions, or the response to and recovery from a terror attack or other disaster. Cargo is unloaded, staged, and transferred through marine terminals designed to manage different types of cargo—containers, liquid bulk, dry bulk, autos, and so on. Most port authorities lease their marine terminals to terminal operating companies, hence the term "landlord ports"—the analogy is also to a shopping mall and leased retail space. Foreign-based companies operate most container terminals because most of the shipping lines are foreign-based companies, and the largest global terminal operating companies are estimated to handle approximately 80 percent of the cargo worldwide.[4] In 2006 the terminals in the ports of Baltimore, Jacksonville, New Orleans, Houston, Los Angeles, and Tacoma are operated entirely by foreign-based companies. U.S.-based companies operate a small percentage of the marine terminals in Los Angeles, Long Beach, New York, and New Jersey (Fritelli and Lake 2006). Efforts to enhance security affects these port-based participants, who are concerned with speed, efficiency, and profit as well as security.

Other key participants in the ports include the 42,000- member International Longshore and Warehouse Union—which represents the men and women who handle all cargo through the marine terminals of ports in California, Oregon, Washington, Alaska, and Hawaii—and the International Longshoremen's Association of the AFL-CIO, representing the 65,000 longshoremen working in ports on the Atlantic Coast, the Gulf Coast, the Great Lakes, and other inland waterways.[5] In the early nineteenth century, men would respond to the call "Men along the shore!" to unload essential cargo from clipper ships. As city populations, ports, and commerce grew, work along the shore became more dangerous and often exploitative. Unions sought protection and pay increases for these dangerous jobs, and the clipper call was shortened to "longshoremen" as a title to represent their interests. In the port security debate, these unions are primarily concerned about worker safety and security in the ports and the safety of areas surrounding the ports where union members live with their families.

Beyond both inland and sea ports, domestic and international interests flow across borders and oceans. Domestic and foreign-based manufacturers and major retailers such as Wal-Mart, Ford Motor Company, and Sears, importing and exporting companies, customs brokers, freight forwarders, consolidated shipping companies, trucking and rail companies, and insurers all are participants in international maritime trade and hence stakeholders in port security. Within this commercial context, individual governments can play a key role in flagging (licensing and regulating) ships and creating a competition for international companies to select one country over another given the most favorable means of doing business—taxes may be lower, wages for ship crews may be lower, and environmental regulations may be more lax (Pluta 2002; Morris 1996; Neff 2007). The competition further blurs borders and the question of jurisdiction for ships that spend

4. For discussions of the 2006 controversy over the management of a U.S. port terminal by Dubai Ports World, a foreign terminal management company, see Flynn and Loy (2006) and Beisecker (2006).

5. Membership information for the International Longshore and Warehouse Union and the International Longshoremen's Association can be found on their respective websites, www.ilwu.org/about/index.cfm and www.ilaunion.org.

minimal time in the country of origin and most of the time on the high seas or in foreign ports, also known as "flags of convenience."

Historically, this blurring of jurisdictions with respect to an individual ship, as well as concerns for safety and for regulating the natural resources of the oceans (from protecting marine populations to preventing oil spills) have led to maritime treaties, the most established being the Safety of Life at Sea (SOLAS) convention, which was established following the sinking of the *Titanic*, in 1912. Overseeing the SOLAS convention is the International Maritime Organization (IMO), a United Nations agency established in 1948 by convention and first convened in 1959 to provide a comprehensive regulatory framework for international shipping to address the major jurisdictional issues (Pluta 2002; International Maritime Organization 1974). Within the IMO, interests and power revolve around "flag" states or "port" states. Flag states register and license ships. Port states primarily receive ships. Voting power in the IMO rests with the flag states—if you do not flag ships, you do not vote. The United States has a small number of flag ships (about 400 in international trade), so it has a vote, but it is primarily a port state whose clout rests in the ability to close access to a flagged vessel or vessels from another country. Before the attacks on New York and the Pentagon on September 11, 2001, the flag states were seeking security from piracy at sea through the IMO, but this issue was not critical for the port states, including the United States. After 9/11 the interest flipped, and major port states such as the United States needed to use the IMO forum to get the flag states to take security measures needed to protect ports and the supply chain more broadly (Englebert 2007).

Ports as Complex Operations Facing Varied Threats

In addition to the multiple participants with varied interests and expectations, ports across the maritime domain present different operating systems to accommodate the types of cargo that transit through the port, and different cargos present different threats to the ports and the broader maritime trading system. Ports such as Los Angeles and Long Beach, for example, are major container ports— together the two ports are the fifth largest hub for container shipments across the globe. These port systems are built around the stability of well-established companies that own and operate the container ships and that operate on fixed routes and schedules. The port infrastructure for unloading and loading ships is also tightly "coupled" with the rail and trucking systems in and out of the port (Harrald, Stephens, and vanDorp 2004). Containers' cargo, however, pose the threat of a "bomb in a box" that could be placed in a container at multiple points in the supply chain (Flynn 2005). Hence, an emerging component of the container systems in ports is radiation detection technology—in LA-Long Beach, radiation portal monitors are in use—to screen containers before they are loaded onto a truck or train for distribution (Customs and Border Protection 2006), and in overseas ports the screening takes place before containers are placed on ships bound for the United States.[6]

Port operations surrounding ferry services, built around different participants and logistical challenges, pose a different set of threats to port security. Regularly published schedules and the accessibility of ferry service to any passenger makes passenger screening a top priority for ensuring the safety of passengers and crew members (Harrald, Stephens, and vanDorp 2004). Similarly, liquid natural gas, bulk cargo, automobiles, and petrochemicals all present ports with different logistical challenges and pose different threats to their operating environment. The diversity of governing arrangements for ports around the globe further diversifies ports as operating systems.

Multiple Security Programs and Missions

A final element of complexity in the maritime environment stems from the existence of multiple government frameworks, programs, and missions, all aimed at enhancing security, but each accompanied by mandates, practices, and interests that can conflict with a broader effort to integrate security concerns. There is potential for integration across many of these programs, and in some cases it is occurring, but there is also the potential for tension and resource competition between approaches that can evolve with distinct and divergent strategies for security.

At the broadest level, the IMO adopted the International Ship and Port Facility Security Code (ISPS Code) in 2002, an international maritime security regime created as an amendment to the SOLAS convention. Motivated by the need for heightened security in the wake of the 9/11 attacks, the core of the ISPS code, implemented beginning in 2004, requires ports, ships, and port facilities to develop and implement security plans to address potential risks and to appoint security officers to oversee plan implementation and maintenance. The IMO has some clout to enforce the code in its ability to withhold an International Ship Security Certificate for vessels that are not in compliance. Many ports will not allow a vessel lacking the certificate to dock, and ships that dock without the certificate can be detained by port authorities until compliance is forthcoming (Fulweiler 2007). In addition, ports with an accepted Port Facilities Security Plan appear on the IMO White List. Ships from ports that are not on the IMO White List are viewed by White List ports as out of compliance with the vessel security requirements as well.[7]

6. A new technology deployed in Hong Kong "can photograph the box's exterior, screen for radioactive material, and collect a gamma-ray image of a box's contents while the truck on which it is carried moves at 10 miles per hour" (Flynn 2005).

7. "International Oceans, Environment, Health and Aviation Law: Establishment of U.S. Antiterrorism Maritime Transportation System." *American Journal of International Law* 98, no. 3 (2004): 588–90.

At this broad level there is integration with the port security framework established in the United States through the Maritime Transportation Security Act (MTSA) of 2002 (Public Law 107-295). As will be seen in the discussion of Coast Guard management of the security network, the Coast Guard led the effort to produce this international and domestic integration of security approaches focused on the individual security efforts of ports, vessels, and facilities. So close are the two security regimes that the Coast Guard refers to its enforcement of the ISPS Code through the implementation of the MTSA. The Coast Guard was responsible for reviewing, approving, and verifying the security plans of 10,000 domestic vessels, 5,000 domestic facilities, and 48 ports and for verifying the security plans for 8,100 international vessels that stop in U.S. ports (O'Rourke 2004)—all incoming ships to U.S. ports require a valid ISPS International Ship Security Certificate, and all ships must provide ninety-six hours' notice of arrival (NOA) (Frittelli and Lake 2006). Under the MTSA, the Coast Guard has extensive enforcement authority, such as the ability to levy fines against ships and facility owners that do not comply with MTSA guidelines.

Where the MTSA is built upon the premise of individualized security plans that meet broad security objectives, a second U.S. mandate, the SAFE Port Act of 2006 (Security and Accountability for Every Port) (Public Law 109-347) approaches security with a primary focus on ports and cargo. The most prominent feature is the requirement that 100 percent of the containers entering the twenty-two largest container ports in the United States had to be screened by the end of 2007 for radiological material (Republican Policy Committee 2006). The goal was to screen cargo containers coming through every U.S. port by the end of 2008. The legislation also codifies two Customs and Border Protection programs focused on the security of cargo. The Container Security Initiative (CSI) targets high-risk containers in fifty-eight foreign ports for inspection by CBP personnel working with partner customs agencies. The Customs Trade Partnership against Terrorism (C-TPAT) is aimed at improving supply chain security by enrolling partner companies that agree to baseline security standards. Only companies in compliance with the ISPS Code are eligible to participate in the program, which promises shorter wait times for customs processing in and out of ports (United States Coast Guard 2004). The act also provides $400 million in port security grants and requires the Department of Homeland Security to develop a plan for resuming trade in the event of a port- or water-based terrorist attack.

One fundamental divide between the MTSA and the SAFE Port Act rests with the framing and targeting of "security." The MTSA focuses on the participants in the international maritime arena, and the SAFE Port Act focuses on the physical ports and containers—the exception being C-TPAT, which builds on the MTSA approach. Both approaches are vulnerable, however, given the need for verifiable information to be effective. In the case of the MTSA, security plans for ports, vessels, and facilities must be approved and vetted. In the case of the CSI and the C-TPAT, CBP relies upon information provided primarily by shippers and manufacturers, as well as on incoming intelligence, to identify containers that are high risk and thus require inspection. The CBP operates by a twenty-four-hour rule under which manifest information must be filed with the agency twenty-four hours before cargo is loaded onto a ship in a foreign port. As discussed in a later section, the challenge of securing accurate information is crucial to managing the networked approach to maritime security.

The final source of program complexity is "legacy"—established approaches to maritime security used prior to passage of the MTSA. Historically, maritime security has focused on combating piracy, human and drug trafficking, and smuggling and on protecting marine resources. The Coast Guard, CBP, Immigration and Customs Enforcement (ICE), and multiple other government agencies continue to focus resources on these important "legacy" elements of security, and the need to focus on potential terror attacks as well, and on ports' resilience in response to a terror attack, puts an added strain on the resources. In some cases, the capacities associated with legacy missions carry over to support broader maritime security concerns. For example, the Coast Guard's Strike Team, established to respond to oil spills and chemical discharges, was used very effectively in responding to anthrax attack sites in Florida and Washington, D.C., and the strike team was on the scene at Ground Zero to manage the hazardous materials after the collapse of the Twin Towers. But the compatibility is not always evident. In the immediate aftermath of 9/11, "The Coast Guard redirected many of its offshore fisheries, drug and migrant law enforcement assets into security operations for ports and waterside transportation and energy infrastructure. Assets performing other functions, such as aids to navigation and marine safety, were similarly redirected" (Underwood 2002, 4). Between FY 2001 and FY 02, expenditures for port security grew from 1 percent of the Coast Guard budget to 58 percent (Greene 2005). Much of the balance between these missions has been restored, but port, waterway, and coastal security continues to demand between 20 and 26 percent of the Coast Guard budget.[8]

These tensions and complexities define the maritime security environment within which the United States Coast Guard is working to build a network to ensure port security. In the next section we present questions confronting managers of a maritime security network and describe the approach the Coast Guard has taken to address the questions and pursue the challenge.

The Network Questions

The Coast Guard confronts several questions in the effort to build and sustain a network aimed at enhancing port security that is global in its reach. At the core,

8. See United States Coast Guard Snapshots for FY 06, 05, and 04: www.uscg.mil/top/about/doc/2006%20coast%20guard%20snapshot.pdf; www.uscg.mil/d8/sector/lwrmsrvr/forms/snapshot05.pdf; www.uscg.mil/d8/sector/lwrmsrvr/forms/snapshot04.pdf.

the questions are about what maritime security means and how it is operational-ized. As the Coast Guard takes steps to partner with the private sector maritime community and other government agencies, it must ask, "What are the policy goals the agency hopes to fulfill, and how do these goals dictate what members of the network should do" (Goldsmith and Eggers 2004, 56). Indeed, questions like this confront managers across the homeland security policy arena (Kettl 2004; Khademian 2006). This big question can be broken down into a series of more specific questions.

First, what logic or approach should frame the maritime security effort? For exam-ple, should the focus be on eliminating threats or reducing the probability of a terror attack or mitigating the consequences of one by estimating different risks and allocating resources accordingly? The effort to screen 100 percent of the con-tainers coming into the United States using radiation detection equipment or large-scale X-ray or gamma ray equipment represents the former approach; the prioritization of critical resources and infrastructure and the allocation of resources according to the most significant threat represent the latter.

Second, what should the focus be of a networked security effort? Should the objects of the supply chain such as containers and ports be the focus of the security effort, or should the focus be on practices that fill, move, and transport the containers to and from ports? Again, targeting the container by scanning the contents or physically inspecting the contents represents the former approach. However, reg-ulators could look "to the manufacturer or supplier overseas, his manufacturing and supplier processes, how and where he or a consolidator somewhere loads the container, when and how it was sealed, how it was moved, who touched it, who paid for it—and even where it might be going once the cargo reaches the United States. For the most part, every bit of that data is available . . . before the cargo ever gets loaded onto a ship bound for a U.S. port" (Quartel 2002, pp. 2–3). This latter approach, described by the security consultant Robert Quartel in testimony before Congress, relies upon the effective collection of data, which are not read-ily given up by private sector shipping interests. Hence, fundamental to this lat-ter approach is the question of how information regarding the manufacturer, the loading of goods into a container, its transport, and means of payment will be gathered, packaged, and provided to a variety of end users.

Third, how should the variety of possible threats be incorporated within the pro-grams and policies intended to protect the supply chain? Should security programs focus on small boats that come quickly in and out of ports, as well as waterside terminals that are not part of the nation's 361 ports? Or should the focus be on the largest vessels that pose the greatest risk in the event of an explosion, sinking in the harbor, or ramming another ship?

Fourth, how might established practices aimed at controlling illegal immigration, drug smuggling, and piracy be used to enhance international port and supply chain security? The Coast Guard, Customs and Border Protection, State Department,

Drug Enforcement Administration, and many other agencies have long worked together at the operational and policy levels of government to address these traditional security concerns. These established partnerships could provide capacity for port security efforts as well.

Fifth, how should the priorities of trade and efficiency be weighted against security? Security is an important concern for shippers, financiers, manufacturers, and all participants in the maritime trade system, and some improvements in security can translate into improvements in the bottom line. Yet concerns about speed and cost have driven the development of the just-in-time system, and will continue to do so in the future. Public and congressional outrage over the news that Dubai Ports World (a terminal operating company owned in part by the government of the United Arab Emirates) would provide stevedore services (loading and unloading containers from ships) and manage terminals (oversee the flow of cargo from ships to other transportation) in U.S. ports prompted a close look at the business of managing port activities in the United States and approving foreign company participation in a U.S. port. Although the political focus was on the United Arab Emirates and the connection between two of the 9/11 hijackers, overlooked in that process were the business efficiencies that Dubai Ports World could have supplied as a large port operator in multiple ports. Dubai Ports World eventually agreed to have a U.S. subsidiary run the U.S. port operations, but the processes for approving such deals has not changed. What was lost in the debate was the potential for actually achieving improved security when large companies such as Dubai Ports World run operations in multiple ports and are able to take advantage of economies of scale that might allow security investments elsewhere (Beisecker 2006).

Finally, where should the responsibility rest for developing, implementing, enforcing, and paying the cost of these security networks? What role should the government play in ensuring the security of processes that are mainly privately owned and operated? And what financial support, if any, should the private sector receive for taking on security responsibilities?

The Coast Guard and a Port Security Network

The Coast Guard is the lead agency in building a network aimed at reducing the threats posed to ports in the United States, and it approaches port security by adopting a broader focus on maritime security. The Coast Guard has addressed the five network questions just posed, and engages the complexity of the maritime security environment with what we describe as a three-pronged strategy:

—Shared responsibility for security across the public and private sectors in the maritime world by adhering to collective commitments and balancing authority with participation

—Risk reduction as a network goal and a benefit, flexibility in how risk is reduced

—Leveraging of established frameworks, strategies, and practices

Implementation of this strategy has required a management approach that is inclusive, to encourage deliberation and information sharing, and experimental, to adapt the regulatory effort to the vagaries of the maritime trading environment. These practices are exemplified by the efforts of Coast Guard captain Suzanne Englebert.

Shared Responsibility for Security

After the attacks on the Twin Towers in New York City on 9/11, the Port of New York was closed for two days. The closure and consequent losses focused the maritime community's security concerns on the port, a shift from the long-held view that security was a flag state, not a port state, issue. As the largest port state in the IMO with a small number of flagged ships, the United States needed help focusing regulatory attention on protecting the ports. Before going to the IMO, however, Captain Suzanne Englebert and a team of Coast Guard officers initiated a broad-based discussion at a two-day workshop in Washington, D.C., in 2002. Invitations were sent to 200 representatives of shipping companies, port authorities, vessel owners, and state and local governments, and 350 people attended. This was the first step in broadening the base of responsibility for port security beyond the Coast Guard and other government agencies and developing a port security strategy with broad support among U.S.-based constituents in the maritime arena before going to the IMO.

The workshop built momentum for an approach that gave responsibility for developing and implementing security plans to vessel and facility owners with Coast Guard approval of the plans, and flexibility in achieving established security goals in each case. Larger ships and facilities would also have the responsibility for developing and implementing security plans, but with greater Coast Guard oversight—larger ships pose a larger security threat with the potential for bigger explosions, more casualties, and greater blockage of a port if it sank. One Coast Guard port security liaison officer stated (Schneider 2006):

> Discussions from these meetings and comments from other interested organizations aided the USCG in determining the types of vessels and facilities that posed risks of being involved in a transportation security incidents, and in identifying security measures and standards to deter such incidents.

This strategy was then the guide for IMO negotiations, which were successfully led by the Coast Guard, and the blueprint for the MTSA and the subsequent development of implementing regulations. The MTSA continued the strategy of shared responsibility with the mandate to create Area Maritime Security Committees tasked with supporting the captain of the port in assessing operations to mitigate threats and planning to respond to any type of catastrophe (Government Accountability Office 2006).

To share the responsibility for port security effectively among port, vessel, and facility owners, several management practices were evident. First, commitments that evolved through broad-based discussions needed to be honored. The workshop was fundamentally about identifying what port security would mean for people working on ships, in ports, and throughout the transportation system, vessels, and facilities. Participants broke into groups of fifty to seventy to discuss the topics of port personnel, vessels, facilities, and public policy consequences, generating technical and experience-based knowledge to begin framing a regulatory approach. Each group left the workshop with "homework" to continue the discussion and the process of developing a regulatory framework following the anticipated passage of the MTSA. Through these ongoing discussions, commitments emerged that required Coast Guard recognition and incorporation. Most important was the commitment to decentralize decisionmaking to the local levels. Concern about the uniqueness of each port and the knowledge of individual captains of the port and area maritime security committees drove the commitment to localized approval for vessel and facilities plans. Captain Englebert noted that many innovative and interesting approaches to security had developed organically, or at the local level. The trade-off, as Captain Englebert recognized, was the potential for a less knowledgeable COTP in all security matters and the need for rigorous training of current and future captains with respect to plan approval and the overall security goals.

Shared responsibility rested not only upon these commitments but also on the ability of the Coast Guard to balance its regulatory authority with its role as a partner in the regulatory effort. Two examples illustrate this effective balance. The first is the ability of the Coast Guard to host broad deliberative forums that moved the debate forward. Participants in the 2002 workshop knew that ultimately regulations for port security would be mandated by the MTSA, but in a significant deviation from traditional regulatory practices whereby rules are promulgated by agencies and then vigorously challenged by those affected by the new rules, the workshop was aimed at building relationships and developing new ideas on port security. Coast Guard leadership was not comfortable with what they feared might be a "circus," but Captain Suzanne Englebert, in particular, had a sense of the potential the workshop held for building a partnership with the private sector interests and providing the Coast Guard with essential information that might not be forthcoming in a traditional regulatory effort (Weber and Khademian 1997). She could not guarantee that the workshop would not turn into a circus, but she could offer processes for the deliberations and an explanation of the importance of utilizing broad participation in developing an effective regulatory approach. The success of the forum rested with an ability of the Coast Guard to be a participant, as well as to run the workshop effectively with some authority.

When Congress gave the Coast Guard a "pass" on compliance with the Administrative Procedures Act to speed the issuance of regulations, the persistence of Captain Englebert and others to pursue seven public forums prevailed. Where Congress supported quick action without the delay of a public forum for national security reasons, the Coast Guard saw open forums as essential to national security. As described by one Coast Guard officer (Schneider 2006):

> To ensure that crucial security concerns were addressed, the USCG included all port stakeholders in the rule making process. For example, seven MTSA outreach and feedback sessions were held throughout the U.S. Discussions from these meetings and comments from other interested organizations aided the USCG in determining the types of vessels and facilities that posed risks of being involved in a transportation security incident, and in identifying security measures and standards to deter such incidents.

As in the case of the pre-MTSA workshop the forums were framed to be inclusive and to solicit as much input and technical information as possible to guide the regulatory process. Instead of approaching vessel, facility, and port owners with regulations to respond to, the Coast Guard issued invitations that set out questions the agency was grappling with in the course of developing regulations. The "hardest thing about regulation inside the beltway," commented Englebert, is "writing a regulation to prevent something without ever knowing if it will happen, unless it happens" (Englebert 2007).

For the forum Englebert adopted the color-coded card system of "Toastmasters" to enforce a three-minute time limit for each participant to hold the floor and speak. The method created some curious dynamics, with organizations gaming the process by having one organizational member after another speak for three minutes each to prolong the time any one organization held the floor, but the process was accepted and adhered to. In the first meeting, participants giggled at the sign of the first warning card displayed matter-of-factly by Englebert, and thereafter practiced self-enforcement, telling each other the time was up when Englebert displayed the red card. Englebert's effective use of the card system established her credibility, through transparent and open leadership in the IMO negotiations, to pass the ISPS Code and the development of the MTSA, but also the authority of the Coast Guard. The agency was there, creating an open forum, listening, and working with the information offered by participants, but it was ultimately the authority responsible for developing regulations, and effective guidance of the deliberative processes was an essential way to exert that authority without stifling the debate.

Risk Reduction as a Network Goal and Benefit

A second component of the Coast Guard strategy in building a maritime security network is the application of risk management to "reduce the risk of terrorism by prioritizing critical infrastructure and key resources" (Downs 2007, p. 36). The method provides a means to connect participants to security with flexibility in the way risk is reduced, or security is achieved, and it has provided a means to demonstrate the benefits of the regulatory strategy to the Office of Management and Budget (OMB).

The Coast Guard is widely recognized as a leader in the use of risk management (Government Accountability Office 2006). According to Rear Admiral Charles Bone, "The Coast Guard has been aggressively employing risk management to inform decisions at the strategic, operational, and tactical levels." The Coast Guard doctrinal text (United States Coast Guard 2002) lists "managed risk "as one of the seven Coast Guard principles of operation, providing "the strategic foundation for all of the Coast Guard's prevention and response missions and capabilities" (Bone 2007, 4). The Coast Guard employs risk management throughout its operations. Risk management was applied to develop voluntary "go/no go" criteria for the masters of small commercial passenger vessels in the Northwest to help them make decisions whether or not to cross a bar—the dynamic and dangerous mouth of a river—in difficult weather conditions, and risk management is applied to assist search-and-rescue boat commanders in making determinations whether to embark. A system is in place requiring commander responses of "red," "amber," or "green" to questions of crew fitness, supervision, environment, planning, crew selection, and the complexity of the event. The decision process is intended to reduce or mitigate the risk associated with any rescue mission. In addition, risk-ranking tools are used for allocating resources and time, such as deciding what vessels to examine or board in matters of maritime or port security, and to set priorities for wreck and debris removal in the wake of Hurricane Katrina (U.S. Coast Guard 2007).

Risk management, specifically the Maritime Security Risk Analysis Model (MSRAM), is the centerpiece of Coast Guard efforts to regulate port security. Just as the boat commanders use risk management as a decisionmaking tool to assess their crew, equipment, weather, and overall readiness before embarking on a search-and-rescue mission, an early version of MSRAM targeted the decisionmaking of captains of the port to enhance their decisionmaking in assessing port vulnerabilities and potential consequences of maritime-related terrorist attacks (Downs 2007). MSRAM provides some standardization of this process of identifying potential threats and the potential consequences of an attack at a local, regional and national level. This approach to individual and organizational decisionmaking, ranking of priorities, and asset management has provided an effective means of engaging the stakeholders in the vast port security network.

At the most fundamental level, the risk-management approach provides a means for network participants to deal with the massive security challenges posed by the threat of a maritime attack. In a post-9/11 world where the unthinkable becomes thinkable, how do stakeholders prevent and prepare for a vast range of scenarios? The risk-based approach provides a means of focusing preparation by identifying possible threats, considering vulnerabilities in terms of critical infrastructure, ships, facilities, resources, and conditions, and potential consequences, all with the intention of reducing the risk of a terror attack or mitigating the impact of an attack and speeding recovery.

In addition to the provision of a common framework for port security, the demonstration of risk reduction provides a means of demonstrating the benefits of the Coast Guard regulatory strategy to the OMB. In a document with the title "Annual Percent Reduction in Terrorism-Related Maritime Risk that the Coast Guard Is Able to Influence," the Coast Guard puts forth its use of risk reduction as a benefit:

> This measure is a risk-based proxy measure of outcome performance. Maritime attack scenarios are scored with respect to Threat, Vulnerability, and Consequence to define a level of terrorism-risk that exists in the maritime domain. The Coast Guard, using subject matter experts, estimates the portion of that risk that is within its authority to influence, then scores its best estimate of reductions to Threat, Vulnerability, and Consequence that its activities, policies, and initiatives may have accounted for—for each scenario. The estimated percent reduction in risk serves as the proxy for Coast Guard outcome performance. In order to improve the validity and objectivity of the measure in the future, the Coast Guard intends to invite external experts to participate in the evaluation.[9]

OMB acceptance of risk reduction as a benefit in its assessment of the benefits and costs of rules—a first for the OMB—is essential for the longer-term development and stability of the port security network.

Leveraging Established Frameworks and Practices

The final strategy employed by the Coast Guard in building a port security network is the leveraging of established frameworks and practices that can provide capacity in the port security effort. Perhaps most critical has been the simultaneous development of the ISPS Code and the MTSA in 2002, and Captain Englebert was central to these parallel efforts. The 2002 workshop provided a means to build a domestic approach to port security that the Coast Guard could take to the

9. See the Coast Guard's website, Expectmore.gov; also www.whitehouse.gov/OMB/expectmore/detail/10003635.2006.html (accessed September 2007).

IMO later that year. The sense of urgency in early 2002 across the maritime community provided the motivation for addressing maritime security at both the domestic and international levels, and the Coast Guard provided the vision for what that approach might be. Following the 2002 workshop, the Coast Guard went to the IMO in London in May with a proposal that became the basis for the discussions. As Englebert and others worked through formal and informal discussions to build consensus among members of the IMO for a new security regime, they held conversations with staff in Congress working on the Maritime Transportation Security Act (Public Law 107-295) to ensure parallel development. Passage of the MTSA provided the Coast Guard with a compatible approach to the ISPS Code, but with regulatory enforcement teeth.

Another point of leverage used by the Coast Guard for building the port security network are the lessons learned in implementing the 1990 Oil Pollution Act (OPA 90). Like the passage of the MTSA in 2002, the OPA 90 was passed in response to a major catastrophe—the oil spill of the *Exxon Valdez*. Implementation of OPA 90, which dramatically increased Coast Guard authority in preventing and responding to oil spills, posed a number of challenges for the Coast Guard. Most significant, OPA 90 established a unilateral position for the United States vis-à-vis the international community, one requiring negotiation and work with the international community after the fact to implement the legislation. In the case of the MTSA, the Coast Guard had been working with the International Maritime Organization prior to the passage of the MTSA and had built domestic as well as international support to the risk-based, results-oriented approach. The lesson learned was to work closely with domestic stakeholders and the international community to develop a cohesive regulatory approach. However, the OPA 90 legislation also provided a format that could be leveraged in the case of the MTSA. The legislation placed responsibility on vessel owners and facility owners to elaborate response plans and incorporated a tiered response from vessel to port to state to national response, depending upon the needed response level for an oil spill. Responsibility is similarly placed with vessel and facility owners to create security plans, with the Coast Guard playing a more prominent role as the size of the facility and ship, and hence potential impact of an act of terror, increases.

Before 9/11 the focus of security issues was limited mostly to criminal activities such as drug smuggling, trade fraud, cargo theft, and stowaways. The President's Interagency Commission on Crime and Security in U.S. Ports, established in the late 1990s, produced a report on criminal and security issues (Interagency Commission on Crime and Security in U.S. Ports 2000; MTSNAC 2001). Terrorism was on the agenda, but the threat was considered low. The report noted,

> The FBI considers the present threat of terrorism directed at any U.S. seaports to be low, even though their vulnerability to attack is high. The Commission believes that such an attack has the potential to cause significant

damage. Some port organizations expressed frustration with not being made aware of specific threat information on an ongoing basis.

Chapter 4 of the report did contain findings and recommendations regarding seaport security and the threat of terrorism. The utility of risk management and the assessment of port vulnerabilities were central to the findings and recommendations. Today the primary security concern is terrorism, and the interagency report became the basis of the MTSA. Before 9/11, Senator Ernest Frederick Hollings (D-S.C.) introduced legislation based upon the report, which did not pass. It had a criminal focus and emphasized coordination between agencies. After 9/11, the legislation was pumped up with an emphasis on terrorism, and it passed unanimously as the MTSA.

Finally, the Coast Guard leveraged long-standing relationships with the maritime community to build a port security network. As a 26-year veteran of the Coast Guard, and current port security official, explained in a 2005 interview with one of the authors:

> The Coast Guard is perceived as an honest broker, not hostile. . . . I have seen other agencies where "it's my way or the highway for enforcement. . . . Here are the rules, or else." Not the Coast Guard. . . . With drug interdiction, there is no collaboration—those customers are not happy to see the Coast Guard. But with safety, fisheries, and so on, the Coast Guard works with people. You depend on other folks. . . . The Coast Guard always played, but not with a heavy hand. In 26 years [with the CG] I have learned don't be heavy handed, do what's best for everyone. . . . It's a Solomon-like approach.[10]

The consensus-building efforts engaged in by the Coast Guard to develop and now implement the MTSA reflected this approach. It is time-consuming but has facilitated the network building needed to implement port security. The legislation has a big financial impact on domestic and international companies, but the Coast Guard has not had many complaints or industry people going to the Congress or the White House to complain. Maritime interests, however, do frequently go to the Coast Guard to get assistance with the technical challenges of implementation, and the Coast Guard works openly and closely to resolve those issues.

Conclusion

Port security is pursued in a context of contrasting expectations and circumstances. The uniqueness of each port, and hence the need for localized decisionmaking, is challenged by the understanding that there is no security unless everyone is secure.

10. Representative of the Coast Guard Office of Port and Vessel Security, Directorate of Port Security, interview by Anne Khademian, July 13, 2005.

The amazing flexibility and efficiency of just-in-time maritime trade, made possible in large part by the development of the standard shipping container, is challenged by the threat the shipping container poses as a potential vehicle for terrorism and the need to scan and inspect as many containers as possible. Flag states have a long history of demanding security in the face of piracy, drug smuggling, and contraband activity, now challenged by port states, such as the United States, which are anxious to prevent ships posing a threat from entering their harbors.

The United States Coast Guard has entered this context with a three-pronged strategy for building a port security network, whose aim is to keep American ports safe but which is dependent upon the sweep of participants in the vast maritime arena. The first prong is to pursue shared responsibility in developing and implementing plans for security. Broad, open forums with opportunities for participation, maintained by the imposition of procedures for engagement and a commitment to decisions accomplished in the small groups, have guided this part of the strategy. The second is to rely on risk reduction as a means of engaging the threat of terrorism and to set security goals while decentralizing the "how" of security. And third, the Coast Guard has leveraged existing frameworks and partnerships to continue to build network capacity.

Assessments of the effectiveness of the maritime network are mixed. Some note the progress on a number of fronts, from improvements in maritime domain awareness to enhanced coordination among state, local, and federal organizations. Critics point to the vulnerabilities and gaps that remain, including the small number of containers scanned before they enter a U.S. port, the use of ports and terminals across the United States by tankers with liquid natural gas or other explosive material, and the delays in implementing a port worker ID program (Flynn and Wein 2005; Flynn 2005; U.S. Department of Homeland Security, Office of Inspector General 2006). They also point to the need for improvement in funding for port security programs, and so on (Wrightson 2005). The reach of the network is vast, the participants, many, and the responsibilities, shared. The Coast Guard continues to focus on the quality of the information that is generated and shared, and the quality of the relationships that facilitate a focus on security through risk reduction.

References

Allen, Thad. 2006. "The Water is Different." Speech at the United States Naval Institute Port Security Conference, Commandant, United States Coast Guard, June 7, 2006.

Beisecker, Randall. 2006. "DP World and U.S. Port Security. Nuclear Threat Initiative." Issue Brief (file:///c:/Coast%20Guard/background%20on%20Dubai%20Ports%20World. htm).

Bone, Charles C. 2007. "Assistant Commandant's Perspective." *Proceedings* (Spring): 4.

Bonner, Robert. 2002. "U.S. Customs Commissioner Robert C. Bonner." Speech at the Center for Strategic and International Studies, Washington, D.C., January 17.

Congressional Budget Office. 2006. "The Economic Costs of Disruptions in Container Shipments." March 29 (www.cbo.gov/ftpdocs/71xx/doc7106/03-29-Container_Shipments.pdf).

Customs and Border Protection. 2006. "Success of Radiation Portal Monitor Program Remains Undiminished," US Customs and Border Protection Today (May) (www.cbp.gov/xp/CustomsToday/2006/may/radiation_portal.xml).

Downs, Brady. 2007. "The Maritime Security Risk Analysis Model." *Proceedings* (Spring): 36–38.

Englebert, Suzanne. 2007. "International Port Security an the Coast Guard." Presentation at Port Security Forum (Network Performance Project), Fels Institute of Government, University of Pennsylvania, March 23.

Flynn, Stephen. 2005. "U.S. Port Security and the Global War on Terror." *American Interest* 1, no. 1: 92–96.

Flynn, Stephen, and James Loy. 2006. "A Port in the Storm over Dubai." *New York Times*, February 26 (www.cfr.org/publication/9976/port_in_the_storm_over_dubai.html).

Flynn, Stephen, and Lawrence Wein. 2005. "Think inside the Box." *New York Times,* November 29 (www.iht.com/articles/2005/11/29/opinion/edflynn.php).

Frittelli, John, and Jennifer Lake. 2006. "Terminal Operators and their Role in U.S. Port and Maritime Security." Congressional Research Service (file:///c:/Coast%20Guard/overview.htm).

Fulweiler, John. 2007. "There's a Lot to Know about the ISPS Code." *Police Link: The Nation's Law Enforcement Community,* May 31 (www.policelink.com/training/articles/1851-theres-a-lot-to-know-about-the-isps-code).

Gerencser, Mark, Jon Weinberg, and Don Vincent. 2003. *Port Security War Game: Implications for U.S. Supply Chain.* Booz Allen Hamilton, Inc. (www.boozallen.com/media/file/128648.pdf).

Goldsmith, Stephen, and William Eggers. 2004. *Governing by Network: The New Shape of the Public Sector.* Brookings.

Government Accountability Office. 2005. *Risk Management: Further Refinements Needed to Assess Risks and Prioritize Protective Measures at Ports and Other Critical Infrastructure.* GAO-06-91. Washington.

———. 2006. "Maritime Security: Information Sharing Efforts are Improving." Statement of Stephen Caldwell before the Subcommittee on Government Management, Finance, and Accountability, Committee on Government Reform, House of Representatives.

Greene, Lawrence. 2005. "The U.S. Coast Guard Reorganization: Why Merging the Field Units is not Enough to Remain *Semper Paratus* (Always Ready)." Ph.D. dissertation, Naval Postgraduate School.

Harrald, John, Hugh Stephens, and Johann Rene vanDorp. 2004. "A Framework for Sustainable Port Security." *Journal of Homeland Security and Emergency Management* 1, no. 2: 1–20.

International Maritime Organization. 1974. "International Convention for Safety of Life at Sea." November 1, 32 UST 47, 1184 UNTS 276 (SOLAS) (www.imo.org/Conventions/contents.asp?topic_id=257&doc_id=647).

Interagency Commission on Crime and Security in U.S. Ports. 2000. *Report of the Interagency Commission on Crime and Security in U.S. Ports* (www.securitymanagement.com/archive/library/seaport1200.pdf).

Kettl, Donald. 2004. *System under Stress: Homeland Security and American Politics.* Washington: CQ Press.

Khademian, Anne. 2006. "The Politics of Homeland Security." In *The McGraw Hill Homeland Security Handbook,* edited by David Kamien. New York: McGraw-Hill.

Lim Fang Jau, Irvin. 2002. "Not Yet All Aboard. . . . But Already at Sea over the Container Security Initiative." *Homeland Security,* November (www.homelandsecurity.org/newjournal/articles/jau.html).

Loy, James M., and Robert G. Ross. 2002. "Global Trade: America's Achilles' Heel." *Journal of Homeland Security,* February (www.homelandsecurity.org/newjournal/articles/lorossglobaltrade.htm).

Morris, Jim. 1996. "Flags of Convenience Give Owners a Paper Refuge." *Houston Chronicle,* August 21 (www.chron.com/content/interactive/special/maritime/96/08/22/part5.html).

MTSNAC (Maritime Transportation System National Advisory Council). 2001. "Security Team Meeting Executive Summary." New York Shipping Administration, 2 World Trade Center, New York, April 26.

Neff, Robert. 2007. "Flags That Hide the Dirty Truth." *Asia Times* online, April 19 (www.globalpolicy.org/nations/flags/2007/0419dirtyflags.htm).

O'Rourke, Ronald. 2004. *Homeland Security: Coast Guard Operations—Background and Issues for Congress.* July 4, 2004.

Parfomak, Paul, and John Fritelli. 2007. *Maritime Security: Potential Terrorist Attacks and Protection Priorities.* Washington: Congressional Research Service (January 9).

Pluta, Paul. 2002. "Vessel Operations Under Flags of Convenience and National Security." Statement before the House Armed Services Committee Special Oversight Panel on the Merchant Marines, June 13.

Public Policy Institute of California. 2006. "Securing the Nation's Seaports: Multiple Goals, Uncertain Results." *Research Brief* 106 (www.ppic.org/content/pubs/rb/RB_606JHRB.pdf).

Quartel, Robert. 2002. "Securing Our Ports against Terror: Technology, Resources and Homeland Defense." Testimony before the United States Senate Committee on the Judiciary, February 26.

Republican Policy Committee, United States Senate. 2006. Highlights of the Conference Report to Accompany HR 4954—Security & Accountability for Every (SAFE) Port, September 29, 2006 (http://rpc.senate.gov/public/_files/Oct506HR4954SafePortActLB.pdf).

Schneider, T. 2006. "Maritime Security: A Collaborative Responsibility." Presentation at the International Conference on the Accession of Bulgaria to the European Union, November 17 (http://64.233.169.104/search?q=cache:yHIcH-S3dHsJ:www.port.bg/conference/presentation/16.Schneider.doc+schneider+%2B+%22port+security+liaison+officer%22+%2B+isps&hl=en&ct=clnk&cd=1&gl=us&client=firefox-a).

Underwood, James. 2002. Responses to Questions by the U.S. Commission on Ocean Policy to RADM James Underwood, Commander, Seventeenth Coast Guard District (file:///c:/Coast%20Guard/Underwood%202002.htm).

United States Coast Guard. 2002. "U.S. Coast Guard: America's Maritime Guardian." Coast Guard Publication 1. Washington.

———. 2004. "Secure Seas, Open Ports: Keeping our Waters Safe, Secure and Open for Business." June 21, 2004. www.piersystem.com/posted/586/DHSPortSecurityFactSheet_062104.41841.pdf

———. 2007. "Risk Management." Special journal issue. *Proceedings: The Coast Guard Journal of Safety and Security at Sea* (Spring).

U.S. Department of Homeland Security, Office of Inspector General. 2006. "DHS Must Address Significant Security Vulnerabilities Prior to TWIC Implementation." Redacted. Washington (http://epic.org/privacy/surveillance/spotlight/0706/ dhsig_0706.pdf).

U.S. Department of Justice, Office of Inspector General. 2006. "The Federal Bureau of Investigation's Efforts to Protect the Nation's Seaports." Audit Report 06-26 (file:///c:/Coast%20Guard/OIG%20report.htm

Weber, Edward, and Anne Khademian. 1997. "From Agitation to Collaboration: Clearing the Air through Negotiation." *Public Administration Review* 57, no. 5: 396.

Walsh, Don. 2002. "Tourism and Terrorism: A Difficult Journey Ahead for the Cruise Ship Industry." Arlington, Va.: Navy League of the United States (www.navyleague.org/sea_power/dec_02_51.php).

Wrightson, Margaret. 2005. "Port Security Issues." Testimony before the Senate Committee on Commerce, Science and Technology, May 17.

8

Dark Networks and the Problem
of Islamic Jihadist Terrorism

H. BRINTON MILWARD AND JÖRG RAAB

Naturally the enemy has adapted. As you capture a Khalid Sheik Mohammed, an Abu Faraj al-Libbi rises up. Nature abhors a vacuum."

Frances Fragos Townsend, presidential adviser on terrorism,
on the need for a review of U.S. antiterrorism policy

Most writers advocating networks have ignored the nature of the problem networking is supposed to solve. It is usually argued that networks are better than hierarchies for solving nonroutine, nonstandardized, ill-structured (Simon 1973), or "wicked" (Rittel and Webber 1973) problems. There is little attention to how problems respond to attempts to solve them, however, and if actors who are a part of these problems are resistant to measures to solve them, it is assumed that those groups or organizations can be co-opted in one way or another (Selznick 1949). Few researchers have looked at cases in which the problem is not an unorganized set of poor or cognitively impaired clients but another network—perhaps engaged in illegal activity such as drug or human trafficking,

Earlier versions of this chapter were presented at the EGOS conference June 29 to July 2, 2005, "Subtheme 21: The Control of Legal and Illegal Networks," in Berlin, and the Eighth Public Management Research Conference at the School of Policy, Planning and Development at the University of Southern California, Los Angeles, September 29 to October 1, 2005. The authors would like to thank Matthew Kennedy, a former graduate student at the School of Public Administration and Policy, University of Arizona, for his help in researching this paper.
Epigraph: Susan B. Glasser, "Review May Shift Terror Policies," *Washington Post,* May 29, 2005, p. A1.

arms and diamond smuggling, or terrorism—making use of the alleged comparative advantage of networks. Such networks are, in principle, able to adapt their structures and behavior or even transform themselves altogether to react to attempts to destroy them. Earlier research found that covert networks will be more likely to survive and be "successful" the more flexible their structures are and the more quickly they can adapt to changing pressures from nation-states seeking to destroy them (Raab and Milward 2003).

In this chapter we take a fresh look at this proposition in the wake of the evolution of Islamic jihadist terrorism in the years since the attacks on Washington and New York on September 11, 2001. They triggered a massive response to destroy the al Qaeda terrorist network,[1] yet despite this massive campaign, which undoubtedly severely damaged the organizational structure that was al Qaeda's in September 2001, the number of terrorist attacks by groups claiming a militant Islamic background has steadily increased in number and geographical scope. Today, al Qaeda and its affiliates—from the border between Pakistan and Afghanistan to Iraq to North Africa, Indonesia, and even Europe—are very much alive.[2]

This analysis begins by looking first at the problem characteristics (Islamic jihadist terrorism), second at the changing conditions in which terrorists have to operate, and third at the organizational responses that they presumably made in order to react to these changing conditions. The goal of this analysis is to contribute to the discussion on how to control illegal and covert, or "dark," networks, to analyze "dark networks as problems" in order to broaden understanding of these organizational forms, and to evaluate what could be learned about networks in general by comparing "bright" and "dark" networks.

"Dark" refers to networks that are both covert and illegal according to the social and political environment they act in. "Bright" refers to networks that are overt and whose actions are in accordance with the legal framework of states they reside in. In reality the distinction is often less clear-cut than the heuristic might imply, and there is a large gray zone in the middle. Legal and illegal networks sometimes come together in a gray zone, or they are confronted with the fact that what is legal in one country is illegal in another. Moreover, legal networks also happen to engage in legally doubtful operations, such as the clandestine transfer ("rendition") of al Qaeda suspects by the U.S. Central Intelligence Agency (CIA) and other international security forces to countries in which their interrogation is not bound by legal restrictions usually applied in the West. The assessment of

---

1. The term "Islamic jihadist terrorism" is freighted with normative baggage, but it simply means that it is terrorism by those whose motivations are rooted in their interpretations of Islam. Terrorist acts by Islamic jihadists have included airline hijacking, beheading, kidnapping, assassination, roadside bombing, and suicide bombing of both military and civilian targets.

2. For the frequency, type, results, location, and attribution of terrorist attacks see U.S. Department of State (2008).

Figure 8-1. *Dimensions in the Universe of Networks*

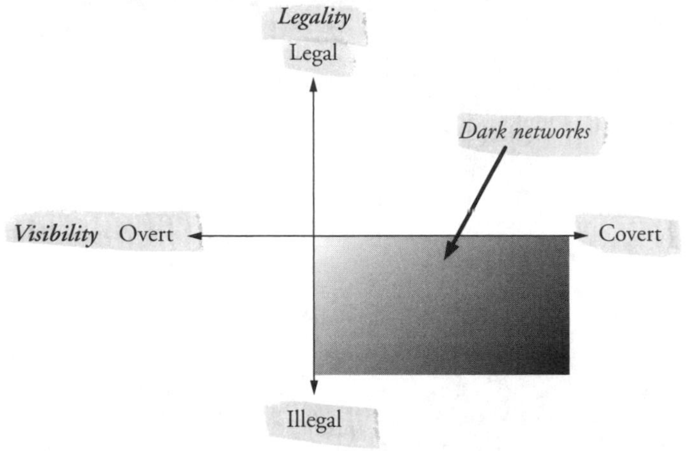

Source: Author.

whether a network is "bright" or "dark" is therefore not a normative but an empirical question.

Figure 8-1 depicts how dark and bright networks could be classified. If there are two dimensions, *visibility* (overt or covert) and *legality* (legal or covert), dark networks fall into the bottom right quadrant, which is both illegal and covert. Of course, in the real world networks often defy categorization. For instance, a dark network such as the Irish Republican Army (IRA) had a legal and overt element, the Irish political party Sinn Fein. In this case the network would actually blend between these two quadrants. The legal and covert quadrant would include intelligence agencies and security services for which covert activity is a defining element of their operation. The illegal and overt quadrant is illustrated by Serbia under Slobodan Milosevic where a gang became a state, and criminals operated quite openly.

"Networks as problems" refers to the fact that networks that are part of problems are in principle able to adapt their structures and transform themselves to react to changing conditions in their environments, just like a network seeking to alleviate a problem. This is a change in perspective, because first, problems had usually been regarded as socially nonreactive and, second, networks were on the basis of normative assumptions almost exclusively seen as solutions to problems, not as problems themselves. Figure 8-2 depicts a problem surrounded by a network and a network within the problem space, illustrating the observation that it "takes a network to fight a network" (Arquilla and Ronfeldt 2001). In this case, connections can be seen between the dark network and the bright network surrounding it, illustrating the role of infiltrators (in both directions) as well as double agents. Although this chapter looks only at what happens to dark networks

Figure 8-2. *Problems and Solutions: "It Takes a Network to Fight a Network"*

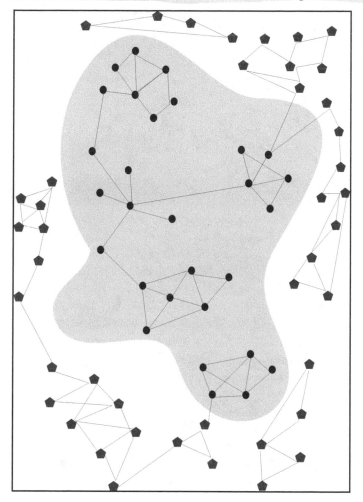

Source: Adapted from Bryson and Crosby (1992, p. 6).

under pressure, a true picture of the relationship between dark and bright networks would include time, which would capture one network's adapting to the moves of another in a strategic contingent fashion. In an earlier paper the authors attempted to model how a dark network would attempt to adapt to attempts to destroy it (Milward and Raab 2006). Adaptation to threat is also the theme of Michael Kinney's recent book, *From Pablo to Osama* (2007), where he compares how Colombian cocaine cartels and al Qaeda attempt to adapt to efforts to destroy them in a strategic-contingent fashion.

It is hoped that this research will contribute to the growing body of knowledge about social and interorganizational networks as well as to the discussion on different forms of network governance (Provan and Kenis 2008). "Network" is a frequently used term, and it is often not clear exactly how it is being used. First, network analysis is a methodology for analyzing social systems from the perspective of actors (individuals or organizations) and their relations, rather than on the basis of categories such as race and gender. Second, a network is a specific social structure characterized by a preponderance of informal communication relations, a horizontal as opposed to a hierarchical pattern of relations, and a decentralized pattern of actors' positions (Kenis and Schneider 1991, p. 32). Third, "network" can refer to a form of governance sometimes seen as a mixture of markets and hierarchies, sometimes as a unique form of actor coordination (Powell 1990).

The general credo among network scholars until the end of the 1990s was that networks are especially effective in complex problem situations in which the ownership of the problem by single organizations and their capacities to alleviate it are not congruent. Solving the problem would also require a diverse body of knowledge, a relatively quick reaction, and the capacity for collective decision-making through negotiations. Because networks were seen as flexible, loosely coupled structures consisting of autonomous actors that are "lighter on their feet than hierarchies" (Powell 1990), they seemed to be the solution for many social, economic, and political problems societies had to face at the end of the twentieth century. Figure 8-3 depicts four organizations collaborating with each other through the mutual links they have forged. The network brings together diverse knowledge, resources, and skills in the context of collective decisionmaking that gives collaborative networks their comparative advantage.

In discussions about networks it was usually assumed that networks were coordination devices used for the benefit of people. However, in looking at the conditions in which they are expected to work well, it should not come as a surprise that parallels to networks and actors that pursue criminal ends can easily be found. This "dark network" research project seeks to combine evidence from different types of dark networks, compare it with research on bright networks, and begin to integrate what is known about managing legal and illegal networks (Raab and Milward 2003; Milward and Raab 2006; Bakker, Raab, and Milward 2008).

Raab and Milward (2003) compared three cases of dark networks: al Qaeda, heroin trafficking networks, and various networks engaged in smuggling arms and diamonds in West Africa. The organizational conclusions were as follows:

—Covert networks, like overt networks, come in all forms and shapes. Dark networks must have a very flexible structure, one that enables them to react quickly to changing pressures from nation-states and other opponents in order to survive.

—Dark networks need a territorial base to be effective. These bases are usually in regions torn apart by civil war and dominated by current or former warlords and where no state with a legitimate monopoly of coercive power exists.

Figure 8-3. *Organizations and Problems*

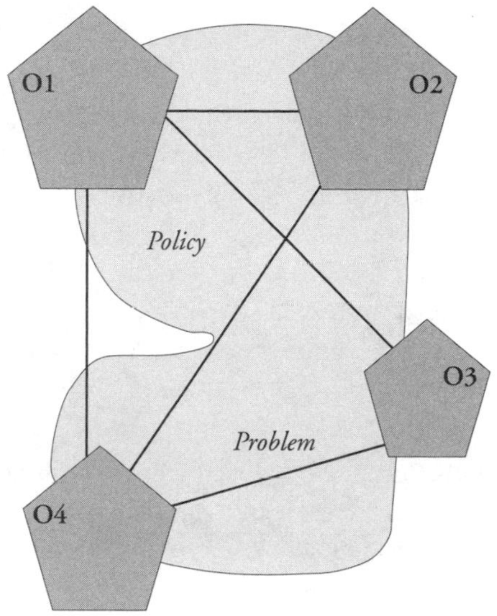

Source: Adapted from Hjern (1992, p. 4).

—Dark and bright networks face similar challenges in terms of differentiation and integration. However, dark networks, as covert and illegal entities, have to find different answers to these challenges because their activity is under constant risk of detection. To enforce their claims and compel adherence to their goals, they have only physical force and coercion, not law.

We reexamine these conclusions in this chapter, in the wake of the evolution of Islamic jihadist terrorism since 9/11. Despite a massive campaign that damaged the organizational structure of al Qaeda as it stood in September 2001, a reconstituted al Qaeda and its affiliates remain the chief threat to the United States and its partners.[3] To conclude that efforts to destroy al Qaeda have not been effective would, however, be premature. To try to reach a balanced view, we analyze the problem of controlling al Qaeda by looking first at it as the object of control, second at the changing conditions terrorists have to operate under, and third at the organizational responses that presumably occurred in order to react to these changing conditions.[4]

3. Ibid., chapter 1, p. 1.
4. In this chapter we do not discuss the organizational characteristics and control strategies of the network of Western security agencies, militaries, or police organizations and how they changed their strategies and structures after September 11; we will examine this important issue in a future publication.

Conclusions Revisited

The first conclusion reached in "Dark Networks as Problems" (Raab and Milward 2003) is that "covert networks, like overt networks, come in all forms and shapes." Dark networks must have a flexible structure that enables them to react quickly to changing pressures from nation-states and other opponents in order to survive. Are there any commonalities among the structures of dark networks? Are the structures they adopt to cope with the need for secrecy necessitated by the illegal nature of their operations similar to one another? Have these dark networks invented new organizational forms?

Looking at al Qaeda, various observers and scholars claim that it has a number of different forms temporally and spatially. The pre– and post–September 11 al Qaeda seem to be quite dissimilar. The al Qaeda network responsible for the October 12, 2002, Bali nightclub bombing and the localized network responsible for the March 11, 2004, Madrid subway bombing may have been structured totally differently. Given the spatial differentiation of what observers claim to be al Qaeda, it may make more sense to talk about it as a network of networks. Though recognizing the limitations of a single case, much can be learned by focusing on a single dark network that has an amazing range of forms and shapes and is tied to a worldwide cultural, religious, and political movement in the Middle East, among Muslims in South Asia, and among the Islamic diaspora in Europe.

To listen to leading scholars, journalists, and intelligence officials describe how al Qaeda is designed and organized is to be reminded of the blind men describing an elephant. Each describes the part he can touch but none is able to comprehend the whole. Some have called al Qaeda a "foundation" that funds terror. Others have said that it is tightly organized in project teams. Others say it is diffuse, more like a social movement than a network. There is even some reason to think it does not exist as a terrorist network except in an iconic way that leads dispersed groups of terrorists to claim that their work was "inspired by" al Qaeda. It may also be a franchise, as Abu Musab al-Zarqawi, the late leader of the insurgency in Iraq, claimed when he said that he represented "al Qaeda in Iraq."

Currently, debate is raging among two of the most influential figures in the world of terrorism studies. Bruce Hoffman (2008), author of *Inside Terrorism* (2006) argues that al Qaeda has regrouped, has reconstituted itself in the border regions of Pakistan, and is very dangerous. He is backed by a recent National Intelligence Estimate (Office of the Director of National Intelligence 2007) and by academics such as Bruce Riedel (2007).

Marc Sageman, author of *Understanding Terror Networks* (2004), *Leaderless Jihad* (2008a), and an influential article in *Foreign Policy* (2008b), has concluded that the greatest Islamic jihadist terrorist threat is from "bunches of guys" who have been radicalized by the Internet or local mosques or clubs and not from a resurgent al Qaeda Central based in the North-West Frontier Territories of Pakistan. Hoffman (2008) has charged that Sageman's research is faulty, that his conclusions about leaderless jihad are wrong, and that accepting this perspective is extremely dangerous. The implications of this debate for policy are huge. Should the United States continue investing billions in a global war against terror fought in places like the Afghan-Pakistani border region, or is this fight against terror a task of "preventing attacks by small bands of zealots in the garages and basements just off Main Street or the alleys behind Islamic madrasas?"[5] If the latter, this is more a job for the local police and the FBI than for Special Operations Forces.

From the authors' perspective, if al Qaeda is a network of networks, this debate is pointless. There is nothing inconsistent in a worldwide ideologically united movement's taking different forms in different parts of the world, depending on the threats and opportunities faced by local radicalized groups. Recruitment can be from below, as Sageman claims, as local cells radicalize themselves through discussion and information they see on the Internet. It can also be top-down with madrasas in South Waziristan drilling a message of hate and jihad into the minds of young children and following this up with camps to turn recruits into mujahidin. Thus, recruitment could result either from the push of local conditions or the pull of organizations created to recruit the next generation of Islamic jihadists. In this chapter, we analyze what is known about al Qaeda from two different perspectives: the political and the organizational.

Political Component

Al Qaeda is the product of the political milieu of Islamic jihadism. In the beginning, al Qaeda's leadership grew out of the shared training and combat experience in Afghanistan, Bosnia, and Chechnya. Like Moammar Gaddafi's Libyan terrorist training camps in the 1970s and 1980s (Raab and Milward 2003, p. 426), these combat theaters produced the environment in which al Qaeda was born and developed. The leadership and fighting skills developed by these leaders would be useful to an organization that wanted to confront the West, particularly the United States, for its policies toward the Islamic world. However, al Qaeda could also draw on a broad recruiting base.

> [The] networked core of the bin Laden organization could draw recruits from another looser social network that had emerged during a widespread process of "re-Islamization from below," under way since the 1980s. From London to Lahore, this network of mosques, madrassahs, and pietist associations implemented a "honey-combing of small areas of society through space and time." . . . The combination of shared experience in war and shared values inculcated by the network and through this far-flung Islamic

---

5. Elaine Sciolino and Eric Schmitt, "A Not Very Private Feud over Terrorism," *New York Times,* Week in Review, June 8, 2008, pp. 1, 8.

religious network furthered coordination without a bureaucratic hierarchy. (Kahler 2002, pp. 9–10)

Terrorist networks are conventionally divided between a core and periphery (Williams 2002, p. 18). In the case of the Basque separatist organization ETA, there are actually three levels—a core and two peripheral levels that constitute the political component. The organizational component consists of a group of between 100 and 150 terrorists who blow up targets and assassinate opponents (it is believed that the IRA was the same size at its peak). The political component that gives active support to the terrorists consists of a much larger group of supporters and sympathizers who provide the terrorists with safe houses, passports, and transportation. Often, these individuals have limited connections to the armed wing, so they can bank, rent property, and move about a city without arousing suspicion. The outer ring of the political component consists of those who exist in the milieu of the social movement that supports the terrorists' goals.[6] In the case of al Qaeda, the third level consists of a worldwide jihadist movement that is recognizable from Lyon to Kuala Lumpur. Mosques are critical nodes, and ethnic communities serve as cover, support, and sources of recruits (Williams 2002, p. 40).

Finance is critical to the survival of any terrorist network, and al Qaeda is no exception. The overall structure of Osama bin Laden's original business network appeared to be patterned after Yasser Arafat's PLO investment schemes, which have been called the privatization of terror. The investment portfolio seems to have followed the template for successful capitalist investing.[7] Loretta Napoleoni (2003, pp. 162–63) points out,

> Funds are placed in several banks across the world, ranging from the Sultanate of Brunei to European countries. The portfolio contains financial investments with different degrees of risk and return. . . . Short-term speculation on Western stock markets is regarded as a favourable and efficient way of accumulating funds in the West without using bank transfers, which are more easily traceable.

However, since the passage of stringent new anti-terrorism banking laws after 9/11, local cells of al Qaeda have begun to self-finance, using low-level criminal scams and various trafficking schemes. Members of cells live very thrifty lives and learn to build bombs that are deadly but cheap.[8] As governments adopt new means to fight terror, terrorists adapt as well.

6. Keith B. Richburg, "ETA Aided by Broad Network of Supporters," *Washington Post,* January 19, 2003, p. A23.

7. See Napoleoni (2003) and Farah (2004) for detailed descriptions of how Al Qaeda developed its financial base.

8. Craig Whitlock, "Al-Qaeda Masters Terrorism on the Cheap," *Washington Post,* August 24, 2008, p. A1.

Organizational Component

According to Simon (1973) and Perrow (1984), networks under attack must be loosely coupled if they are to survive, so that "knock-on or cascading effects are limited and damage to one part of the network does not undermine the network as a whole. Loose coupling also preserves more diversity in response options, offering considerable latitude in the decision of which parts of the network should respond to the threat (Williams 2001, p. 80).

This is particularly true the more a terrorist network takes the form of a multihub or "spider's web" design, with multiple centers and peripheries. To the extent that this is the pattern, the more redundant and resilient the network will be, and the harder it will be to destroy. The more the terrorist network resembles a small world network of personal acquaintances as opposed to a hierarchical network, the more resilient and resistant it is to fragmentation, because it is highly interconnected. A significant fraction of nodes can be randomly removed without much impact on its ability to function effectively (Barabasi 2002, p. 140). The way to attack a small world network that is scale-free is through its hubs.[9] "If enough hubs are destroyed, the network breaks down into isolated, noncommunicating islands of nodes" (Sageman 2004, p. 140).

Sometimes what seems to be a small world network results from the seeming destruction of a hierarchical predecessor network through the decapitation of its leadership. By analogy, when Napster's activities were curtailed by legal action in the United States, it led to more free music being downloaded and shared by loose peer-to-peer networks. In a more direct comparison, the killing of Pablo Escobar and the dismantling of the powerful Colombian cocaine cartels during the 1990s led to drug smuggling by small, loosely organized networks that specialized in only one aspect of the production or transportation of the drug. Collectively these networks, linked together in a bilateral chain, continue to flourish and are able to import as much cocaine into the United States as the cartels did. The question for authorities trying to combat illegal networks is whether small, more nimble networks are harder to combat than the central network that was destroyed (Arquilla and Ronfeldt 2001, pp. 364–65; Kinney 2003, pp. 191–92; Raab and Milward 2003, pp. 420–21).

It is easy to state with some assurance that al Qaeda is a network, or perhaps a network of networks, but the relevant question is, what kind of network or networks is it? Is it a chain, hub, or all-channel network, or perhaps a combination of all three? Do bridges and brokers connect the network to additional actors? The answers to these questions are important because the configuration of a network gives it different competencies and vulnerabilities.[10]

9. A scale-free network is one in which, as the size of the whole network increases, some nodes become hubs that are much better connected than would be expected to occur randomly. These hubs make it easier to move from one part of the network to another. They are also the network's vulnerable points.

10. David Ronfeldt, "Al Qaeda and Its affiliates: A Global Tribe Waging Segmental Warfare," *First Monday*, 10, no. 3, March, 2005 (http://firstmonday.org/issues/issue10_3/ronfeldt).

Many believe that al Qaeda is highly distributed, characterized by semi-autonomous cells. This is a structure that encourages local entrepreneurial actions, with guidance from the center rather than central control. This structure creates fleeting targets for counterterrorism and limits the ability of potential targets to take special defensive measures (Davis and Jenkins 2002, pp. 31–32).

The loss of al Qaeda's base in Taliban-controlled Afghanistan may have been a blessing for them. Without the sunk costs of a physical infrastructure, which adds significantly to their vulnerability, al Qaeda operatives can migrate from areas where risks of attack are high to areas where the risks are much lower. Because of its transnational character, al Qaeda, like any transnational criminal network, can exploit differences between different countries' legal systems by engaging in jurisdictional arbitrage (Williams 2001, p. 71). If Germany's legal system provides more protection of privacy than France's, it may provide a locational advantage.

Al Qaeda also has shown a facility for merging with other ideologically compatible networks. "The fluid nature of al-Qaeda's core leadership—its ability to merge or ally with other organizations that shared its core Islamic precepts and world-view—was an important element in its network identity" (Kahler 2002, p. 11). Examples are the merger between al Qaeda and Ayman al Zawahri's Egyptian Islamic Jihad before 9/11 and the alliance between al Qaeda and Abu Mus'ab Al-Zarqawi's organization—"al Qaeda in Mesopotamia"—after the U.S.-led invasion and occupation of Iraq in 2003.

The technological prowess of the United States and other Western governments is arrayed against al Qaeda, but the network, too, has gained significantly from the information revolution:

> They can harness information technology to enable less hierarchical, more network designs—enhancing their flexibility, responsiveness, and resilience while in turn, information technology can enhance their offensive operation capabilities for the war of ideas as well as for the war of violent acts. (Zanini and Edwards 2001, p. 29)

The effectiveness of the training available on the Internet is debatable, but there is no debate over the massive amount of materials available from al Qaeda and its affiliates from websites specializing in Islamic jihadist terrorism, constituting a

> dynamic online library of training materials—some supported by experts who answer questions on message boards or in chat rooms—covering such varied subjects as how to mix ricin poison, how to make a bomb from commercial chemicals, how to pose as a fisherman and sneak through Syria into Iraq, how to shoot at a U.S. soldier, and how to navigate by the stars while running through a night-shrouded desert. These materials are cascading

across the Web in Arabic, Urdu, Pashto and other first languages of jihadist volunteers.[11]

How rational is al Qaeda? Can it, as Considine (2002) conjectures, be assumed that al Qaeda's leaders have been well trained in the structural contingency theories made popular in the best business schools and have learned to shape an organization's internal structure to reflect the structure of its environment? Does al Qaeda follow a strategically rational mode of operation or do organizational or psychological factors cloud its strategic logic? Assuming rationality, in their battle against the state, terrorists have the advantage of being able to see what they want to attack, but they have a limited ability to attack what they see. A government, in contrast, has an advantage in its ability to attack the terrorists (often with overwhelming force) but has a limited ability to identify the terrorists it wishes to destroy. Terrorist groups enjoy an information advantage; the state enjoys a force advantage. This simple asymmetry defines the strategy that a terrorist group or a state is able to employ. Carried one step further, the terrorist group can strike, perhaps even a civilian target, in the hope that it will provoke the government to strike indiscriminately at targets it cannot see. Terrorist atrocities are deliberately calculated to produce counter atrocities redounding to the advantage of the terrorist group. The strategic aim of the terrorist group is to force the government to engage in broad-based repression, thus exacerbating its unpopularity with the population of the state (McCormick 2003, pp. 10–11). Another way of understanding terrorist networks, in contrast to the rational strategic approach, is by using the assumptions of the organizational model pioneered by what is known as the Carnegie school of organization theory, which emphasizes the importance of organizational routines and internal politics in decisionmaking (March and Simon 1958; Cyert and March 1963), popularized by Graham Allison (1971). The assumptions of this theory of decisionmaking depart from the rational strategic model and suggest that terrorist networks can be understood only by looking at factors inside the network (McCormick 2003, p. 12). Organization routines, culture, and internal politics affect all organizations (networks included) to some degree. One goal of further research is to try to identify what these routines and cultural elements are and how they may affect al Qaeda's decisionmaking. This chapter assumes that organizational networks operate on the basis of both theories (sometimes more, sometimes less rational); unless al Qaeda is a unique organizational network, it is unlikely that it operates in a completely strategic fashion.

One thing that all terrorist networks must do is operate in a covert and clandestine way. If they fail to maintain secrecy, they will pay a heavy price. From this

11. Steve Coll and Susan B. Glasser, "Terrorists Turn to the Web as Base of Operations," *Washington Post,* August 7, 2005, p. A1.

perspective, the work of the Carnegie school scholars may be germane because it focuses on suboptimization and sequential attention to goals. It is unlikely that al Qaeda could treat its terrorist plans in chessboard fashion because it is constantly balancing the need to maintain secrecy in order to survive with the need to attack the enemy. Both goals require serious trade-offs. Morselli, Giguere, and Petit (2007) found that different types of dark networks make different trade-offs between these competing goals. They found that networks with political, as opposed to greed-driven, goals adopt a risk-averse strategy, avoiding risks that endanger their survival in the course of achieving their goals of attacking and damaging their enemy. This risk-averse strategy is conditioned by the level of uncertainty about the terrorist network's ability to survive after an attack and affects its decision to engage in an attack in the first place (Bakker, Raab, and Milward 2008).

Their willingness to attack may be conditioned by the initial adoption of a "script" on which they pattern their actions.[12] Is that script tailored to their specific requirements of operational and strategic objectives or is it a general template taken from prior terrorist organizations (McCormick 2003, p. 13)? Does it contain a set of routines that they follow? To the extent that their actions are not predictable and the terrorists learn from their mistakes, surviving mistakes increases their survival possibilities. One factor going against this ability to learn is the need to act, as Morselli, Giguere, and Petit (2007) point out. Terrorists need to act to back up their words and are impatient for results, which can lead them to discount the future (McCormick 2003, p. 13).

Strategy is a two-sided game. After employing a strategy of capturing and killing al Qaeda leaders since 9/11, the Bush administration is moving toward a broader strategy of combating the rise of Islamic extremism. This shift recognizes two things: first, al Qaeda has adapted and become a more amorphous, diffuse, and difficult-to-target organization since the initial attacks of September 11, 2001. Second, the policy discussion in Washington has focused on how to deal with the rise of a new generation of terrorists, some schooled in Iraq over the past five years. "Top government officials are increasingly turning their attention to anticipate what one called 'the bleed out' of hundreds or thousands of Iraq-trained jihadists back to their home countries throughout the Middle East and Western Europe."[13] Although this assertion contains an element of truth, it wildly overstates the number of foreign fighters with ties to Western Europe who might return there. It is sobering, however, to realize that a terrorist network of several

12. See Bakker, Raab, and Milward's (2008, pp. 21–22) description of the script created by the MK, the armed wing of the African National Congress, to give internal and external legitimacy to their struggle against apartheid.

13. Glasser, "Review May Shift Terror Policies."

hundred members such as the IRA or ETA can do a great deal of damage and force a country to spend billions of dollars fighting them.[14]

The second conclusion reached in "Dark Networks as Problems" (Raab and Milward 2003) was that "dark networks need a territorial base to be effective." These bases are usually in regions torn apart by civil war and dominated by current or former warlords, where no state exists with a legitimate monopoly on coercive power. After finishing writing "Dark Networks as Problems," the authors were more certain of their conclusions about the nature of failed states and their role in fostering dark networks than about any of the other conclusions. Since the U.S. invasion and occupation of Iraq, it has become apparent that failed states are both multifaceted and constitute a continuum of different degrees of failure. It has also become apparent that a terrorist network does not need a failed state as a sanctuary. Developed and developing states can serve as sanctuaries just as well, as long as the state tolerates the terrorists' existence. Transatlantic population movements during the period of globalization prior to World War I allowed anarchist and Communist revolutionaries to find safe havens in both Great Britain and the United States, whence they planned violent deeds elsewhere (Kahler 2002, p. 8). Until recently, the IRA used the United States in the same fashion. The resources to continue the IRA's battles with Great Britain often were generated by IRA fundraisers from the Irish community in the United States.

The issue of failed and failing states is receiving a great deal of attention from policymakers as civil strife, resource wars, corruption, economic collapse, and governmental incapacity have created great concern in the international community. For the last four years, *Foreign Policy* magazine and the Fund for Peace, an independent research nonprofit, have developed a "Failed States Index" using twelve indicators of social, economic, political, and military development. These indicators are applied to 177 states "in order of their vulnerability to violent internal conflict and social deterioration."[15] It is no surprise that Somalia, Sudan, Zimbabwe, Chad, and Iraq lead the index of failed states. On the plus side, progress has been made in Ivory Coast, Liberia, and Haiti where U.N. peacekeepers are stationed.

In addition to failed and failing states, terrorist networks take advantage of what Takeyh and Gvosdev (2003) call "brown zones" in Western societies as secondary bases of operations. Whereas a failed state such as Afghanistan under the Taliban may serve as a training base and redoubt against its enemies, the Islamic diaspora in Western Europe provides an area where the writ of the legitimate government

14. For a reassessment of the effect of Iraq as a terrorist incubator see Elaine Sciolino, "Fears of Iraq Becoming a Terrorist Incubator Seem Overblown, French Say," *New York Times*, April 8, 2008 (www.nytimes.com/2008/04/08/world/europe/08terror.html?_r=l&en=2bab).

15. "Failed States Index," *Foreign Policy*, July–August 2008, p. 66.

is weak due to a failure to integrate Muslim populations into the larger society. Many European states have tightened previously lax asylum laws and immigration procedures and started to give serious scrutiny to what goes on in mosques and Islamic philanthropic organizations. In the meantime, al Qaeda and its affiliates have stepped up their efforts to recruit completely assimilated second- or third-generation Muslims or converts to their ranks so they will attract less attention and move more freely between Western nations without attracting undue attention (Takeyh and Gvosdev 2003, p. 99).

Thus, the failure of European societies to fully integrate their Muslim citizens and residents may be considered an example of partial state failure (Kahler 2002, p. 35). Saudi Arabia represents partial state failure as well. Until recently the government used a "no-go" space it had created in the wake of the Saudi government's tacit agreement to acquiesce in the activities of groups and financial interests that provided support to Osama bin Laden and the al Qaeda network (Kahler 2002, p. 34). There is some evidence that this "no go" space has become much smaller in the wake of all of the terrorist attacks in the Saudi kingdom and efforts to rehabilitate militant jihadists.[16]

Failed States and State Failure

There are a number of different types of state failure. One type consists of states such as Colombia and Pakistan, where there are pockets of instability—failed areas—but the government still controls most of the country. This would include the North-West tribal areas of Pakistan or the FARC-controlled areas of Colombia (until recently), where the government cedes control of remote areas to tribal groups or guerrillas turned narco-terrorists.

When the United States and its allies in Afghanistan defeated the Taliban and killed and captured a number of al Qaeda fighters, what was left of the al Qaeda network found refuge across the Pakistani border in the Federally Administered Tribal Territories of the North-West Frontier Province. Following the example of the British when they were colonial overlords, the government of Pakistan granted a great deal of autonomy to Pashtun tribal leaders and exempted these areas from direct control by Pakistan's police, military, and courts. This autonomy, along with extremely forbidding topography, make it an ideal place for al Qaeda to hide.

A second category of state failure would be states such as the Sudan, where the central government and rebel groups are engaged in brutal civil wars bordering on genocide such as the one in Darfur and southern Sudan. There the state is incapable of delivering anything but spoils to its supporters and death to its opponents.

A third category would be collapsed states such as Somalia today or Liberia under Charles Taylor, the warlord turned president. These collapsed states have

---

16. Jason Burke, "Saudis Offer Pioneering Therapy for Ex-Jihadists," *The Guardian,* March 9, 2008 (www.guardian.co.uk/world/2008/mar/09/saudiarabia.terrorism/print).

been completely exhausted by civil war and warlords, who operate like gangsters and are reduced to a Hobbesian war of each against all for survival.

Any one of these types of failing or failed states can serve as both a breeding ground and a sanctuary for terrorists (Napoleoni 2003, pp. 139–40). Different types of state failure provide different opportunities for terrorist networks like al Qaeda and for criminal networks as well. A collapsed state is not the same as a failed state: it has no international legitimacy, there is no functioning government, and it has no foreign policy recognized by other countries. A collapsed state is generally less useful to terrorist networks than a failed state. A weak state deteriorating into a failing state or a failed state is more useful to terrorists, since such a state often has a shell of legitimacy left, even if it cannot control its borders, as in Sudan or Afghanistan under the Taliban (Napoleoni 2003, pp. 142–43). In addition, failed states maintain diplomatic relations to some extent (Afghanistan under the Taliban had relations with Pakistan, Saudi Arabia, and a few other Muslim countries) and can still purchase weapons, if no UN sanctions apply, issue passports, and register ships and aircraft (Liberia has one of the largest "flags of convenience" in the world with its international shipping registry).

All these elements of sovereignty can be extremely useful to a terrorist or criminal network. Weapons can be transferred with impunity from the state to terrorists. Once criminals or terrorists gain a measure of control, they can set up training camps or bases to protect themselves. Nature may abhor a vacuum, but terrorists and criminals love them. The failed state can easily become a transshipment point for narcotics, weapons, dirty money, blood diamonds, or illegal immigrants (Napoleoni 2003, p. 143; Raab and Milward 2003, pp. 427–29). For example, during the civil war in Bosnia, Islamic radicals carved out areas where they could operate with little scrutiny.

Control over a part of a state not only establishes an institutionalized presence but also allows for the creation of legal or illegal businesses to support the armed struggle. For example, al Qaeda developed gum arabic plantations in Sudan (Takeyh and Gvosdev 2003, p. 96): "Like a multinational corporation whose product was violence, al Qaeda saw failed states as the ideal 'corporate headquarters,' offering weakness with 'a veneer of sovereignty' that warded off external intervention. Al-Qaeda and its terrorist allies found those conditions in Albania, in the Sudan and with the Taliban regime in Afghanistan" (Kahler 2002, p. 31).

Perhaps calling a failed state an ideal corporate headquarters goes too far. Though the use of failed states as bases for terrorists and criminal networks is indeed frustrating to legitimate states, from the perspective of a terrorist network like al Qaeda, a failed state is a distinctly second-best option. Communications, the economy, transport, and connections to the rest of the world are all limited in failed states like Sudan or Afghanistan: "Al-Qaeda operatives apparently bridled at the technological constraints of the host country: Europe seemed a far more suitable base of operations" (Kahler 2002, p. 35).

What is the process whereby a terrorist group or criminal gang takes over all or part of a failed or failing state? One of the most compelling findings in social network theory is that "birds of a feather flock together," which is known as the "homophily principle" (Watts 2003, p. 57). Terrorists go where they believe they will be welcomed or tolerated by people with whom they have some things in common. Their interpretation of Islam may be the same as those who control the state, as with the Taliban. They may simply count on the rapacity of a gang that has become a state and could not turn down a lucrative offer, as in Liberia, where al Qaeda is thought to have traded dollars for diamonds (Farah 2004; Raab and Milward 2003). They may also offer their services as fighters during a conflict, as in Bosnia or Chechnya. In these conflicts, al Qaeda forces would offer their fighters from prior conflicts. They would bring short-handed armies or guerrilla forces—men, equipment, and money. Once on the ground, they could exchange their military skills for residency (Takeyh and Gvosdev 2003, p. 96).

In summary, terrorist networks need failed and failing states for the following reasons:

—They provide the opportunity to acquire territory on a scale much larger than a collection of scattered safe houses—enough to accommodate entire training complexes, arms depots, and communications facilities.

—Failed states have weak or nonexistent law-enforcement capabilities, which allows terrorist groups to engage in smuggling and drug trafficking to raise funds for operations.

—Failed states create pools of recruits and supporters for terrorist groups.

—Failed states retain the outward signs of sovereignty. (Takeyh and Gvosdev 2003, pp. 96–97)

—Failed states with a measure of sovereignty make it difficult for the United Nations or a coalition of states to intervene.

When the authors originally wrote about failed and failing states, these countries were viewed as safe havens and training facilities (Afghanistan) or places to acquire weapons or launder money (Liberia). The authors did not realize that partial state failure, as in Pakistan's North-West Frontier Province, or the failure of European countries to fully integrate their Muslim citizens, facilitated the operation of terrorist networks to the degree that they do.

Similar Challenges, Different Answers

The third conclusion reached in "Dark Networks as Problems" (Raab and Milward 2003) was "Overt and covert networks face similar challenges in terms of differentiation and integration." Covert networks have to find different answers to these challenges than overt ones because their activity is under constant risk of detection, and institutionalization is rather weak, yet they tend to revert to physical force and coercion to compel adherence to their goals.

As argued by Lawrence and Lorsch (1967) in relation to organizations and Milward and Raab (2006) to dark networks, social systems are likely to be more effective if they manage to balance differentiation and integration, that is, reap the benefits of (functional) specialization by maintaining a high level of coordination. However, as explained by Lawrence and Lorsch (1967), the stronger the functional differentiation is, the more complex the integration mechanisms need to be to achieve or maintain the capacity to act. Especially strong functional differentiation requires direct coordination through communication by e-mail, regular mail, phone, couriers, or face-to-face meetings. For dark networks, the dilemma is that the more complex the integration mechanisms have to be to deal with an uncertain task environment and functional differentiation, the more susceptible dark networks are to discovery and attacks. Every communication link increases the probability of discovery because it might be intercepted, endangers covertness, and gives the government the chance to roll up the network. Thus, as Krebs (2001) has shown in connection with the network structure of the terrorists who attacked New York and Washington in 2001, dark networks try to function with as few ties as possible and try to maintain global coordination with transitory shortcuts that connect different groups within a network and are activated only from time to time. Consequently, to survive, dark networks have to build in redundancies in skills, which weakens functional differentiation and is relatively inefficient.

Discussion

So far in this chapter the organizational choice al Qaeda faces as a network has been discussed, but a critical question has not yet been answered in the discussion of the original three conclusions: How is al Qaeda organized as a network? What are its strengths and potential weaknesses? How is it connected to other networks that it seems to be affiliated with. Given that al Qaeda is an illegal and covert network, it is not surprising that this is a difficult question to answer. It is not likely that analysts of dark networks would have any luck penetrating a terrorist network, or, if they did, would live to tell the tale.

Though it is clearly a second-best option, scholars are working to visualize the connections between known members of terrorist networks and their connections to terrorist events. Using Marc Sageman's book *Understanding Terror Networks* (2004), and additional data that Sageman collected on 366 members of what he calls "the Global Salafi Jihad (GSJ) network," Jennifer Xu and Jialun Qin (2004) of the Artificial Intelligence Lab at the University of Arizona have used structural analysis software to create a visualization of the GSJ network.[17] This

---

17. Their analysis consists of centrality measures to identify leaders, gatekeepers, and outliers. They use hierarchical clustering to partition a network into nested clusters and block modeling to extract patterns of interaction. In addition they use Web community–mining algorithms to determine the overall structure of the terrorist network to give the visualization independence from Sageman's data.

network is roughly equivalent to al Qaeda's network of networks at the time of their analysis, 2004. They find that the GSJ network consists of four "clumps" based on geographic location:

—A central staff with Osama bin Laden as the network hub

—A core Arab group with Khalid Sheikh Mohammed (now in U.S. custody) as the network hub

—A Maghreb Arab, or North African, group

—A Southeast Asian group

Xu and Chen (2004), in a separate analysis of the data, found that together these "clumps" constituted the GSF network, which had both small-world and scale-free network characteristics.[18] The small-world network has a high tendency to form groups and is very efficient at communication. In the scale-free network there are a small number of nodes with many links (high-degree centrality) and many nodes with just a few links (low-degree centrality). From a strategic perspective, scale-free networks are very robust and rarely succumb to random failure. However, they are vulnerable to targeted attacks on central nodes, especially on the bridges and hubs connecting different communities. Although it is important to be able to visualize what the known parts of al Qaeda look like, doing so reveals nothing about its strategic plan, order of battle, and tactical objectives.

A fact of life in researching dark networks is that knowledge often comes secondhand and after the fact from newspaper accounts, court records, truth and reconciliation hearings, and declassified documents from intelligence services. However, some lessons can be learned from this kind of analysis. A dark network like the MK (Umkhonto we Sizwe), the armed wing of the African National Congress, was able to rebound from a disastrous shock early in its life when almost the entire central command was captured by the South African government. It slowly rebuilt its capability using safe havens in neighboring countries, demonstrating formidable resilience until it was unbanned in 1990 when apartheid was dismantled in South Africa (Bakker, Raab, and Milward 2008).

From a strategic perspective, would it be more effective to attack the hubs and bridges and try to fragment the network? Does allowing al Qaeda to continue to have some central direction serve a strategic purpose for Western countries seeking to destroy it? If the perspective is accepted that terrorism is unlikely to go away and that it can only be managed better or worse, it may be preferable to allow some central direction that can potentially be monitored instead of attacking all its central nodes and seeing the network differentiate and fragment in unpredictable ways. Using the drug example mentioned earlier in the chapter, is it better to know who the opposition is and be able to estimate its capabilities rather than to see networks recede into terrorist cells that are isolated from each other?

18. A small-world network has a significantly larger clustering coefficient than a random graph model. Scale-free networks are characterized by the power law degree distribution.

Conclusion

The authors of "Dark Networks as Problems" (Raab and Milward 2003) compared al Qaeda, heroin-trafficking networks, and illegal weapons and diamond smuggling networks in West Africa. They came to three conclusions about the characteristics and behavior of dark networks, as opposed to bright networks that deliver health care and operate in the light of day. By studying dark networks, the authors hoped to broaden understanding of networks in general. Publicly available data on al Qaeda were used to track its evolution over time, from before 9/11 until 2008. A significant change was found in the structure of the network, not least due to pressure from the United States and its allies in the war on terror. It is now generally assumed that al Qaeda itself has become much more "networky" and has linked up with other Islamic terror organizations worldwide. The question therefore is whether it is conceptually useful to talk about one global Islamic terror network or, rather, of a network of loosely affiliated networks. Furthermore, the terror network seems to be embedded in a global jihadist movement that functions as a support structure. A serious limitation for the analysis, however, is the still limited availability of data in open sources about the inner workings of al Qaeda and the frequent impossibility of corroborating it.

Developments over these years clearly reveal the important role of failed or failing states for the future of the conflict between the West and Islamic terror groups. In "Dark Networks as Problems," the authors recognized that these networks can take great advantage of failed states as territorial bases for their activities. However, they learned that different forms of state failure and their implications for terror networks have to be much better differentiated than heretofore and that state failure is not an absolute condition but instead there is a continuum of degrees of state failure.

Given that Islamic terrorism has become truly global, learning much more about how to control terror networks is extremely important. Containment is still probably the best option for the foreseeable future (Kinney 2007). Even if the assumption is correct that al Qaeda, for the moment, is unable to launch attacks similar to 9/11, the danger of attacks of the type experienced in Madrid and London should warrant great efforts to control terror networks—especially if global Islamic jihadism continues to be able to recruit new mujahidin to replace those killed or captured.

References

Allison Graham. 1971. *The Essence of Decision: Explaining the Cuban Missile Crisis.* Boston: Little Brown.

Arquilla, John, and David Ronfeldt, 2001. *Networks and Netwars.* Santa Monica: RAND.

Bakker, René, Jörg Raab, and H. Brinton Milward. 2008. "A Preliminary Theory of Dark Network Resilience." Working Paper. Tilburg University (Netherlands), Department of Organizational Studies.

Barabasi, Albert-László. 2002. *Linked: The New Science of Networks.* Boulder: Perseus.

Bryson, John M., and Barbara C. Crosby. 1992. *Leadership for the Common Good.* San Francisco: Jossey-Bass.

Considine, Mark. 2002. "Joined at the Lip? What Does Network Research Tell Us about Governance?" In *Knowledge, Networks and Joined-Up Government.* Proceedings of the International Political Science Association research conference, pp. 153–68. University of Melbourne, Centre for Public Policy.

Cyert, Richard M., and James G. March. 1963. *A Behavioral Theory of the Firm.* Upper Saddle River, N.J.: Prentice Hall.

Davis, Paul K., and Brian Michael Jenkins. 2002. *Deterrence and Influence in Counterterrorism.* Santa Monica: RAND Corporation.

Farah, Douglas. 2004. *Blood from Stones: The Secret Financial Network of Terror.* New York: Broadway Books.

Hjern, Benny. 1992. "Illegitimate Democracy: A Case for Multiorganizational Policy Analysis." *Policy Currents* 2, no. 1: 1–5.

Hoffman, Bruce. 2006. *Inside Terrorism.* Revised edition. Columbia University Press.

———. 2008. "The Myth of Grass-Roots Terrorism." *Foreign Affairs* 87, no. 3 (May–June): 133–38.

Kahler, Miles. 2002. "Networks and Failed States: September 11 and the Long Twentieth Century." Paper presented at the annual meeting of the American Political Science Association, Boston, August 29–September 1.

Kenis, Patrick, and Volker Schneider. 1991. "Policy Networks and Policy Analysis: Scrutinizing a New Analytical Toolbox." In *Policy Networks: Empirical Evidence and Theoretical Considerations,* edited by B. Marin and R. Mayntz, pp. 25–62. Boulder and Frankfurt: Westview Press and Campus Verlag.

Kinney, Michael. 2003. "From Pablo to Osama: Counter-Terrorism Lessons from the War on Drugs." *Survival* 45, no. 2: 187–206.

———. 2007. *From Pablo to Osama: Trafficking and Terrorist Networks, Government Bureaucracies, and Competitive Adaptation.* University of Pennsylvania Press.

Krebs, V. E. 2001. "Mapping Networks of Terrorist Cells." *Connections* 24, no. 3: 43–52.

Lawrence, P. R., and J. W. Lorsch. 1967. "Differentiation and Integration in Complex Organizations." *Administrative Science Quarterly* 12: 1–47.

Lennon, Alexander T. J., ed. 2003. *The Battle for Hearts and Minds: Using Soft Power to Undermine Terrorist Networks.* MIT Press.

March, James G., and Herbert A. Simon 1958. *Organizations.* New York: John Wiley.

McCormick, Gordon H. 2003. "Terrorist Decision Making." *Annual Review of Political Science* 6: 473–507.

Milward, H. Brinton, and Jörg Raab. 2006. "Dark Networks as Organizational Problems: Elements of a Theory." *International Public Management Journal* 9, no. 3: 333–60.

Morselli, C., C. Giguere, and K. Petit. 2007. "The Efficiency/Security Trade-Off in Criminal Networks." *Social Networks* 29, no. 1: 143–53.

Napoleoni, Loretta. 2003. *Modern Jihad: Tracing the Dollars behind the Terror Networks.* London: Pluto Press.

Office of the Director of National Intelligence. 2007. *National Intelligence Estimate: The Terrorist Threat to the U.S. Homeland.* Washington: July.

Perrow, Charles. 1984. *Normal Accidents.* New York: Basic Books.

Powell, Walter W. 1990. "Neither Market Nor Hierarchy: Network Forms of Organization." *Research in Organizational Behavior* 12: 295–336.

Provan, Keith G., and Patrick Kenis. 2008. "Modes of Network Governance: Structure, Management, and Effectiveness." *Journal of Public Administration Research and Theory* 18, no. 2: 321–45.

Raab, Jörg, and H. Brinton Milward. 2003. "Dark Networks as Problems." *Journal of Public Administration Research and Theory* 13, no. 4: 413–39.

Riedel, Bruce. 2007. "Al Qaeda Strikes Back." *Foreign Affairs* 86, no. 3 (May–June): 24–40.

Rittel, Horst W. J., and Melvin M. Webber. 1973. "Dilemmas in a General Theory of Planning." *Policy Sciences* 4: 155–69.

Sageman, Marc. 2004. *Understanding Terror Networks.* University of Pennsylvania Press.

———. 2008a. *Leaderless Jihad: Terror Networks in the Twenty-First Century.* University of Pennsylvania Press.

———. 2008b. "The Next Generation of Terror." *FP: Foreign Policy,* March–April, pp. 37–42.

Selznick, Phillip. 1949. *TVA and the Grass Roots.* University of California Press.

Simon, Herbert A. 1973. "The Structure of Ill-Structured Problems." *Artificial Intelligence* 4: 181–201.

Takeyh, Ray, and Nikolas Gvosdev. 2003. "Do Terror Networks Need a Home?" In *The Battle for Hearts and Minds: Using Soft Power to Undermine Terrorist Networks,* edited by Alexander T. J. Lennon, pp. 94-107. MIT Press.

U.S. Department of State. 2008. *Country Reports on Terrorism.* Washington: Office of the Coordinator for Counterterrorism, April 30 (www.state.gov/s/ct/rls/crt/2007/103704).

Watts, Duncan J. 2003. *Six Degrees: The Science of a Connected Age.* New York: Norton.

Williams, Phil. 2001 "Transnational Criminal Networks." In *Networks and Netwars,* edited by John Arquilla and David Ronfeldt, pp. 61–98. Santa Monica: RAND Corporation.

———. 2002. "The Changed Landscape: From Slime Molds to Terrorism." Presentation at Kent Center Conference, Central Intelligence Agency Headquarters, Langley, Virginia, May 23–24.

Xu, Jennifer J., and Hsinchun Chen. 2004. "The Topology of Dark Networks." Unpublished paper. University of Arizona, Department of Management Information Systems.

Xu, Jennifer J., and Jialun Qin. 2004. "Terrorist Network Analysis." Presentation of the Artificial Intelligence Lab, University of Arizona, June 9.

Zanini, Michele, and Sean J. A. Edwards. 2001. "The Networking of Terror in the Information Age." In *Networks and Netwars,* edited by John Arquilla and David Ronfeldt, pp. 29–60. Santa Monica: RAND Corporation.

9

Networked Government: Survey of Rationales, Forms, and Techniques

MARK H. MOORE

In recent years, practitioners and scholars of public management have looked to the concept of "networked government" to guide improvements in government performance.[1] At the core of this idea is the belief that the old organizational form of government—a centralized executive branch consisting of large, hierarchical organizations, each with its own distinct, well-defined mission, its own appropriated funds, and its own structure of accountability—is simply not up to the substantive challenges confronting contemporary governments. To improve the performance of government—to create more public value from available assets—it is necessary to overlay that rigid, highly differentiated hierarchical structure with "networks" specially designed to scoop resources from different parts of government and society at large and focus them on achieving desired social outcomes.

This book has offered some case studies that describe the circumstances in which networked government arrangements arise, how they are constructed, how they seem to perform, and how they can be developed and sustained. In this concluding chapter I offer some commentary, based on these cases, on the prospects for networked government. First, to show the nature of potential conflicts, I identify possible sources of tensions among the primary aims of networked govern-

---

1. For a basic introduction to these concepts, see Goldsmith and Eggers (2004), Milward and Provan (2006), and Agranoff (2007).

ment arrangements and also explore other important public values that have to be reflected in the operations of government.[2] Second, I review the cases to see what they reveal about the form networks take, how well they seem to perform, and how they are constructed, operated, and maintained. Finally, I develop lessons from the cases that will be useful to government managers who seek to improve their performance by creating and using networked government arrangements.

Networked Government: Justifications and Challenges

"Networked government" is a term that encompasses (or overlaps with) many other ideas about how government performance might be enhanced through improved coordination among organizations positioned to contribute to the solution of social problems. Initially, government looked for the potential for improved coordination within operating relationships among different *government* organizations—for example, "integrating human service operations" or treating the different agencies involved in criminal justice as a highly integrated "criminal justice system" rather than as organizations pursuing their own distinct and independent missions.[3] The potential for improving operating relations via networks was also seen in improving coordination across levels of government to take advantage of the strengths of each level of government.[4] Soon, the concept of "networked government" included not only effective coordination across government organizations but also the possible integration of both for profit and nonprofit private sector organizations into production systems designed to achieve public purposes. Thus, "networked government" came to include the "privatization of government services," the development of "public-private partnerships," and fostering "collaborative governance."[5]

Standard Criticisms of Government Operations

The various interpretations of networked government emerged in response to a particular critique of government operations, rooted in the frustration of ordinary citizens interacting with government at two different levels: first as impatient

2. Examples of the aims of government arrangements are increased innovativeness, enhanced responsiveness to citizens' aspirations, sharpened focus on achieving desired social results, improved coordination among separate agencies contributing to the same desired results, and more extensive and creative use of private motivations and capabilities in the pursuit of public purposes. Examples of public values are tight accountability over the use of government assets, reliability in performance, and fairness in the handling of individual cases.

3. On operating relationships among government organizations, see Bardach (1998); "integrating human service operations": Weiss (1981); "distinct and independent missions": President's Commission on Law Enforcement and the Administration of Justice (1968).

4. Donahue (1997).

5. On "privatization of government services": Donahue (1989); "development of public-private partnerships": Brooks, Liebman, and Schelling (2004); "collaborative governance": Donahue and Zeckhauser (forthcoming 2009).

clients of government operations who longed for the kind of service quality they received as customers in the private sector; second as disappointed citizens and taxpayers who had paid money into a collective enterprise in hopes that some desired social outcomes would be achieved, only to be disappointed in the results that occurred.[6] This critique was powerfully influenced by an unfavorable comparison of government's performance with the remarkable capacity of the market to satisfy customer desires, and to deliver high levels of efficiency and effectiveness in operations. This stance eventually acquired a certain ideological valence (a preference for small government and market-oriented solutions to public problems) as well as a practical side. Taken together, the practical and ideological challenge to government performance cohered into an oft-repeated set of charges. Bureaucratic government—long held up as the ideal of a rational, fair, efficient, and effective government—had failed in four crucial respects:

1. Government organizations were (and are) insufficiently innovative. It seemed to many that government organizations could neither keep up with newly emerging public problems, nor find ways to reduce costs while maintaining or increasing the volume and quality of government output, nor quickly exploit the potential of emerging technology. Government agencies seemed to rely on the same old policies, same old processes, and same old technologies even as they faced new problems such as fighting terrorism and curbing global warming. They failed to experiment with new methods for teaching children to read and write or delivering benefits to clients in entitlement programs, even though new technologies seemed admirably suited to these tasks.

2. Government organizations were (and remain) inflexible and unresponsive, failing to adapt to local, unique, or unusual circumstances. Government organizations traditionally emphasized strict consistency in implementing policies and procedures, for three different reasons. First, because it was easier for overseers to monitor government activities than the results they achieved, the demand for accountability focused on the faithful execution of established policies. Second, because established policies were thought to embody the best professional knowledge about how an organization might deploy its assets to achieve desired results, compliance with policies and procedures was deemed important to ensure consistently high performance. (If, however, the policies and procedures were based on outdated knowledge, and produced mediocre results, pressures for compliance would have the opposite effect: they would keep government organizations from innovating and searching for the boundaries of their "production possibility frontier," which exacerbated the problem of insufficient innovation described above.) Third, government organizations followed standard procedures because consistent responses to similar cases produced a kind of fairness that was considered important in govern-

6. For a discussion of the key distinctions among the concepts of citizens, clients, and taxpayers see Moore (1995, chapter 2).

mental operations. (Consistency in operations ensured that like cases would be treated alike, but it also caused government agencies to ignore an equally important idea of justice and fairness that insisted that cases that differed from one another in some morally or practically significant way should be treated differently. Relying too much on one-size-fits-all solutions opened the door to accusations of unresponsiveness, poor performance, and unfairness.)

3. Government organizations could not (and still cannot) integrate their separate activities to make a whole greater than the sum of their parts. Interorganizational cooperation often proves elusive because each government agency has a distinct mission and is held strictly accountable for the use of its assets in the service to that mission. Rules designed to advance the specific purposes of particular organizations determine "appropriate" actions in a given case. The difficulty of getting different government organizations to work together often shows up at street level when various agencies try to provide overlapping or contradictory services to individuals and families in need, or when various regulatory agencies show up to inspect particular businesses for slightly different but fundamentally interrelated purposes. It also shows up at the agency level when organizational jealousies and competition for limited resources lead law enforcement agencies to refuse to cooperate with one another in criminal investigations, or lead intelligence agencies to withhold information that would enrich the picture held by other agencies. The fact that public organizations reward performance strictly along hierarchical lines also undermines the will of public officials to contribute to the purposes of other government organizations.

4. Government organizations did not (and still do not) harness and manage private capacities effectively in service of their goals. Just as demands for accountability in mission achievement challenge interorganizational cooperation, demands for organizational integrity and focus make it hard for government organizations to engage private organizations effectively. Of course, government often contracts with private organizations to provide particular services. Government also regulates the behavior of private organizations, and in doing so deploys the authority of the state to mobilize private actors to contribute to public purposes. But these purchases of services and regulations of private conduct are generally tightly circumscribed to ensure there is no corruption or favoritism in procurement or in enforcement. Most government agencies are discouraged from informal discussions or consultations with either vendors or the objects of regulation, lest the procurement officers or the regulatory agents be unduly influenced by the interests of the private actors. The private actors are discouraged from suggesting ways they might help the government achieve its goals. In such tightly circumscribed encounters it is hard for government to discover how its goals might be achieved at a lower production cost or with a lighter regulatory burden. It also means that public managers cannot easily capitalize or build legitimacy and support for what they are doing from potential private sector contributors.

The Allure of the Private Sector: Innovation, Flexibility, and Tight Accountability

Ironically, these performance problems stem in part from citizens' persistent, urgent demands for government accountability. The bureaucratic forms that seem so inimical to performance when one is concerned about innovation, responsiveness, effective coordination, and mobilization of additional assets are generally the preferred method for ensuring strict accountability in the use of government money and authority and the achievement of highly consistent, reliable perform ance in government operations. To the degree that strict accountability was judged to be an important driver of performance excellence, these forms were thought to improve, not degrade, government performance.[7]

As the performance problems in government mounted, however, many citizens began to look longingly to the private sector as a better model for combining their desire for strict accountability with a high degree of innovation, responsiveness, and performance. Private companies seemed to be highly accountable to shareholders and consumers yet also managed to be innovative, adaptive to niche markets, and able to mobilize and combine capacities from different suppliers to assemble complex products that satisfied their customers' diverse desires. If only government's social problem-solving efforts could come to resemble the dynamic, fluid processes of private markets and operate less like the rigid, apparently mindless bureaucracies so characteristic of government!

Key Differences between the Private and Public Sectors

Citizens, academics, and practitioners realized that government could never operate entirely like a market.[8] After all, the driving force of markets is a collection of heterogeneous customers, all with their own needs and desires and money to spend satisfying them. In a market, individual customers with money to spend are the engines that fuel productive efforts and the arbiters of the value that is produced. Their desires create a market opportunity for any entrepreneur or supplier who can imagine and deliver products and services to meet these desires at a price consumers are willing to pay. A little success allows private companies and entrepreneurs to raise funds from private investors. Thus, socially consequential decisions about how assets can be turned into products and about which products meet the tests of the market are not made all at once by a single decisionmaker but cumulatively, over time. Failures to read the market correctly are swiftly punished, and success is quickly rewarded. Private sector organizations can also take advantage of a much smaller group of constituents (its investors and customers as

7. Herbert Kaufman may have been the first to identify this fundamental tradeoff between the desire for accountability and consistent performance on one hand and responsiveness on the other. See Kaufman (1963).

8. Moore (2000).

opposed to the public at large) and a much more focused set of expectations (financial growth and customer service as opposed to hard-to-pin-down social values such as fairness, opportunity, and quality of life).

In contrast, the driving force in the public sector is not a collection of individual consumers making individual choices to spend their own money to buy products and services they value for themselves but is instead a single, large, collective consumer that chooses to buy a particular social outcome for every citizen and taxpayer. That collective actor is the public as a whole telling the government what it wants to buy (or otherwise achieve) through the imperfect processes of representative government. The government does not exist to maximize the satisfactions of individual customers; it exists to pursue the collective judgments and goals of the society it simultaneously serves and governs. Its financial and material wherewithal come from a collective choice by the public to tax and regulate itself in order to produce the desired results. These collective political processes occasion the creation of a particular government agency to pursue a desired objective, and they provide both the resources necessary to achieve the desired result and the social justification for the agency's activities.

The public, deciding to tax and regulate itself as a collective to achieve a broad social purpose, can never quite act like a simple aggregation of individual consumers in a market, all giving varied signals about what they want produced and how much each one would pay for it. Individual citizens, taxpayers, and clients with stakes in the use of government money and regulatory authority have to spend a lot of time talking and arguing before the choice is made; and then the choice is made all at once and for many individuals. Once made, the choices tend to persist, and large volumes of resources are poured into achieving the authorized results through the authorized means. In most bureaucracies, responding to individual clients' desires and needs takes a backseat to executing the collectively established public policies as reliably and consistently as possible. These bureaucracies do not have competitors pushing their activities to the production possibility frontier. They do not have access to venture capital. All they have is a mandate, a rulebook, and a zillion forms to prove to any of their millions of constituents that they are playing by the rules they established.

Special Values to Be Protected and Advanced in the Public Sphere

Because the broader public acts not in the marketplace but in a political forum, it makes choices that reflect collective, public values. These collective, public values differ in important ways from the values that guide the allocation of resources and production in the market sphere.

ACHIEVING SOCIAL GOALS. Government, acting as an agent of society as a whole, is less interested in satisfying individual desires than achieving socially desired outcomes. Central to this argument is that there can be a collective will that can be expressed as a statement of the values that the collective seeks to achieve through the agency of government. Legislation that authorizes government action or appropriates tax funds to the agency usually specifies the purposes that the collective hopes to achieve through the authorizations and appropriations. Administrative rules likewise usually define the purposes they seek to achieve through the regulatory authority they deploy in specific regulations. And all government organizations suppose that they have some "mission" they are trying to pursue on behalf of the public. From a theoretical and practical perspective, we all understand how difficult it is for any collective to become articulate as to its purposes. But if one is operating as a government manager using the collectively owned assets of government to achieve specific concrete results, one has to believe that there is some kind of collectively defined goal that justifies and guides one's action. And often that is embodied in a particular "social outcome" one is supposed to achieve.

As government has sought to make itself more innovative, adaptive, and re sponsive, it has turned to the private sector for inspiration. Emulating private sector models, government has tried to improve the quality of service to its customers (the clients of its many agencies), and measures of client satisfaction have appeared in efforts to evaluate government operations. At the same time, government agencies increasingly have been made accountable for achieving desired social outcomes, an idea often mistakenly considered virtually identical to satisfying the government's clients. But it does not take much reflection to see that achieving social outcomes is very different from satisfying government clients. In welfare, drug treatment, and other public-service delivery activities, the usual goal is not to make clients happy but to provide services that will cause the clients to make themselves better off and to contribute to particular outcomes thought important by the rest of society. A welfare program nudges clients toward financial independence, which society thinks would be better for them and society overall than continued dependency. A drug treatment program attempts to enable and encourage clients to stop using drugs, stop committing crimes, get a job, and support their families. In both these cases, society is the arbiter of value, not the individual client, and society wants the achievement of tangible social conditions, not the satisfaction of individuals.

LEGITIMACY AND ACCOUNTABILITY. Because government agencies use the collectively owned assets of the state, they have to legitimate their actions by making themselves accountable to both political oversight and the rule of law, not just to their clients.[9] When government acts to produce publicly desired results, it (generally) uses either tax dollars or regulatory authority. These state assets are owned collectively by the public. They can be used only with the consent and for the benefit of the public, and, to ensure this result, the public managers who use these assets are made accountable to the public as a whole. They are accountable

9. Moore (1995, chapter 2).

in the first instance to elected overseers in the legislative and executive branches of government and in the second instance to the courts, which are particularly interested in cases in which government officials have abused their discretion by pursuing purposes not authorized by law or have violated individual rights to due process. As a practical matter, both political authorization (public policy mandates enacted through legislation or other kinds of policy declarations) and bureaucratic rules that seek to limit official discretion exist to meet the challenge of ensuring that government action both reflects and serves the public. Traditionally, the legitimacy of government operations has been ensured by the continuity of intent, from citizen aspiration through political authorization to operating policies and programs guided by bureaucratic rules that were thought not only to embody the most efficient and effective ways of using government assets to achieve desired results but also to ensure certain kinds of fairness and justice in the implementation of government policy. In the last two decades or so, government agencies have been called to account for efficiency and effectiveness in achieving the desired results and responding to the demands and needs of individuals and the interests of political groups that are smaller than the polity as a whole. This shift in public expectations toward the achievement of social outcomes and responsiveness to the needs of individuals and smaller groups is transforming the process of legitimating government action. Legitimacy is rooted not only in lawful compliance with established policies but also in bureaucratic efforts to satisfy and respond to many diverse interests that may not have been adequately represented in the established policy mandate, and in the achievement of desired social results independent of the means used in their pursuit.

GOVERNMENT AND RISK. Generally speaking, government is less authorized than its private sector counterparts to take risks with untried and untested initiatives and therefore is less able to innovate and adapt. It is not true, however, that government has no mechanisms for creating innovation.[10] To no small degree, democratic politics provides a continuing incentive and capacity to innovate in the use of government-owned assets. Politicians ceaselessly campaign for change, and in so doing create an environment in which policy and programmatic innovations become authorized throughout government. Policy entrepreneurs are constantly developing new ideas about the purposes that government should pursue or the means they should rely on to achieve traditional goals. Bureaucracies are forever creating "pilot programs" to see if their assets could be more effectively deployed. Even the media give special standing to new initiatives, often at the expense of monitoring the less glamorous issues of routine operations. Still, despite these pressures for innovation, government is restrained from high rates of innovation by the widespread view that it should not gamble with taxpayers' money. When government uses the authority and money of the state in order to

10. Altshuler and Behn (1997).

produce meaningful improvements in the well-being of others, it should have a high degree of confidence that its efforts will succeed. If there is significant uncertainty about the likely results, particularly if outcomes might be worse than the government's current performance, a prudent government manager will refrain from taking such risky action.

GOVERNMENT AS AGENT OF SOCIETY. Acting as an agent of society as a whole, government is interested in fairness and justice—in deciding what individuals deserve, how benefits could be fairly distributed, and how burdens could be fairly allocated—as well as efficiency and effectiveness.[11] Because government uses the collectively owned assets of the state—its powers to tax and regulate, money raised through taxation, and the material assets entrusted to the state for the future good of the public—it has to give assurances to citizens who have been asked to give up their liberty and their money to the state. Those assurances can be made through arguments that the assets are to be used for the common good and that the means chosen to pursue societal goals are known to be efficient and effective. Government usually also has to be able to claim that its purposes are just, not merely good—that the government-delivered private benefits are guided by social conceptions of what particular individuals need and deserve as well as what they want, and that the benefits of government action are being distributed according to some principle of fairness as well as the (potentially competing) principles of efficiency and maximum impact. Government also has to be able to offer assurances that the burdens of the collective action are being distributed according to some commonly recognized principle of justice and fairness, as well as efficiency.

JUSTICE AND FAIRNESS AS GOVERNMENT GOALS. Justice and fairness are important government goals in themselves, not just constraints on means. Government, acting as an agent of society as a whole, is able to use its authority to achieve particular results. When it does so, concerns about justice and fairness take on a special prominence. Unlike private producers, government can use its authority as well as its money to produce socially valuable results. In fact, in many cases, even the money that government uses to achieve its results is raised through the use of authority. In a democracy, the authority of the state is subject to conditions of use that differ from the rules for use of privately held money. The authority of the state cannot be used for any purposes except those sanctioned by the body politic. Even then, its use is limited by the existence of some individual rights vis-à-vis the state. Concerns about the fairness and justice of the government's use of public money, whether it is being used to pursue just conditions in the society, and the means being applied emerge as important public values to be protected in government operations.[12]

11. Mashaw (1983).
12. Ibid.

SHAPING RELATIONSHIPS. Government, acting as an agent of society as a whole, is often interested in trying to shape relationships to achieve the goal of a just, orderly, and sociable community, as well as achieving material results for individuals. Society entrusts government with the task of assigning responsibilities and duties to particular individuals and conferring privileges and rights. This assignment originates in individuals' needs for some way of peaceably adjudicating disputes. Disputes arise when one person feels unjustly or unfairly treated by another, and the second person disagrees with the first person's view. They need a third party to settle the dispute fairly and authoritatively. Dispute resolution may be the most obvious instance of state intervention to structure relationships among individuals in the society, but the state's role in structuring societal relationships is more pervasive than that. In its every rule regulating the conduct of one social actor to another, the state seeks to establish and enforce a "right relationship" among the social actors. The content of that right relationship is specified in the duties imposed and the privileges conferred on the social actors. Though conferred on individuals, the duties and privileges are guided by or entail a social idea of right relationships among citizens in a society and an idea of what each social actor owes another. When the government uses state power to structure and enforce these relationships, it is trying to move a society toward more amicable, equal, and just relationships—for example, when it establishes a rule that makes it a crime to willfully deceive the investing or consuming public or to knowingly expose workers to hazardous conditions; when it requires parents to care for their children; when it outlaws discrimination or makes hate speech a crime; when it gives new political rights to women; and when it punishes tax evaders or corrupt officials. Of course, there are limits to what the state can do in seeking to create certain kinds of relationships in society. The law cannot change the human heart, but it can and does often insist that social actors present in their behavior an outward manifestation of a right relationship with others.[13]

Networked Government as a Balance between Government and Markets?

These basic expectations of government in democratic societies tend to produce considerably more rigid operational production systems than does a private market. Yet the hope persists of finding a better balance between the values democratic governments are politically and constitutionally required to protect and the adaptability and flexibility that is required to allow government to adapt to an environment that is both heterogeneous and dynamic in its demands. If only the boundaries of government could be softened a bit . . .

Perhaps the idea of networked government solutions could provide the answer. Instead of pursuing democratic accountability to the point of blotting out all variation and flexibility, perhaps the governmental system could be rigid with

13. Moore (1997).

respect to the protection of core values but be allowed a significant amount of variability in the means chosen to advance those broad ends. Perhaps the preferences of different political communities and differently placed individuals could be given more standing in the collision of publicly defined purposes and local community or individual variation. Perhaps government could allow midlevel managers to take locally responsive and innovative initiatives and use that variability to improve its performance. Perhaps if government could make itself more responsive in the detailed purposes it sought, and especially in the means it used, it could attract more voluntary private assistance. Private parties might volunteer to accomplish purposes chosen together, accepting their duties gracefully and pursuing them aggressively. This is the idea of networked governance—a network in service to public purposes, but more innovative, adaptable, nimble than the traditional organizational form.

This sort of thinking is illustrated in table 9-1. It depicts a continuum with the extremes of market and hierarchical government at either end and networked government around the middle.[14] Of particular importance in this conception are two ideas.

First, a key difference between a market and a network has to do with how much central authority exists to guide network operations. "Central authority," however, turns out to be a complex idea. It is a functional capacity that describes how much the actions of different parts of a network can be explicitly directed and controlled by some central governing authority. It is also a normative idea about the particular institution or process that serves as the socially appropriate "arbiter of value." As noted earlier, in markets both production and consumption decisions are highly decentralized, and the individual customer is the arbiter of value. In government, production and consumption decisions are collectivized and the public, acting through the processes of representative government, is the arbiter of value.

In some networks the government has not exerted its full powers of command and control as an arbiter of public value and organizer of production; instead, it has invited other social actors to contribute to the definition and solution of public problems. In these instances, government has given up some of its capacity to control network operations and perhaps also some of its powers to define the ends to be pursued. This is the price of engaging, negotiating with, and using the resources of other independent actors in a combined and coordinated, but not centrally directed, enterprise. This loss of some operational control and the monopoly over the definition of public value is partially mitigated by the acknowledgment of shared goals and objectives and the creation of specific, more or less enforceable agreements among network members about how they will act together to achieve results all agree are better than the current conditions. In other

14. In this passage I follow the lead of Woody Powell (1991).

words, an implicit or explicit contract among the parties replaces hierarchical authority. It is the deal that governs, not the government; and the government is merely a party to the deal.

Further, because the idea of central authority over network operations is complex and exists in varying degrees, networks created by public officials or otherwise incorporating government assets take on many different forms. At one end of the spectrum are government-dominated networks; at the other are privately constructed networks in which government plays a small role in either the network's creation or its continued management. The question of central authority in network operations also brings into sharp focus the idea that a network could be conceived as a nested set of more or less explicitly negotiated deals and could be evaluated according to the degree to which the agreed deals protect and advance the public values that democratic government is charged with protecting. Indeed, one of the important challenges of networked government is to develop oversight mechanisms that allow public vetting of the deals made to create networked government arrangements, to be sure that important public values are protected and that government assets have not been improperly subordinated to private purposes.

How Broad Is the Need?

In this account networked governance emerges as a response to the challenge of improving government's innovativeness, its ability to focus government resources on the achievement of socially desired outcomes, and its ability to mobilize assistance from the private sector while remaining true to core values of democratic government. An important and as yet unanswered question is how broad and pervasive the need is for networked government. Will networked government need to take over 10 percent of the government's work, or 60 percent?

One way to answer this question is to revisit the reasons governments are reaching out for networked government solutions. If the occasions requiring networked government are understood, estimating how often it would be needed might be possible. There are at least three different views on the extent of the need for networked government.

First, networked government can be seen as always the best way to organize government efforts to solve public problems. According to this view, these techniques were not used in the past because people erred in imagining that bureaucratic government could perform as well as networked government. The benefits of imposing a tight, centralized bureaucratic structure on government operations were simply overestimated and the costs underestimated. One result was increased control and accountability, which boosted government performance in some ways, but too great a price was paid for that gain in terms of lost innovativeness, responsiveness, and capacity to focus all available social resources on the solution of public problems. In this view, had the principles of networked government been figured out and applied long ago, there would be far fewer public problems today. The

Table 9-1. *Networked Government as a Balance between Markets and Government*

Aggregating mechanism	*Form of Social Organization*				
	Market	*Loose network*	*Tighter network*	*Government*
Common purpose among network actors?	None; aggregate effects emerge from different goals.	Loose; no glue binds network together.	Common purpose among independent social actors is important part of glue holding network actors together and shaping joint action.	Clear common purpose established in government-formed policy mandate.
Sovereign or central authority guiding network activities?	None.	Authority in network rests in tacit agreements and negotiated deals.	Network actors have established governance structure that provides some collective authority, and a forum within which purposes and means can be discussed.	Overarching central, sovereign authority over network operations.
Degree of explicit, mutually agreed upon agreements among independent social actors?	None.	Very little; coordination structured by ad hoc deals.	Some coordination created by combination of shared goals, existing governance structure, and a clear, agreed-upon network mission.	Explicit coordination and control to achieve given purposes flow from authority and funding and are guided by an agreed-upon network mission that assigns tasks to social actors.

Relationship of aggregate results to original central intentions?	None. Aggregate results emerge from decentralized purposes and decisions.	Little. Despite some common purposes and awareness of interpendence, goals to be advanced will be determined by the accumulation of decentralized deal making.	Closer relationship between results and central intentions, produced by combinations of shared purposes, shared governance, recognized interdependence, and the creation of explicit and widely shared guidance as to who will do what.	Close relationship of results to intentions, produced by power of central actor to define purposes and assign roles to social actors.
Driving forces behind organization and production of material results by the organization of social actors?	Individual customers with desires and money to spend, and individual suppliers with the goal of making money by satisfying customer desires.	Social actors seeking to achieve goals through exchange and cooperation with other social actors to whom they have little formal relation.	Social actors seeking to achieve goals through exchange and cooperation with other social actors with whom they have strong relationships built on shared purposes, a common structure of governance, recognized interdependence, and accustomed interactions.	Social actors seeking to use government assets for some desired public purposes.

Source: Author.

implication of this viewpoint is that nearly 100 percent of government-controlled resources and activities should come to be governed by networked relationships and agreements and removed from hierarchical bureaucratic structures. Bureaucracies should be the substratum of government; government operations should be guided by networked agreements.[15]

A second, more restrictive, viewpoint is that networked government arrangements are needed for only a select number of governmental functions, where the connection between the old government structure and the problems it sought to address has disintegrated over time. The idea is that the old responses seemed adequate—bureaucratic government continued to work well—for some problems that had long been assigned to government and that had changed little over time. Only in areas where the problems previously assigned to government were changing in ways that rendered the old governmental structure ineffective would networked government solutions have to be sought. Networked government solutions would be needed to adapt the performance of government because old agencies could not simply be scrapped and new structures built; instead, capacities present in both the existing government and private sector would have to be cobbled together to solve these problems. Networked government emerges as a kind of temporary prosthesis to cope with a growing misfit between old structures and the changing character of today's problems while moving toward a more satisfactory permanent structure. This perspective suggests that networked government would not be needed everywhere—only for tasks that had changed in ways that stymied the effectiveness of existing governmental arrangements. Furthermore, networked government might not be needed permanently but only on an interim basis, while policymakers figured out how to adjust the existing permanent structures.[16]

The third, most restrictive perspective on networked government arrangements is that they are needed only for a select group of problems with special characteristics that required network solutions. The idea here is that the complexity of certain governmental tasks—protection against global terrorism, coping with environmental change, managing global health threats—makes any bureaucratic structure less effective (particularly the old ones) than networked government arrangements. According to this view, networked government is

---

15. Sometimes it seems that this is the position of Goldsmith and Eggers (2004): government performance can always be improved by thinking more about building networks of capacity to achieve desired outcomes than focusing narrowly on the performance of a single organization in its assigned mission.

16. Viewing networked government arrangements as a temporary adaptation of government structures and processes to deal with a growing mismatch between old structures and either changing problems or new problems reminds us that the alternative to networked governance is often a major structural reorganization of government. There is a great deal of evidence to suggest, however, that wholesale structural reorganizations of government do not work very well. See, for example, Moore (1978). Consider also the problems that government now faces in realizing the potential of the reorganized Department of Homeland Security, or the reorganized intelligence community. See Kettl (2003) and G. Edward DeSeve (chapter 6 this volume).

needed only where governments cannot solve problems by traditional government means.[17]

Creating Networked Government Arrangements

However pressing the need for networked government arrangements seems to be, if we are interested in exploiting the potential of networked government arrangements we have to think a bit about the processes by which such arrangements come into existence. Broadly speaking, it seems that networked government is called into existence through two different mechanisms: formally, from the top down, when a top-level government decision is taken to create a network to deal with an observed performance problem; or informally, from the bottom up, as individual officials, struggling to achieve their assigned purposes, realize that they need to supplement the capacities they directly control with assets and capabilities held by independent social actors and then seek to enroll them in some kind of mutually satisfactory networked government arrangements. Examples of top-down efforts to create governmental networks include the appointment by federal, state, or local governments of "drug czars" to coordinate governmental and private action to reduce drug abuse, or the appointment of a terrorism coordinator to plan for a society-wide effort to prevent or mitigate harm from terrorist attacks, or the initiation of an interagency, intergovernmental, cross-sector planning process to reduce teen pregnancies.[18] In each of these cases a central-government actor acts to create a networked form of government that can call on the capacities of existing public and private organizations and, in so doing, outperform the existing bureaucratic structures.

Examples of bottom-up efforts to create networked government arrangements that can outperform existing bureaucratic structures are not hard to find. A police precinct commander who finds that he or she cannot control youth violence without assistance from the local community in identifying the most serious offenders may be motivated to create a small networked government arrangement to control and prevent youth violence.[19] It may occur to a state social services commissioner who cannot find enough adoptive parents in minority communities that the development of a partnership with minority churches might help locate and recruit parents to fill the gap, and he or she will consider creating a networked government solution.[20] A Coast Guard officer charged with guaranteeing the security of U.S. ports quickly realizes that he must try to construct a networked government

17. This seems to be the claim of Milward and Raab with respect to Islamic terrorism (see chapter 8, this volume).

18. Reduce drug abuse: Buntin and Heymann (1998); terrorist attacks: de Vries (2008); reduce teen pregnancies: Sarhill and Harmeling (2000).

19. Scott and Zimmerman (2007).

20. Altshuler, Warrock, and Zegans (1988).

arrangement not by the use of top-down authority but by the process of persuasion, coalition building, and taking advantage of existing organizations that seem interested in the same goal.[21]

Given the potential importance of networked government arrangements for improving government performance, there is no need to choose between these two different ways of building networked government arrangements. Networks constructed both from the top down and from the bottom up can probably be used. However, in planning for evolving to a world with more networked government arrangements it might be particularly important to keep in mind the importance of networks that emerge from the bottom up. Government officials trying to do their jobs well discover over and over again that they need these new networked arrangements to achieve their assigned tasks. Underscoring the importance of these arrangements will increase the number and guarantee the immediate utility of the networks created.

Further, to support the development of bottom-up networks, managers will have to be authorized to do this work and equipped with the required skills.[22] Thus, government managers would have to be asked to feel accountable not only for deploying the assets and directing the activities of the organizations they lead but also for recognizing when they need to supplement their capacities with those of other social actors. They would also have to be trained in the skills of leadership and negotiation in addition to the traditional skills of direct supervision and management of hierarchical organizations.

A little reflection also suggests that the problems of government performance are not solved by the creation of a single new networked governmental solution. The newly created network often needs to be adapted and further developed over time. And new problems requiring new networks will always arise. Thus, in a governmental system that has come to understand the virtues of operating in networks, both very senior and less senior government officials will have to learn the skills of recognizing when networks are needed, and then building, sustaining, and adjusting the networks as they go along.

The Cases: Examples of Networks and Networkers

All the cases in this book describe problems that government is trying to solve, and most also describe the institutional structures and processes that government relies on to alleviate the problem. Most of the government responses described take the form of a networked government solution, but there are two significant exceptions: H. Brinton Milward and Jörg Raab (chapter 8) examine the role of terrorist networks in creating problems for government but not the government's

---

21. See Anne M. Khademian and William G. Berberich (chapter 7, this volume).

22. This seems to be the conclusion reached by the Department of the Interior. See William Eggers's discussion of the DOI's "Cooperative Conservation Initiative" (chapter 2, this volume).

methods for combating the networks, and William D. Eggers (chapter 2) looks at how a single organization turned itself into a school for training government officials to become network builders but does not present much detail on any of the networks those individuals have gone on to build.

In a conclusion to a book that presents so many different insights about the relationship of networks to government, the challenge is to decide whether to try to summarize everything offered or to narrow the focus of the summary to two key operational questions: (1) what do these cases reveal about the conditions under which networked government arrangements will outperform traditional bureaucratic structures, and (2) how can such arrangements be constructed, sustained, and operated to improve governmental performance. I have chosen the second, narrow-focus, course at the risk of neglecting some important insights contained in the individual cases.

Moreover, since there are only seven cases, and not all of them focus on the two questions under consideration, any claims I make about the issue have to be treated as tentative hypotheses rather than definitive conclusions. As more cases of networked government are developed, hypotheses can be tested and understanding improved. This book begins with what is in hand.

A Schematic Review of the Networks Described in the Cases

A starting point would be to simply catalog some features of the networks described in the cases. That seems straightforward, but in application, care has to be taken describing the network that is the focus of each case.

THE COOPERATIVE CONSERVATION INITIATIVE (CHAPTER 2). The case of the cooperative conservation initiative formed around the Detroit River offers evidence that networked government has become the preferred mode of operation for at least the Department of the Interior, and perhaps for the Environmental Protection Agency as well. It is remarkable to see the degree to which the DOI in particular has shifted its mode of operations from a command-and-control regulatory regime to one that seeks to build collaborative governance capacity as the solution to particular environmental problems. Ultimately, however, the main object of analysis is not a specific network per se but rather one organization, the EPA, and how it turned itself into an entity committed to doing its work through networked government arrangements. The case describes how the EPA is training its operating officials to build and use these networks, and the government-wide initiative to encourage other regulatory agencies to use these same techniques. A key use of this case would be to explore the methods the organization relies on to train individuals to build networks.

CALIFORNIA ENVIRONMENTAL POLICY NETWORK (CHAPTER 3). The case of the California environmental policy network is about the challenge of developing a state-level coordinating network that can improve the performance of a series of localized or special-purpose networks that have sprung up in California to deal with specific issues. This emergent network of networks is described as a "first-in-the-world comprehensive program."

CHESAPEAKE BAY PROGRAM (CHAPTER 4). In the Chesapeake Bay Program, the relevant network is the body of social actors with interests and capacities to shape the ecological and economic character of the Chesapeake Bay region.

STATE BENEFITS ELIGIBILITY SYSTEMS (CHAPTER 5). The chapter on state benefits eligibility systems describes three somewhat different networks. The first is the network of individual local offices, delivering more or less standardized services, that exists within a unified, state-level agency. The second is the broader network of private sector collaborators whose expertise in information systems could help speed up, standardize, and customize the process of eligibility determination. The third is the national network of state agencies that are joined by a common set of federal regulations and a shared professional community. The case primarily concerns the second network and how the privatization of the eligibility-determination function improved the system's performance.

INTELLIGENCE COMMUNITY (CHAPTER 6). Here, the network consists of the assorted government agencies that collect and analyze intelligence about threats to the security of the United States, particularly the threat of terrorist attack. The challenge is to protect the integrity of each organization while seeking improved performance through better collaboration across the network.

PORT SECURITY (CHAPTER 7). In the case of ensuring port security, the network seems straightforward enough: it depends on the mobilization of a set of actors with the interests and capacities to protect U.S. and world ports from becoming either a target of terrorism or a conduit through which terrorist arms could pass easily.

ISLAMIC TERRORISM (CHAPTER 8). The chapter on Islamic terrorism describes not a network of government agencies dealing with a problem but the network of more or less independent actors that constitute the terrorist organization, network, or movement that is creating a major threat to governments around the world.

The Chesapeake Bay Program and the port security initiative look like classic networked governance arrangements in that they seek to organize the efforts of many disparate groups—some governmental, some not—that are trying to deal with a common problem. The logic of including a specific social actor in a network rests on the interest and capacity of that actor to contribute materially and practically to the solution of a specific public problem.

The California environmental policy network also looks like a classic example of networked government in that it illustrates the emergent need for a network to coordinate and focus the actions of independent government entities. The distinguishing feature of this network, however, is that it is a network of smaller networks that were created to solve problems that single organizations working alone could not solve, not of single established organizations. These smaller, more local, more specialized networks were created from the bottom up by a "virtual army of policy entrepreneurs." Thus, the "first-in-the-world comprehensive environmental program" is not a network of organizations but of networks.[23]

These three cases seem best to exemplify the arrangements one would expect to see in networked government. They describe successful efforts to combine capacities from different government organizations and from the private sector, to build a capacity to perform that did not exist until the new networked relationships were built.

The case of the state eligibility system looks like a classic privatization effort, particularly if one concentrates on the state-level efforts to contract this key function out to the private sector. As such, it is a narrower kind of networked government case than those described above: fewer actors have to be knitted together to achieve the desired result. Moreover, the limited network can be dominated by government insofar as government is prepared to use its financial power and its contracting power to specify what it wants produced. There need not be much negotiation about what is to be produced, only about the price for doing the work.

The Chesapeake Bay, port security, California environment, and state benefits eligibility standards cases all describe networks built from independent organizations or, in the case of California environmental protection, from independent networks. Running through the list, however, one could argue that the governance of the networks is getting thicker and tighter. There are fewer players; the purposes of the network are being more centrally defined by higher levels of government. They are drifting toward hierarchical government relationships.

This shift continues in the networks described in the intelligence community and in the cooperative conservation initiative cases. The intelligence community case looks more like an effort to develop more effective coordination among distinct governmental organizations facing similar, highly interdependent tasks. The means for building that coordination include not only efforts to create a shared sense of mission and better mechanisms for cooperation but also the creation of a coherent central authority to insist on as well as merely encourage cooperation. And, as noted earlier, the case of the cooperative conservation initiative looks less like a network per se than a case of an organization that has decided to operate through networks, and has focused its attention on training network builders.

23. The "virtual army" of social entrepreneurs who created the small-scale networks that become the focus of the "world's first comprehensive approach" can be seen in two quite different lights. They could be seen (and applauded) as busy networkers who, acting independently but within the same broad domain, were laying the basis for networks that would allow each to solve its own problem and enable all of them together to make progress on solving the big problems that none of them alone could handle. Or they could be seen as the problem itself that someone operating at a higher level of governmental authority and with a wider perspective would have to resolve.

Finally, the case of Islamic terrorism is certainly about networks. In the context of this book, this case serves a very important cautionary purpose, reminding us that networks in themselves are neither good nor bad; their value depends on the purposes the networks are enabling. It also suggests the potential urgency of developing network capacities in government. If it is true that "it takes a network to combat a network," then the government will have to be able to construct a network to deal effectively with terrorism. To see the networked government arrangements that are being constructed to confront this network, one could go back to the cases on port security or intelligence.

The Chesapeake Bay project, port security, the statewide California environmental system, and the state eligibility guidelines cases seem particularly relevant for analyzing when networked government arrangements are appropriate, and how they might be constructed, largely because in those networks no central authority guides the work and because the networks reach out across many different boundaries. The intelligence community also retains enough network-like characteristics to justify treating its operations as the result of networked rather than hierarchically organized government, despite efforts to give the intelligence network a centrally directed and thus hierarchical character.

Table 9-2 shows these five networked government arrangements along four dimensions that are useful in characterizing the form the network takes and what occasioned its development. Each of the five networks is described in terms of four dimensions. The first dimension is the stage of the network's development. One of the defining characteristics of networks is that they are ever-changing rather than fixed and determined, so no network can ever be "fully established," but some distinctions can be made nevertheless: (1) between networks with relatively fixed membership and those still recruiting new members; (2) between networks in which the sense of interdependence and common cause is still emerging and those in which the actors have grown accustomed to thinking of themselves as interdependent; (3) between networks that have accomplished some important tasks and those that have not yet done much but talk; (4) between networks still developing most working relationships and those with established strong, trusting relationships. Viewed in this way, none of the networks examined in this book can be considered well established—they are all in the state of "becoming"—so it is hard to evaluate their performance or say how established networks can be managed well. These cases say more about starts than finishes.

Second, the networks are described in terms of their scope. A network's scope can usefully be presented in terms of geographic scale and of the number and type of boundaries crossed. Networks dealing with national security are global in scale; they are concerned with actions and conditions on an international stage, scooping up resources and capacities from social actors around the world and taking action in many different parts of the world. The environmental networks, by contrast—for example, the California and Chesapeake Bay cases—are more local in geographic scope.

Sectoral and organizational boundary crossings are also significant in the scope dimension. Boundary crossing is one of the defining characteristics and unique challenges in creating a network. If all the social actors within a network are subject to a close-by and active common authority, they really belong to an "organization" rather than a "network." By definition, a network combines assets and capacities from social actors that do not have a common, authoritative superior or cannot easily call upon that authority because it is distant or distracted. This fact makes network coordination and operation more a matter of recognizing shared interests and negotiating working agreements than of appealing to a common authority. The more boundaries crossed, the more complex the network. The wider the cultural divide is among actors, the more challenging are the border crossings and negotiations. Viewed from this perspective, the network with the most borders to cross is the port security network. The one with the fewest might be the cooperative conservation initiative, at least when it operates simply to create networking-inclined public officials, because all the processes are within the same organization. The intelligence network is a challenge. Even though it looks as though it is run by a common authority and therefore is not a network at all, given the agencies' historic independence and the practical necessity of tightly controlling information flows, it is quickly apparent that it is in fact closer in form to a network than a single organization because its loosely coupled agencies have to be persuaded to act together.

The third dimension on the table is the driver of development: whether the drive for network development came from the top down or the bottom up. Top-down development means the network came into being at the behest and with the active leadership of someone in a position of authority to mandate the creation of a network that could supersede the authority of the existing organizations. Bottom-up development means that the network emerged from the entrepreneurial efforts of individuals or informal groups of individuals in less lofty hierarchical positions. These people, seeing a functional need for a network so they can do their jobs, begin to develop network capacity without any particular authorization to do so. Here the cases seem to divide neatly. The top-down cases are the California environmental case, the benefits eligibility standards case, and the intelligence community case. The "bottom-up" cases are port security and the Chesapeake Bay Program.

The fourth dimension is the "thickness" of its internal operations. In a thin network contacts among network members are limited, perhaps only taking place among the individuals at the top of the organizations in the network. In a thick network, the social actors in the network are more extensively involved with one another—individuals at many different levels of the networked organizations talk frequently and act together. A related idea is that a thick network moves reasonably

Table 9-2. *Five Cases of Networked Government Described on Four Dimensions*

Dimension	Port security	Intelligence community	Chesapeake Bay Program	California environmental policy network	State benefits eligibility systems
			Case		
Stage of development	Early	Old structure being redeveloped	Established and operating	Conditions for networking present, not yet developed	Varied, but mostly in development
Scope	International, cross-sectoral, cross-organizational boundaries	National, cross-governmental organizations	Local, cross-sectoral, cross-organizational boundaries	State, cross-governmental organizations, cross-government levels, cross-sectoral	State, cross-government, public-private
Driver of development	Bottom up	Top down	Bottom up	Top down	Top down
Thickness of network	Becoming thick	Thick	Thick	Thin	Thick

Source: Author.

quickly from talk to action, and from policy to implementation. In essence, a thick network begins to look more like an organization in operational terms, even though its ownership and control functions remain distributed across organizational boundaries.

There is a close relationship between the thinness or thickness of a network and the network's stage of development (the first dimension in the table.) Almost certainly a thick network takes more time to develop than a thin one, and it would be natural to say that a thicker network is more developed than a thinner network. However, some networks even when fully developed do not have to be particularly thick to be effective. The case of Islamic terrorism, for example, suggests that this particular network is becoming more effective as it is becoming thinner, precisely because it is less interdependent, making the whole network less vulnerable to a successful attack on a part of the system. Much depends on how often and in what ways individual actors, placed on the opposite sides of organizational boundaries, have to recognize an interdependence, pool separately held assets in a common pot, and act in highly coordinated ways to achieve the network goals. If the social actors in a network can operate independently, they do not need a thick network; if they have to make frequent, unpredictable boundary crossings, they do. In terms of its requirements for operational coordination, a relatively thin but useful port security network could possibly be produced. The main function of the network might be nothing more than keeping the attention of the key actors focused on taking steps on their own to enhance port security. In contrast, it is almost inconceivable that the intelligence community could be successful without a very thick network.

Conditions under Which Networks Seem to Arise

What, then, do these cases reveal about the conditions that might encourage networks or about the places where networks might be needed? There may or may not be an important relationship between the conditions that foster networks and the places where they are needed. Although it is tempting to imagine that the need for a network might be one of the conditions favoring its development, this is only true if some agent perceives the need and takes actions that help create the network. A description of the kinds of problems for which networks might be the best answer might yield a predictive theory about where they will arise. In any case, it reveals a normative theory about where someone might want to create networks.

From a review of both the general theory of networked government and the cases, one could hypothesize that the following conditions could be favorable to the development of networks:

—Government's performance problems are glaring (crisis).

—The technical requirements for dealing with a problem and the institutional arrangements governing the social response are out of sync.

—Some features of a problem could best be attacked by a loosely coupled network rather than by a large, hierarchical organization.

GLARING PERFORMANCE CRISES. Perhaps the single most important factor favoring the development of networked government solutions is undeniable evidence of major performance problems in government—a crisis of some kind. Because government organizations do not typically go bankrupt, resources can long remain committed to failures. Bankruptcy in the private sector, though bad for a company and its investors, stops the continued waste of resources by freeing them up from old commitments.

The closest analogs to bankruptcies in the public sector are glaring crises of performance: the destruction of the World Trade Center by terrorists or an environmental regulatory dispute that runs twenty years without any improvement in the environment. Crises create an opportunity to establish a new way of doing business.[24] That opportunity consists of several key elements: a sense of urgency about a task; the discrediting of old structures and solutions so that they can no longer make compelling claims on resources; an implicit authorization for anyone with an idea about how to proceed to make a suggestion; and both top-down and bottom-up searches to invent new ways of proceeding. As a practitioner colleague once explained, "A crisis collapses all the existing structures and creates an opportunity to build something new with resources regained from the old failed solution."[25] This seems to be a perfect description of the functional equivalent of a private sector bankruptcy.

The difficulty is in establishing as an incontrovertible fact that government organizations are failing badly in some critical task. The question of how well a government organization performs is not answered by objective evidence of financial performance; it is always a politically contested claim. Some people allege government failure and crisis even when it is not evident. Making an undeniable claim that a government operation has dramatically failed is a political task. Some highly visible event, or the publication of some key statistic, has to be amplified by means of political action. When this occurs, the chances of reorganizing or reconstituting government's efforts, particularly from the top down, increase.

The troubles that create occasions for declaring public sector bankruptcies vary a great deal. In the cases in this volume, all the following events and conditions provide the occasion for a major reorganization and the creation of networked arrangements:

—A series of intelligence failures ranging from the failure to anticipate terrorist attacks to faulty intelligence about weapons of mass destruction in Iraq

—A recognition that the nation's ports were both a tempting target for terrorists and a portal through which they or their matériel might have to pass

—A decades-long stalemate on the environmental regulation of a key natural resource

24. Moore (1969).
25. Ed Hamilton (Kennedy School of Government), personal communication, 1972.

—Aggravated environmental conditions left unresolved by fragmented and stalemated environmental policy initiatives

It takes little imagination or research to come up with many more triggers for the creation of networked government arrangements. The severe acute respiratory syndrome (SARS) epidemic, economic development of abandoned parts of cities, enhanced security for residents of dangerous urban environments—all present the same kinds of urgent conditions that collapse existing institutional forms and create both the need and the opportunity to form new governmental responses. Joseph Schumpeter's "gale of creative destruction" does not happen only in the private sector; it appears in a more muted and restrained form in the public sector.[26] In such turbulence, opportunities to build networked government arrangements occur.

Mismatch between Problems and Organizational Structures. A second factor contributing to the development of networked government is a substantial misfit between the technical requirements for dealing with a given problem and the institutional arrangements governing the social response. This factor and the performance crises described above overlap significantly because irrefutable evidence of performance problems often reveals a wide mismatch between significant problems and institutional arrangements for their mitigation. On many occasions "insiders" understand that there is a bad mismatch between problems and institutional means for solution, but the public at large does not know about it. In these cases the drive to create networked government solutions will probably come from the bottom up, with midlevel public officials struggling to improve structures and processes without help from top-down authorization. When the wider public comes to understand the mismatch between a problem and government's response, the initiative to create a networked government solution will often become top-down as public concern triggers the action of the higher-level officials who can mandate, rather than negotiate, networked arrangements.

A mismatch between problems and structures can take many forms. For instance, if government faces a task with changing characteristics, it may be challenged to innovate, adapt, and maintain a variety of responses instead of clinging to "tried and true" measures. That challenge seems to have prompted the Department of the Interior to try to codify a set of practices that would allow their bureaucrats to custom-tailor responses to conservation disputes involving public lands.

Another possibility is that government may face a problem where close coordination across organizational boundaries is necessary to achieve its desired goals. The distinct organizations may have been established to develop specialized expertise of one kind or another, but that expertise has value primarily when it is closely aligned operationally with other technical expertise located in different

26. Schumpeter (1976, 1994).

organizations. If the organizations do not have any well-oiled means of operational coordination, there will be a misfit between operations and performance. This seems to have been the case with the U.S. intelligence community.

Another possibility is that the government seeks to solve a problem without commanding enough resources for the job. The most obvious limitation is usually money. Theoretically, if the government had enough money it could buy solutions to problems through direct production and contracts with private suppliers, but government's assigned tasks are usually much bigger than the funds available. That means that the government must find ways to mobilize other actors who control useful or necessary assets. It can use its regulatory authority to require private actors to contribute to public purposes or use its bully pulpit to exhort individuals to make voluntary contributions to the public purpose. Both regulatory authority and exhortation depend crucially on government's standing and legitimacy in the eyes of those being compelled or asked to contribute to public solutions. But government may lack legitimacy as well as money or regulatory authority. If government is to succeed it must find a way to combine its money with its regulatory authority and its legitimacy to mobilize a wide set of actors to contribute to a common goal. The only way to do this is through consultation, consensus building, and continuing pressure to focus on a problem that many actors have to deal with but no one actor feels responsible for solving. It was this situation that seems to have animated and guided the development of both the Chesapeake Bay Program network and the gradual emergence of the port security solution.

SPECIAL CHARACTERISTICS OF PROBLEMS. A third factor encouraging or facilitating the development of a networked government solution would be a problem that had some specific features that a network could better address than a large, hierarchical organization. There are some features of substantive problems that might make networked government arrangements particularly useful.

First, the symptoms of problems could show up in places that are relatively distant from the causes of the problem. Most governments are spatially organized within geographical boundaries, but the material and social conditions that generate problems do not necessarily respect these boundaries. A problem can appear in jurisdiction X but originate in jurisdiction Y. A higher-level government unit Z that includes both X and Y could theoretically solve this problem, but suppose, as in the case of international port security, there is no Z. Or there might be a Z, but the problem between X and Y is not important enough to rank high on Z's agenda. Or suppose that Z's recommended solution is worse than many solutions that X and Y could develop together. In all these cases it might make more sense for X and Y to see if they can make a deal themselves, with or without the help of Z.

Second, the big problem to be solved could be an aggregation of many different smaller problems that are distinct in their location, causes, and solutions. The set of smaller, independent problems may include problems of many different sizes, ranging from pretty big problems, cutting across existing boundaries, to small problems located in a single jurisdiction. To deal with a large social issue like a "national crime problem" or an "obesity epidemic," a single action at the national level will not suffice. There are certainly actions worth taking at the highest level, but many small, local actors must be mobilized to attack the many small, local problems that constitute the big problem. This often requires efforts to build and maintain political pressure to work on the problem. Some causes of a problem may be structural and general, but it should not be assumed that all such problems are best handled by means of large-scale, structural solutions. There may be many big problems that can be eliminated only by first solving the many smaller component problems.

This seems to be the characteristic of both the environmental and the national security problems discussed in this volume. The deteriorating natural environment is a problem that is dislocated geographically from its causes. It is also a big problem that is made up of many smaller, more or less independent problems. And it is this characteristic of environmental problems that gives us the familiar slogan "Think Globally, Act Locally." But the converse, "Think Locally, Act Globally," might also make sense in some situations. The tension between allowing decentralized action to accumulate to aggregate results on the one hand, and structuring a large-scale effort to make progress on local issues on the other plays out in the California environmental regulation case.

Some Principles for Network Designers and Managers

So we see that the conditions under which networked government arrangements arise are at least partially determined by functional requirements. Networks arise when they seem necessary because of dramatic performance failures or a misfit of problem to structure, or when a problem has features that make networked responses seem particularly appropriate. But this hypothesis may be overly optimistic. Networked government arrangements could also arise because they have become a management fad. Worse, they might fail to develop in cases where they are needed because there is no explicit authorization to create them or no enterprising managers to see the need and to create them.

These observations are a reminder that networked government arrangements do not arise spontaneously, even when there is a need. They arise when officials at the top or midlevels of government act to create and use networks rather than organizations to achieve their purposes. This means that much depends on whether officials are authorized and encouraged to become networkers and whether they have the appropriate skills for this work.

Because the cases in this volume reveal more about networks than about the networkers who design them from the top down or build them from the bottom up, there is still much to learn about the leadership and management skills that go into their creation. Learning about these issues will have to await a set of cases focused on managerial action to create, sustain, or operate within networks. In anticipation of this work, we offer some ideas and hypotheses that can be tested in future research.[27]

The Role of Leadership and Management in Creating Networks

The cases reveal networks at different stages of becoming. An important question to consider in understanding both the past history and future prospects of these networks is which particular actors are doing the work of creating these networks. Without a doubt there are individuals in particular positions making specific efforts to transform working relations with others and, through those new relationships, transforming the real productive capacities of the system as a whole. It also seems obvious that these individuals must explore and invest in the new working relationships as well as discover ways to use those relationships to produce different material results. It also has to be assumed that any given network combines investment and development activities with the operational use of the new working relationships.

However, one should not necessarily assume that the development of a network is under the conscious control of any particular individual or group. The impetus to create the network can come from many different actors and can change over time. The success of the network never depends solely on the strength of a single actor, but depends instead on the latent potential of the network as a whole, the ability of many different actors to recognize that potential, and their willingness to cooperate to build the network.

Consistent with this observation is the further idea that networks can be created both explicitly from the top down and more tacitly and incrementally from the bottom up. It seems likely that top-down networks can be created only when there are significant, highly visible performance problems. In contrast, the networks that are occasioned by structural misfits or special problems may be generated from the bottom up. Those bottom-up efforts will always be aided by some kind of top-down authorization to engage in the work, but the top-down authorizations need not be specifically instructive; they can be generally permissive.

Focus on the Problem Rather Than the Organization

The examples in this book make it clear that one key principle followed by the "networkers" whose actions form the central focus of the cases is to keep their attention riveted on the problem they want to solve rather than on the position they occupy or the organization they lead. This distinction may seem trivial. After

---

27. This discussion follows the path—even retraces the steps—of Milward and Provan (2006).

all, most government operating managers hold positions that make them account-able for the solution of some social problem, or the production of some kind of public value. They have been entrusted with public assets—money and author-ity—to achieve those results, and they often are responsible for managing an organization whose operations have been developed over time to allow them to achieve the desired results. Indeed, it has long been a principle of good public administration that public managers should be given sufficient authority and resources to fulfill the responsibilities entrusted to them. Consequently, it has long been assumed that the idea of a manager's accountability for achieving social objec-tives is closely aligned with the objective of efficient and effective use of assets under his direct control—in other words, with efficient and effective organiza-tional management.

These cases do, however, reveal a mismatch between the problems for which a given manager feels responsible and his ability to solve them with resources directly under his control. The system that assigns public managers the task of achieving desired results often does not give them the authority and resources needed for the task.[28] In this situation, public managers have two options: they can retreat into seeing their problem as managing the assets and organization entrusted to them while knowing that such efforts will be insufficient to deal with the problem, or they can move forward, remaining committed to the solu-tion of the problem and searching for assets not under their direct control that they can use to achieve their purposes. The networkers in these cases take the lat-ter approach. They seek to enlarge the effective scope of their influence to tap into assets they do not directly control. Thus, they can bridge the gap between the problem they think they have been asked to solve and the resources that have been entrusted to their direct control.

It is not clear what moves the entrepreneurial networkers described in these cases to take on this kind of responsibility. There are many reasons for them to take the first rather than the second approach. The traditions and culture of pub-lic administration make it a virtue for public officials to stay narrowly focused on their own responsibilities, a tendency reinforced by the reluctance of other pub-lic officials to have their judgments second-guessed or their turf invaded by a bureaucratic colleague. Tradition and culture also make it a virtue for public offi-cials not to engage in the development of working partnerships with organiza-tions outside the boundaries of government. Close engagement or active negoti-ations with private for-profit or nonprofit groups can suggest corruption. If public

---

28. Usually the problem is "not enough." Sometimes the problem is too much, and or not the right kind. Both present problems. And both reflect the continuing struggle to align fixed structures with a dynamic set of problems and varying opportunities for dealing with the problems. There has to be more flexibility   opportunism   than is usually contemplated by those who would like their systems to be more consistent and reliable.

officials seek to develop a bit of independent political power so that they can negotiate with private actors from a strong position and thus avoid the perception and reality of corruption, they run into norms and rules that discourage them from developing any kind of independent political identity. The only reason for public managers to take the second approach—to seek to widen their scope for action by entering into working relations with other organizations—is that they feel accountable for achieving substantive results, not for doing their duty as it is ordinarily and narrowly understood.

The idea that the duty of public officials includes achieving substantive results beyond the actual capacities of the assets entrusted to them has been bolstered in recent years by a determined effort to focus officials' attention on the achievement of results, not simply on organizational activity. Organizations have come under strong pressures to measure their performance in order to enhance both their accountability and performance. Those pressures have urged managers to go beyond measuring organizational activity and output to measuring the degree to which the organization achieved the social outcome that provided its ultimate raison d'être. These social outcomes often occur far down a causal chain from the organization's own activity, so many factors other than those under the control of the organization could come into play to shape the organization's ultimate success. Consequently, it is natural for organizational managers to begin thinking about how they could get more control over the factors that influence the success of their organization but are not directly under their control. The natural result of that kind of thinking is to consider the development of a network that extends the influence of the organization to factors that are now beyond its control. Thus, the pressure to achieve social outcomes creates both a pressure and a justification for organizational managers to create wider networks of capacity that allow them to have a broader, deeper, and more durable impact on the social conditions they seek to change.[29]

Imagining the Network

The ability to imagine how to piece together a valuable network is a key skill to develop and deploy in the process of creating networked government solutions. A relatively simple method, called "mapping backward," in principle is useful for producing effective networks.[30] The method involves the following steps:

—Imagine the social outcome sought.

—Formulate a set of actions that could produce the desired result.

—Identify the existing social actors who could plausibly take the required actions and the motivations that might encourage them to do so.

The key idea is to use the idea of reverse engineering—the logic of manufacturing production—to identify the specific social actors to be recruited to the

29. Moore (2002).
30. Allison and Moore (1978).

network because of their control of assets or capacities that are necessary or help-ful to produce the desired result.

In practice, using this reverse-engineering logic to visualize the required net-work is more difficult than it first appears. A major part of the difficulty is that as an analyst begins "mapping backward" from a desired social result to the required action of social and government agents, the analysis tends to sprawl out of control. Once a desirable social outcome is defined, the real work starts. A way of producing the result has to be imagined. But there are often many different ways, and each method leads to a focus on a different set of social actors. If all possible methods are investigated, the analysis very quickly gets very complex. Finally, the empirical work has to be done to identify the social actors who can contribute to the solution of the problem, and to figure out how they might be motivated to do so. This last step is particularly difficult because the effects of the actions of a particular social actor engaged in a productive network are not always limited to the targeted problem, which forces a redefinition of the prob-lem to be solved.

Although it is difficult to do a complete analysis of the network actors needed to achieve a desired result, it is not hard to use this logic to get started on the task of imagining and building the network. The key is to look beyond the capacity of one's own organization to see who else can make a useful contribution.

Organizing and Aligning the Network

Once the network is imagined according to a logic of production, the next step is to think about how best to call the network into existence so that its latent poten-tial to produce desired social results can be activated and ensured. A person who holds a powerful position in a social or institutional hierarchy and thus can exert strong political pressures to improve results can easily imagine a top-down ap-proach to creating a network. Indeed, a new organization designed to achieve the desired result might simply be formed by fiat, dispensing with the necessity of network creation altogether!

More commonly, though, individuals trying to build an efficacious network from a weak position must start negotiations with potential network participants. There is much to be learned about how to carry out such negotiations: the role that shared goals can play in facilitating the negotiations; the extent to which agree-ments should be explicit and written down versus left implicit and generally under-stood; the sequence in which network participants might best be approached; deciding when there are enough actors in the network to be able to begin produc-ing results and the likely impact of the network's existing capacity on future nego-tiations; and others. The important thing to understand is that the network is likely to develop through a series of more or less explicit deals struck among net-work participants—partly to achieve the common goal of improving network per-formance and partly to achieve other goals of the social actors. The participants will all have their own mix of reasons for joining, staying in, and operating on behalf of the network.

Animating, Driving, and Disciplining the Network

Eventually, networks in the process of development have to act to produce the desired results. Let's assume that the negotiations among the actors have provided a general rationale for joint action, identified the actors' key contributions to the common goal, and created specific incentives for particular actors to do their part in the network. If that skein of deals works, the network will perform. In the real world, however, things rarely go this smoothly, and most networks do not perform as expected, so they suffer crises of confidence and erosions of trust. The bonds that hold them together get tested and have to be recreated.

Thus, an important test of a network and an important focus of someone trying to create a network has to be the development of mechanisms that protect the operational discipline of the network and allow for resolution of the conflicts that inevitably arise. These mechanisms could be thought of as the network's governance process, which guides the recruitment of new actors into the network, keeps track of the implicit and explicit deals, seeks to mediate or arbitrate disputes among members of the network, and so on. Learning how networks get through difficulties as well as how they are created should be a key focus of future research.

Evaluating the Performance of the Networks: The Idea of Leverage

The final principle for network designers and managers to put into practice is the evaluation of network performance.[31] From an academic point of view it is important to see whether the dividends delivered by the networked government arrangements match predictions. Practically, evaluation is important to the designers and builders of networks because it provides assurance that they are moving in the right direction and measures their contribution to the solution of public problems.

Indeed, one of the most important tools to sustain and discipline a network is a continuing capacity to monitor its performance and accomplishment. Negotiated arrangements among network participants, tracked by performance measurement and evaluation systems, can produce a functional equivalent for centralized authority in disciplining and focusing the actions of the network. If networks are held together and act through a set of negotiated deals within which the overall performance is one large part of the motivation to stay in the network, it is important to network members' morale and continued enthusiasm for them to see the imagined results of their action realized. Agreement about shared goals combined with a performance measurement system provides a record as to whether the desired results are being achieved and whether particular actors are doing their agreed part, and the agreements and measurement systems stand in for central

31. For a start, see Provan and Milward (2001).

authority. An organization that has a central authority, a core identity, and accustomed patterns of interaction can get along largely on tradition and the repetition of past actions. A network, in contrast—lacking the support of a central authority, a shared culture, and a history of joint action—has to be held together through a continuous demonstration of the network's value to each independent network member. Key to demonstrating that value is a strong capacity to monitor the activities and results of the network. Performance measurement may be even more important in networks than in organizations, because it forms much of the glue that keeps the network together.

From an academic perspective, the key evaluative question concerns the degree to which the creation of the network improved government's or society's overall ability to deal with a social problem. How does the network's ability to create net public value compare with that of operations prior to the creation of the network? To measure the degree of improvement, one must imagine what the world would have been like if a particular network had not been developed.

The focus of this evaluation is on improved performance, but the problem is that that the improvement could have been produced in two different ways: (1) via the development of new methods for achieving the old result or a better alignment of existing capacities (that is, programmatic or technical improvements—inventions in products, services, or processes that changed the deployment of a stock of assets to achieve better, more socially valuable results); or (2) via the mobilization of new assets for the solution of the problem. It may be that nothing much changed in how a given problem was approached and that the whole difference lay in finding new resources and assets to apply to the problem.

Both of these sources of improvement could be viewed as socially valuable. It is good if better ways can be found to achieve desired results using the same amount of social resources. It is good if additional resources can be found to help deal with an urgent social problem. The key difference between them is that only the first is unambiguously good. The second is good only if the new resources applied to the problem are not particularly valuable in alternative uses. If the new resources are voluntarily contributed from many decentralized actors without their noticing that they have shifted their attention to the solution of a public problem, the flow of new resources to the solution could be considered relatively "free." If, however, the resources have to be shifted from another urgent social task, the improved performance in dealing with the problem of current interest has to be discounted because it leads to some lost capacity in dealing with other important public problems.

Thus, when we are evaluating network performance, it is not enough to notice whether overall success in dealing with the problem has gone up or not. We must also evaluate how much of the improvement came from the mobilization of new resources and how much value those new resources would have had in alternative uses. Only then can the net value of the network be calculated.

In practical terms the key evaluative question includes the academic question but is not limited to it. At the practical level, the key issue is whether the network helps network participants achieve their desired objectives. Each network participant has some interest in seeing the overall social goals achieved but may have other goals different from the social outcome that an academic evaluator would define. For example, a network participant might want to leverage her assets by engaging the assets of the other network participants. That is one of the motivations that draw participants to the network. Left to herself a network participant may be able to produce only a small impact on a problem. If individual participants can leverage their resources through use of the network, however, their own performance will be much better than when they are acting without the help of a network.

This way of thinking, though helpful to a network practitioner, can lead to misunderstanding. The real social leverage produced by a network is only the net difference observed in overall results, adjusted for the likelihood that they have been achieved partly by applying to the problem previously undeployed resources. There may well be synergies that can be exploited through improved coordination in a network. A network may also be able to tap otherwise unused or wasted resources, and real social performance goes up to the degree that this is true and network members can take credit for better results than they could have achieved had they done nothing but add their own resources to the common pot. But if each member of the network claims for himself the full value of the network, and the social value of the network is reckoned by totaling up each network participant's claims, we may significantly overestimate the value of the network, as each network participant double-counts the contribution made by all the other network participants. Part of being a good network participant is learning to remain humble about one's particular role in network development and operation.

Summary and Conclusions

Much accumulated experience suggests that many of government's most troubling problems cannot be handled by a single government organization acting alone, no matter how efficient and effective the organization and skilled its leader. Problems such as environmental degradation or terrorist threats cannot be met by a single organization located at one level of government. For problems like these and others, action is usually required from different government agencies, operating at different levels of government. Action may also be required from private enterprises, civil society, and nonprofit organizations. Often, action is also required from thousands or millions of ordinary families and citizens mobilized to contribute to a public cause by a complex blend of self-interest and public spirit.

If effective action to deal with an important problem is needed from many social actors distributed across a society, the burden of solving that problem cannot be placed only on effective action by a single organization, led by a single authoritative individual. Instead, a network of capacities has to be developed and exploited to draw assets, connections, knowledge, and motivations from social actors spread across and nestled in key points in the social firmament.

From this understanding grew the idea of networked government as a new and improved approach to handling difficult social problems. This approach is different from and more promising than the conventional approach, which relies on equipping leaders to drive their organizations toward increased efficiency and effectiveness in achieving relatively narrow and well-defined preset missions.

The idea of networked government is intuitively appealing. It is tempting to think that some of government's biggest limitations might be overcome by creating entities with more capacity to mobilize, align, and coordinate the actions of others than to command and control them. Although the theoretical reasons for being enthusiastic about networked government are persuasive, empirical evidence that networked government arrangements outperform traditional arrangements is still scant. Networks are being formed, and their potential for improving performance is promising, but so far no networked government arrangements that have been in place for a long time have been solidly evaluated. Equally important is the lack of any strong empirical base to guide the actions of public officials wanting to design networks from the top down or build them from the bottom up.[32]

The seven cases presented in this book sharpen and focus conceptual understanding of why networked government might be important and when it is particularly urgent. They also raise important questions about the conditions in which networked government arrangements are likely to be created, about how network designers might think of going about it, and about how best to evaluate established networks. This is a large accomplishment for one volume, and much more work remains to be done to lay a solid empirical basis for gauging the potential of networked government and understanding how public officials can spot and exploit that potential.

References

Agranoff, Robert. 2007. *Managing within Networks: Adding Value to Public Organizations.* Georgetown University Press.

Allison, Graham T., and Mark H. Moore. "Implementation Analysis." *Public Policy* 26, no. 2 (special issue, Spring 1978): 153–56.

Altshuler, Alan A., and Robert Behn, eds. 1997. *Innovations in American Government: Challenges, Opportunities and Dilemmas.* Brookings.

32. An extremely valuable start has been made by Eugene Bardach (2008) in the context of intergovernmental relations.

Altshuler, Alan, Anna Warrock, and Marc Zegans. 1988. "Finding Black Parents: One Church, One Child." Kennedy School of Government Case 856.0. Harvard University, Kennedy School of Government.

Bardach, Eugene. 1998. *Getting Agencies to Work Together: The Practice and Theory of Managerial Craftsmanship.* Brookings.

————. 2008. "Developmental Processes: A Conceptual Exploration." In *Innovations in Government: Research, Recognition, and Replication,* edited by Sandford Borins, pp. 113–37. Brookings.

Brooks, Harvey, Lance Liebman, and Corinne Schelling, eds. 2004. *Public-Private Partnership: New Opportunities for Meeting Social Need.* Cambridge, Mass.: Ballinger.

Buntin, John, and Philip Heymann. 1998. "A Czar among Bureaucrats. General Barry McCaffrey Considers a Role in the War against Drugs." KSG Case 14206.0. Harvard University, Kennedy School of Government.

de Vries, Jouke. 2008. "Europe's War on Terror: The Leadership Challenge Facing the European Union's COUNTERTERRORISM Coordinator." Parts A and B. Harvard University, Kennedy School of Government, KSG Executive Programs.

Donahue, John D. 1989. *The Privatization Decision: Public Ends, Private Means.* New York: Basic Books.

————. 1997. *Disunited States.* New York: Basic Books.

Donahue, John D., and Richard J. Zeckhauser. 2009 (forthcoming). *The Lever: Private Roles to Lift Public Goals.*

Ghobadian, Abby, ed. 2004. *Public-Private Partnerships: Policy and Experience.* Basingstoke, U.K.: Palgrave Macmillan.

Goldsmith, S. G., and W. D. Eggers. 2004. *Governing by Network: The New Shape of the Public Sector.* Brookings.

Kaufman, Herbert. 1963. *Politics and Policies in State and Local Government.* Englewood Cliffs, N.J.: Prentice Hall.

Kettl, Donald F. 2003. "Contingent Coordination: Practical and Theoretical Puzzles for Homeland Security." *American Review of Public Administration* 33: 253–77.

Mashaw, Jerry L. 1983. *Bureaucratic Justice: Managing Social Security Disability.* Yale University Press.

Milward, H. Brinton, and K. Provan, 2006. *A Manager's Guide to Choosing and Using Collaborative Networks.* Washington: IBM Center for the Business of Government.

Moore, Mark H. 1969. "Crisis Politics." Unpublished paper. Author's collection.

————. 1978. "Re-Organization Plan #2: Problems in Implementing a Strategy to Reduce the Supply of Drugs to Illicit Markets in the United States." *Public Policy* 26, no. 2 (Spring 1978): 229–62.

————. 1995. *Creating Public Value: Strategic Management in Government.* Harvard University Press.

————. 1997. "Justice as a Theory of Right Relationships: The Role of Criminal Justice Agencies in Building Just Communities." Eleventh Annual Sister Virginia Geiger Lecture in Ethics and Society, College of Notre Dame of Maryland, Baltimore.

————. 2000. "The Market versus the Forum." In *Governance amid Bigger, Better Markets,* edited by John D. Donahue and Joseph Nye. Brookings.

————. 2002. "Creating Networks of Capacity: The Challenge of Managing Society's Response to Youth Violence." In *Securing Our Children's Future: New Approaches to Juvenile Justice and Youth Violence,* edited by Gary Katzmann. Brookings.

Powell, W. W. 1991. "Neither Markets nor Hierarchy: Network Forms of Organization." *Research in Organizational Behavior* 12: 295–336.

President's Commission on Law Enforcement and the Administration of Justice. 1968. *The Challenge of Crime in a Free Society*. New York City: Avon.

Provan, K. G., and H. Brinton Milward. 2001. "Do Networks Really Work? A Framework for Evaluating Public-Sector Organizational Networks." *Public Administration Review* 61, no. 4: 414.

Sarhill, John C., and Susan S. Harmeling. 2000. "The National Campaign to Prevent Teen Pregnancy." HBS Case 9-300-105. Harvard Business School, February 7.

Scott, Esther, and Peter Zimmerman. 2007. "Revisiting Gang Violence in Boston." KSG Case 1887. Harvard University, Kennedy School of Government.

Schumpeter, Joseph A. 1976/1994. *Capitalism, Socialism, and Democracy*. 1976; New York: Routledge, 1994.

Weiss, Janet. 1981. "Substance vs. Symbol in Administrative Reform: The Case of Human Services Coordination." *Policy Analysis* 7, no. 1 (Winter): 20–45.

Bibliography

Abramson, Mark A., Jonathan D. Breul, and John M. Kamensky. *Six Trends Transforming Government*. Washington: IBM Center for the Business of Government, 2006.

Agranoff, Robert. "Inside Collaborative Networks: Ten Lessons for Public Managers." *Public Administration Review* 66, no. 1 (2006): 56–65.

———. *Managing within Networks: Adding Value to Public Organizations*. Georgetown University Press, 2007.

———. "Understanding Networks: A Guide for Public Managers." Arlington, Va.: IBM Endowment for the Business of Government, 2003.

Agranoff, Robert, and Michael McGuire. "Multi-Network Management: Collaboration and the Hollow State." *Journal of Public Administration Research and Theory* 1 (1998): 67–91.

———. *Collaborative Public Management: New Strategies for Local Governments*. MIT Press, 2003.

Aspinwall, Richard, and J. Cain. "The Changing Mindset in the Management of Waste." *Philosophical Transactions: Mathematical, Physical and Engineering Sciences* 355 (1997): 1425–437.

Austin, James E. *The Collaboration Challenge: How Nonprofits and Businesses Succeed through Strategic Alliances*. San Francisco: Jossey-Bass, 2000.

Bardach, Eugene. *Getting Agencies to Work Together: The Practice and Theory of Managerial Craftsmanship*. Brookings, 1998.

———. "Developmental Dynamics: Interagency Collaboration as an Emergent Phenomenon." *Journal of Public Administration Research and Theory* 2 (2001): 149–64.

Bardach, Eugene, and Robert Kagan. *Going by the Book: The Problem of Regulatory Unreasonableness*. Temple University Press, 1982.

Barr, Donald A. "A Research Protocol to Evaluate the Effectiveness of Public-Private Partnerships as a Means to Improve Health and Welfare Systems Worldwide." *American Journal of Public Health* 97, no. 1 (2007): 19–25.

Becker, Fred, and Valerie Patterson. "Public-Private Partnerships: Balancing Financial Returns, Risks, and Roles of the Partners." *Public Performance and Management Review* 29, no. 2 (2005): 125–44.

Behn, Robert D. "Management by Groping Along." *Journal of Policy Analysis and Management* 7, Fall (1988): 643–63.

Benkler, Yochai. *The Wealth of Networks: How Social Production Transforms Markets and Freedom.* Yale University Press, 2006.

Bennett, John, and Elisabetta Iossa. "Contracting Out Public Service Provision to Not-for-Profit Firms." CEDI Discussion Paper Series 07-08, pp. 1–31. London: Brunel University, Centre for Economic Development and Institutions, 2005.

———. "Delegation of Contracting in the Private Provision of Public Services." *Review of Industrial Organization* 29, no. 1 (2006): 74–92.

Bingham, Lisa B., and Rosemary O'Leary, eds. *Big Ideas in Collaborative Public Management.* Armonk, N.Y.: M. E. Sharpe, 2008.

Bloomfield, Pamela. "The Challenging Business of Long-Term Public-Private Partnerships: Reflections on Local Experience." *Public Administration Review* 66, no. 3 (2000): 400–11.

Bogason, Peter, and Juliet A. Musso. "The Democratic Prospects of Network Governance." *American Review of Public Administration* 36, no. 1 (2006): 3–18.

Bogason, Peter, and Mette Zølner, eds. *Methods in Democratic Network Governance.* New York: Palgrave Macmillan, 2007.

Bowling, Cynthia J., and Deil S. Wright. "Change and Continuity in State Administration: Administrative Leadership across Four Decades." *Public Administration Review* 58, no.5 (1998): 429–44.

Brenner, Thorsten, Wolfgang Reinicke, and Jan Martin Witte. "Multisectoral Networks in Global Governance: Toward a Pluralist System of Accountability." *Government and Opposition* (2004): 191–210.

Brodkin, Evelyn Z. "Bureaucracy Redux: Management Reformism and the Welfare State." *Journal of Public Administration Research and Theory* 17, no. 1 (2007): 1–17.

Brown, Trevor L., Matthew Potoski, and David M. Van Slyke. "Managing Public Service Contracts: Aligning Values, Institutions, and Markets." *Public Administration Review* 66, no. 3 (2006): 323–31.

Bryson, John M., and Barbara C. Crosby. *Leadership for the Common Good.* San Francisco: Jossey-Bass, 1992.

Bryson, John M., Barbara C. Crosby, and Melissa Middleton Stone. "The Design and Implementation of Cross-Sector Collaborations: Propositions from the Literature." *Public Administration Review* 66, no. 1 (2006): 44–55.

Buchel, Bettina, and Steffen Raub. "Building Knowledge-Creation Value Networks." *European Management Journal* 20, no. 6 (2002): 587–96.

Buskens, Vincent, and Kazuo Yamaguchi. "A New Model for Information Diffusion in Heterogeneous Social Networks." *Sociological Methodology* 29 (1999): 281–325.

Calhoun, Craig. "The Privatization of Risk." *Public Culture* 18, no. 2 (2006): 257–63.

Carlile, Paul R. "A Pragmatic View of Knowledge and Boundaries: Boundary Objects in New Product Development." *Organization Science* 13, no. 4 (2002): 442–55.

Caruson, Kiki, and Susan A. MacManus. "Mandates and Management Challenges in the Trenches: An Intergovernmental Perspective on Homeland Security." *Public Administration Review* 66, no. 4 (2006): 522–36.

Chrislip, David D., and Carl E. Larson. *Collaborative Leadership: How Citizens and Civic Leaders Can Make a Difference.* San Francisco: Jossey-Bass, 1994.

Churchman, C. West. "Wicked Problems." *Management Science* 4, no. 14 (1967): B141–B42.

Coggburn, Jerrell D. "Outsourcing Human Resources: The Case of the Texas Health and Human Services Commission." *Review of Public Personnel Administration* 27, no. 4 (2007): 315–35.

Considine, Mark. "Partnerships and Collaborative Advantage: Some Reflections on New Forms of Network Governance." Background Paper. University of Melbourne (Australia), Centre for Public Policy, 2005.

Considine, Mark, and Jenny M. Lewis. "Governance at Ground Level: The Frontline Bureaucrat in the Age of Markets and Networks." *Public Administration Review* 59, no. 6 (1999): 467–81.

Coulson, Andrew. "A Plague on All Your Partnerships: Theory and Practice in Regeneration." *International Journal of Public Sector Management* 18, no. 4 (2005): 151–63.

Cross, Rob, and Andrew Parker. 2004. *The Hidden Power of Social Networks: How Work Really Gets Done in Organizations.* Harvard Business School Press.

Crosby, Barbara, and John Bryson. "A Leadership Framework for Cross-Sector Collaboration." *Public Management Review* 7, no. 2 (2005): 177–201.

Daniels, Steven E., and Gregg B. Walker. *Working through Environmental Conflict: The Collaborative Learning Approach.* Westport, Conn.: Praeger, 2001.

Denhardt, Robert, and Janet Vinzant Denhardt. "The New Public Service: Serving rather than Steering." *Public Administration Review* 60, no. 6 (2000): 549–59.

Doig, W., and Erwin C. Hargrove. *Leadership and Innovation: Entrepreneurs in Government.* Johns Hopkins University Press, 1990.

Edelenbos, Jurian, and Erik-Hans Klijn. "Trust in Complex Decision-Making Networks: A Theoretical and Empirical Exploration." *Administration and Society* 39, no. 1 (2007): 25–50.

Eglene, Ophelia, Sharon S. Dawes, and Carrie A. Schneider. "Authority and Leadership Patterns in Public Sector Knowledge Networks." *American Review of Public Administration* 37, no. 1 (2007): 91–113.

Erridge, Andrew. "Public Procurement, Public Value and the Northern Ireland Unemployment Pilot Project." *Public Administration* 85, no. 4 (2007): 1023–043.

Farneti, Federica, and David W. Young. "A Contingency Approach to Managing Outsourcing Risk in Municipalities." *Public Management Review* 10, no. 1 (2008): 89–99.

Fedorowicz, Jane, Janis L. Gogan, and Christine B. Williams. "A Collaborative Network for First Responders: Lessons from the CapWN Case." *Government Information Quarterly* 24, no. 4 (2007): 785–807.

Evans, Karen. "Reclaiming John Dewey: Democracy, Inquiry, Pragmatism, and Public Management." *Administration and Society* 32, no. 3 (2000): 308–28.

Fernandez, Sergio. "Developing and Testing an Integrative Framework of Public Sector Leadership: Evidence from the Public Education Arena." *Journal of Public Administration Research and Theory* 15, no. 2 (2005): 197–217.

Fernandez, Sergio. "What Works Best When Contracting for Services? An Analysis of Contracting Performance at the Local Level." *Public Administration* 85, no. 4 (2007): 1119–141.

Fernandez, Sergio, and Craig R. Smith. "Looking for Evidence of Public Employee Opposition to Privatization." *Review of Public Personnel Administration* 26, no. 4 (2006): 356–81.

Fernandez, Sergio, Craig R. Smith, and Jeffrey B. Wenger. "Employment, Privatization, and Managerial Choice: Does Contracting Out Reduce Public Sector Employment?" *Journal of Policy Analysis and Management* 26, no. 1 (2007): 57–77.

Feldman, Martha S., and Anne M. Khademian. "To Manage Is to Govern." *Public Administration Review* 62, no. 5 (2002): 529–41.

Feldman, Martha S., Anne Khademian, Helen Ingram, and Anne Schneider. "Ways of Knowing and Inclusive Management Practices." *Public Administration Review* 66 (special issue, 2006): 89–99.

Fisher, Roger, and William Ury. *Getting to Yes.* Boston: Houghton Mifflin, 1981.

Fleming, Jenny, and Jennifer Wood, eds. *Fighting Crime Together: The Challenges of Policing and Security Networks.* New South Wales University Press (Sydney, Australia), 2007.

Franklin, Barry M., Marianne N. Bloch, and Thomas S. Popkewitz. *Educational Partnerships and the State: The Paradoxes of Governing Schools, Children, and Families.* New York: Palgrave Macmillan, 2006.

Freeman, Tim, and Edward Peck. "Performing Governance: A Partnership Board Dramaturgy." *Public Administration* 85, no. 4 (2007): 907–29.

Gargiulo, Martin, and Mario Benassi. "Trapped in Your Own Net? Network Cohesion, Structural Holes, and the Adaptation of Social Capital." *Organizational Science* 11, no. 2 (2000): 183–96.

Gazley, Beth. "Beyond the Contract: The Scope and Nature of Informal Government-Nonprofit Partnerships." *Public Administration Review* 68, no. 1 (2008): 141–54.

Gazley, Beth, and Jeffrey L. Brudney. "The Purpose (and Perils) of Government-Nonprofit Partnership." *Nonprofit and Voluntary Sector Quarterly* 36, no. 1 (2007): 389–415.

Gerberding, Julie. "Protecting the Public's Health with Small World Connections." James E. Webb Lecture, National Academy of Public Administration, Washington, D.C., November 18, 2004 (www.napawash.org/Pubs/gerberding.pdf).

Goldsmith, Stephen, and William Eggers. *Governing by Network: The New Shape of the Public Sector.* Brookings, 2004.

Gollust, Sarah E., and Peter D. Jacobson. "Privatization of Public Services: Organizational Reform Efforts in Public Education and Public Health." *American Journal of Public Health* 96, no. 10 (2006): 1733–739.

Goodsell, Charles T. "Six Normative Principles for the Contracting-Out Debate." *Administration and Society* 38, no. 6 (2007): 669–88.

Graddy, Elizabeth A., and Bin Chen. "Influence on the Size and Scope of Networks for Social Service Delivery." *Journal of Public Administration Research and Theory* 16, no. 4 (2006): 533–52.

Greenway, John, Brian Salter, and Stella Hart. "How Policy Networks Can Damage Democratic Health: A Case Study in the Government of Governance." *Public Administration* 85, no. 3 (2007): 717–38.

Grimsey, Darrin, and Mervyn Lewis. *The Economics of Public-Private Partnerships.* Northampton, Mass: Edward Elgar, 2005.

Grout, Paul A., and Silvia Sonderegger. "Simple Money-Based Tests for Choosing Between Private and Public Delivery: A Discussion of the Issues." *Review of Industrial Organization* 29, no. 1 (2006): 93–126.

Hackworth, Jason R. *The Neoliberal City: Governance, Ideology, and Development in American Urbanism.* Cornell University Press, 2007.

Hall, Thad, and Laurence J. O'Toole. "Shaping Formal Networks through the Regulatory Process." *Administration and Society* 36, no. 2 (2004): 186–207.

———. "Structures of Policy Implementation: An Analysis of National Legislation, 1965–1966 and 1993–1994." *Administration and Society* 31, no. 6 (2000): 667–86.

Hallett, Michael A. *Private Prisons in America: A Critical Race Perspective.* University of Illinois Press, 2006.

Hamel, Gary. "Competition for Competence and Inter-partner Learning within International Strategic Alliances." *Strategic Management Journal* 12 (1991): 83–103.

Handley, Donna M. "Strengthening the Intergovernmental Grant System: Long-Term Lessons for the Federal-Local Relationship." *Public Administration Review* 68, no. 1 (2008): 126–36.

Hansen, M. T. "The Search-Transfer Problem: The Role of Weak Ties in Sharing Knowledge across Organization Submits." *Administrative Science Quarterly* 44, no. 1 (1999): 82–111.

Heclo, Hugh. "Issue Networks and the Executive Establishment." In *The New American Political System,* edited by Anthony King, pp. 88–120. Washington: American Enterprise Institute for Public Research, 1978.

Herranz, Joaquin. "Network Governance: Strategies for Public Managers." Paper presented at the Public Management Research Association conference, Los Angeles, September 30, 2005 (www2.ku.edu/~pmranet/conferences/USC2005/USC2005papers/pmra.herranz.2005.pdf).

Hood, John, Ian Fraser, and Neil McGarvey. "Transparency of Risk and Reward in U.K. Public-Private Partnerships." *Public Budgeting and Finance* 26, no. 4 (2006): 40–58.

Hudson, Bob. "Analysing Network Partnerships: Benson Re-Visited." *Public Management Review* 6, no. 1 (2004): 75–94.

Ibarra, Herminia, and Mark Hunter. "How Leaders Create and Use Networks." *Harvard Business Review* 85, no. 1 (2007): 40–47.

Imperial, Mark T. "Using Collaboration as a Governance Strategy: Lessons from Six Watershed Management Programs." *Administration and Society* 37, no. 3 (2005): 281–320.

Jennings, Edward T., and Jo Ann Ewalt. "Interorganizational Coordination, Administrative Consolidation, and Policy Performance." *Public Administration Review* 58, no. 5 (1998): 417–28.

Jones, Candace, William Hesterly, and Stephen Borgatti. "A General Theory of Network Governance: Exchange Conditions and Social Mechanisms." *Academy of Management Review* 22, no. 4 (1997): 911–45.

Jones, Robert, and Gary Noble. "Managing the Implementation of Public-Private Partnerships." *Public Money and Management* 28, no. 2 (2008): 109–14.

Juriado, Rein, and Niklas Gustafsson. "Emergent Communities of Practice in Temporary Inter-Organisational Partnerships." *Learning Organization* 14, no. 1 (2007): 50–61.

Justice, Jonathan B., and Robert S. Goldsmith. "Private Governments or Public Policy Tools? The Law and Public Policy of New Jersey's Special Improvement Districts." *International Journal of Public Administration* 29, nos. 1–3 (2006): 107–36.

Kedia, B. L., and A. Mukherji. "Global Managers: Developing a Mindset for Global Competitiveness." *Journal of World Business* 34, no. 3 (1999): 230–51.

Kelly, Josie. "Reforming Public Services in the UK: Bringing in the Third Sector." *Public Administration* 85, no. 4 (2007): 1003–022.

Kenis, Patrick, and Keith G. Provan. "The Control of Public Networks." *International Public Management Journal* 9, no. 3 (2006): 227–47.

———. "Towards an Exogenous Theory of Public Network Performance." *Public Administration* 86: forthcoming.

Kenis, Patrick, and Jorg Raab. "What Do Policy Networks Do?" Paper presented at the Conference on Democratic Governance, Copenhagen, May 22–23, 2003.

Kettl, Donald F. "Contingent Coordination: Practical and Theoretical Puzzles for Homeland Security." *American Review of Public Administration* 33, no. 2 (2003): 253–77.

Kettl, Donald F. The Global Public Management Revolution: A Report on the Transference of Governance. Brookings, 2005.

———. "Managing Boundaries in American Administration: The Collaboration Imperative." *Public Administration Review* 86, no. 1 (2006): 10 - 19.

———. System under Stress: *Homeland Security and American Politics.* Washington: CQ Press, 2004.

———. *The Transformation of Governance: Public Administration for Twenty-First-Century America.* Johns Hopkins University Press, 2002.

Khademian, Anne. *Working with Culture: How the Job Gets Done in Public Programs.* Washington: CQ Press, 2002.

———. "The Politics of Homeland Security." In *The McGraw Hill Homeland Security Handbook,* edited by David Kamien. Columbus, Ohio: McGraw Hill, 2005.

Kickert, Walter J. M., Erik-Hans Klijn, and Joop F. M. Koppenjan, eds. *Managing Complex Networks: Strategies for the Public Sector.* London: Sage, 1997.

Kiefer, John J., and Robert S. Montjoy. "Incrementalism before the Storm: Network Performance for the Evacuation of New Orleans." *Public Administration Review* 66 (special issue, 2006): 122–30.

Klijn, Erik-Hans, and Joop F. M. Koopenjan. "Public Management and Policy Networks: Foundations to a Network Approach to Governance." *Public Management* 2, no. 2 (2000): 135–58.

Koliba, Christopher J. "Serving the Public Interest across Sectors: Asserting the Primacy of Networks." *Administrative Theory and Praxis* 28, no. 4 (2006): 593–601.

La Porte, Todd R. "Shifting Vantage and Conceptual Puzzles in Understanding Public Organization Networks." *Journal of Public Administration Research and Theory* 6, no. 1 (1996): 49–74.

Ladd, Darin, and Mark Ward. "An Investigation of Environmental Factors Influencing Knowledge Transfer." *Journal of Knowledge Management Practice* 3 (August 2002) (www.tlainc.com/articl38.htm).

Lave, Jean, and Etienne Wenger. *Situated Learning: Legitimate Peripheral Participation.* Cambridge University Press, 1991.

Light, Paul. "A Government Ill Executed: The Depletion of the Federal Service." *Public Administration Review* 68, no. 3 (2008): 413–19.

———. "The Tides of Reform Revisited: Making Government Work, 1945–2002." *Public Administration Review* 66, no. 1 (2006): 6–19.

Lowndes, Vivien, and Helen Sullivan. "How Low Can You Go? Rationales and Challenges for the Neighbourhood Governance." *Public Administration* 86, no. 1 (2008): 53–74.

MacManus, Susan A., and Kiki Caruson. "Financing Homeland Security and Emergency Preparedness: Use of Interlocal Cost-Sharing." *Public Budgeting and Finance* 28, no. 2 (2008): 48–68.

Markle Foundation Task Force on National Security in the Information Age. "Creating a Trusted Information Network for Homeland Security." Report. New York, 2003.

Martimort, David. "An Agency Perspective on the Costs and Benefits of Privatization." *Journal of Regulatory Economics* 30, no. 1 (2006): 5–44.

Martimort, David, and Jerome Pouyet. "'Build It or Not': Normative and Positive Theories of Public-Private Partnerships." CEPR Discussion Papers Series 5610. London: Centre for Economic Policy Research, 2006.

Mason, Richard, and Ian Mitroff. "A Program for Research on Management Information Systems." *Management Science* 19, no. 5 (1973): 475–87.

Mayer-Schonberger, Viktor, and David Laser, eds. *Governance and Information Technology: From Electronic Government to Information Government.* MIT Press, 2007.

McCartney, Sean, and John Stittle. "'Taken for a Ride': The Privatization of the UK Railway Rolling Stock Industry." *Public Money and Management* 28, no. 2 (2008): 93–100.

McCormack, Tracy Walters. "Privatizing the Justice System." *Review of Litigation Symposium* 25, no. 4 (2006): 735–46.

McGrath, Rita Gunther, and Ian MacMillan. *The Entrepreneurial Mindset.* Harvard Business School Press, 2000.

McGuire, Michael. "Collaborative Public Management: Assessing What We Know and How We Know It." *Public Administration Review* 66, no. 1 (2006): 33–43.

McKinney, Matthew, and William Harmon. *The Western Confluence: A Guide to Governing Natural Resources.* Washington: Island Press, 2004.

McSwite, O. C. *Legitimacy in Public Administration: A Discourse Analysis.* London: Sage, 1997.

Megginson, William L. *The Financial Economics of Privatization.* Oxford University Press, 2005.

Meier, Kenneth, and Laurence O'Toole. *Bureaucracy in a Democratic State: A Governance Perspective.* Johns Hopkins University Press, 2006.

———. "Public Management and Educational Performance: The Impact of Managerial Networking." *Public Administration Review* 63, no. 6 (2003): 689–99.

Miller, Gary J. *Managerial Dilemmas: The Political Economy of Hierarchy.* Cambridge University Press, 1992.

Milward, H. Brinton, Patrick Kenis, and Jörg Raab, "Introduction: Towards the Study of Network Control." *International Public Management Journal* 9, no. 3 (2006): 203–08.

Milward, H. Brinton, and Keith G. Provan. *A Manager's Guide to Choosing and Using Collaborative Networks*. Washington: IBM Center for the Business of Government, 2006.

———. "Measuring Network Structure." *Public Administration* 76 (1998): 387–407.

Milward, H. Brinton, and Jörg Raab. "Dark Networks as Organizational Problems: Elements of a Theory." *International Public Management Journal* 9, no. 3 (2006): 333–60.

Molnár, David M. "The Accountability Paradigm: Standards of Excellence." *Public Management Review* 10, no. 1 (2008):12/–37.

Moore, Mark H., and Jean Hartley. "Innovations in Governance." *Public Management Review* 10, no. 1 (2008): 3–20.

Morse, Ricardo S., Terry F. Buss, and C. Morgan Kinghorn, eds. 2007. *Transforming Public Leadership for the 21st Century*. Armonk, N.Y.: M. E. Sharpe

Moynihan, Donald P. "Learning under Uncertainty: Networks in Crisis Management." *Public Administration Review* 68, no. 2 (2008): 350–65.

———. *Leveraging Collaborative Networks in Infrequent Emergency Situations*. Washington: IBM Center for the Business of Government, 2005

Nahapiet, J., and S. Ghoshal. "Social Capital, Intellectual Capital and the Organizational Advantage." *Academy of Management Review* 23 (1998): 242–66.

Nalbandian, John. 1999. "Facilitating Community, Enabling Democracy: New Roles for Local Government Managers." *Public Administration Review* 59, no. 3 (1999): 187–98.

Nicolini, Davide, Silvia Gherardi, and Dvora Yanow, eds. *Knowing in Organizations: A Practice-Based Approach*. Armonk, N.Y.: M. E. Sharpe, 2003.

Noble, Gary, and Robert Jones. "The Role of Boundary-Spanning Managers in the Establishment of Public-Private Partnerships." *Public Administration* 84, no. 4 (2006): 891–917.

O'Leary, Rosemary, Robert F. Durant, Daniel J. Fiorino, and Paul S. Weiland. *Managing for the Environment: Understanding the Legal, Organizational, and Policy Challenges*. San Francisco: Jossey-Bass, 1999.

Orr, Julian. *Talking about Machines: An Ethnography of a Modern Job*. Cornell University Press, 1996.

Osborne, Stephen P., Celine Chew, and Kate McLaughlin. "The Once and Future Pioneers? The Innovative Capacity of Voluntary Organisations and the Provision of Public Services: A Longitudinal Approach." *Public Management Review* 10, no. 1 (2008): 51–70.

O'Toole, Laurence J. "Treating Networks Seriously: Practical and Research-Based Agendas in Public Administration." *Public Administration Review* 57, no. 1 (1997): 45–52.

Owen-Smith, Jason, and Walter W. Powell. "Knowledge Networks as Channels and Conduits: The Effects of Spillovers in the Boston Biotechnology Community." *Organization Science* 15, no. 1 (2004): 5–21.

Peters, Guy. *The Future of Governing*. University of Kansas Press, 2001.

Peters, Guy, and John Pierre. "Governance without Government: Rethinking Public Administration." *Journal of Public Administration Research and Theory* 8, no. 2 (1998): 223–44.

Pfeffer, Jeffry, and Gerald Salencik. *The External Control of Organizations*. New York: Harper & Row, 1978.

Podolny, Joe, and Karen Page. "Network Forms of Organization." *Annual Review of Sociology* 24 (1998): 57–76.

Powell, Walter. "Learning from Collaboration: Knowledge and Networks in the Biotechnology and Pharmaceutical Industries." *California Management Review* 40, no. 3 (1998): 227–40.

———. "Neither Market Nor Hierarchy: Network forms of Organization." *Research in Organizational Behavior* 12 (1990): 295–336.

Powell, Walter, and Peter Brantley. "Competitive Cooperation in Biotechnology: Learning through Networks?" *Networks and Organizations* (1992): 366–94.

Powell, Walter, Kenneth Kopet, and Laurel Smith-Doerr. "Interorganizational Collaboration and the Locus of Innovation: Networks of Learning in Biotechnology." *Administrative Science Quarterly* 41, no. 1 (1996): 116–45.

Prager, Jonas. "Contract City Redux: Weston, Florida, as the Ultimate New Public Management Model City." *Public Administration Review* 68, no. 1 (2008): 167–80.

Provan, Keith G., and Noshir Contractor. "Understanding and Managing Stakeholder Networks." In *Greater than the Sum: Systems Thinking in Tobacco Control. Tobacco Control Monograph* 18, NIH publication 006-6085. Bethesda, Md.: U.S. Department of Health and Human Services, National Institutes of Health, National Cancer Institute, 2007.

Provan, Keith G., and Patrick Kenis. "Modes of Network Governance: Structure, Management, and Effectiveness." *Journal of Public Administration Research and Theory* 18, no. 2 (2008): 229–52.

Provan, Keith G., Patrick Kenis, and Sherrie E. Human. "Legitimacy Building in Organizational Networks." In *The Collaborative Public Manager,* edited by Rosemary O'Leary. Georgetown University Press, 2008.

Provan, Keith, and H. Brinton Milward. "A Preliminary Theory of Network Effectiveness: A Comparative Study of Four Mental Health Systems." *Administrative Science Quarterly* 40, no. 1 (1995): 1–33.

Provan, Keith G., and Joerg Sydow. "Evaluating Interorganizational Networks." In *The Oxford Handbook of Inter-Organizational Relations,* edited by Steve Cropper, Mark Ebers, Chris Huxham, and Pete S. Ring. Oxford University Press, forthcoming.

Provan, Keith G., Mark A. Veazie, Lisa K. Staten, and Nicolette Teufel-Shone. "The Use of Network Analysis to Strengthen Community Partnerships." *Public Administration Review* 65, no. 5 (2005): 603–13.

Raab, J., and H. Brinton Milward. "Dark Networks as Problems." *Journal of Public Administration Research and Theory* 13, no. 4 (2003): 413–39.

Reich, Robert, ed. *The Power of Public Ideas.* Harvard University Press, 1990.

Rhodes, Rod A. W. "The New Governance: Governing without Government." *Political Studies* 44, no. 4 (1996): 652–67.

Resnick, Mitchel. "Beyond the Centralized Mindset." *Journal of the Learning Sciences* 5, no. 1 (1996): 1–22.

Riccucci, Norma M. *Unsung Heroes: Federal Execucrats Making a Difference.* Georgetown University Press, 1995.

Rittel, Horst, and Melvin Webber. "Dilemmas in a General Theory of Planning." *Policy Sciences* 4 (1973): 155–59.

Roberts, Nancy C. "Public Entrepreneurship and Innovation." *Policy Studies Review* 11, no. 1 (1992): 55–71.

———. "Public Deliberation: An Alternative Approach to Crafting Policy and Setting Direction." *Public Administration Review* 57, no. 2 (1997): 124–32.

———. "Innovation by Legislative, Judicial, and Managerial Design." In *Public Management Reform and Innovation: Research, Theory, and Application,* edited by H. G. Frederickson and J. M. Johnston. New York: Wiley, 1999.

———. "Wicked Problems and Network Approaches to Resolution." *International Public Management Review* 1, no. 1 (2000): 1–19.

———. *The Transformative Power of Dialogue.* New York: JAI Press, 2002.

Root, Franklin R. "Some Taxonomies of International Cooperative Arrangements." In *Cooperative Strategies and Alliances,* edited by Farok J. Contractor and Peter Lorange. Amsterdam: Elsevier, 2003.

Rosenau, James N., and others, eds. *Governance without Government.* Cambridge University Press, 1992.

Savas, E. S. "Privatization in the City: Successes, Failures, Lessons." Washington: CQ Press, 2005.

Scharpf, Fritz. *Governing in Europe: Effective and Democratic?* Oxford University Press, 1999.

Schau, Hope J., Michael F. Smith, and Per Ivar Schau. "The Healthcare Network Economy: The Role of Internet Information Transfer and Implications for Pricing." *Industrial Marketing Management* 34, no. 2 (2005):147–56.

Scott, James C. *Seeing like a State: How Certain Schemes to Improve the Human Condition Have Failed.* Yale University Press, 1998.

Selznick, Philip. *Leadership in Administration: A Sociological Interpretation.* New York: Harper & Row, 1957.

Shaoul, Jean, Anne Stafford, and Pam Stapleton. "The Cost of Using Private Finance to Build, Finance and Operate Hospitals." *Public Money and Management* 28, no. 2 (2008): 101–08.

Snider, Keith. "Expertise or Experimenting: Pragmatism and the American Public Administration, 1920–1950." *Administration and Society* 32, no. 3 (2000): 329–54.

Sørensen, Eva, and Jacob Torfing. "The Democratic Anchorage of Governance Networks." *Scandinavian Political Studies* 28, no. 3 (2005): 195–218.

———. "Network Governance and Post-Liberal Democracy." *Administrative Theory and Praxis* 27, no. 2 (2005): 197–237.

———, eds. *Theories of Democratic Network Governance.* New York: Palgrave Macmillan, 2007.

Standfort, Jodi, and H. Brinton Milward. "Inter-Organizational Relations and Public Sector Service Partnerships." In *The Oxford Handbook on Inter-Organizational Relations,* edited by Steve Cropper, Mark Ebers, Chris Huxham, and Peter S. Ring. Oxford University Press, forthcoming.

Stanton, Thomas H. "Reducing Government Involvement in a Market: Lessons from the Privatization of Sallie Mae." *Public Budgeting and Finance* 28, no. 1 (2008): 101–23.

Susskind, Lawrence. *The Consensus Building Handbook.* London: Sage, 1999.

Tushman, Michael L., and Thomas J. Scanlan. "Characteristics and External Orientations of Boundary Spanning Individuals." *Academy of Management Journal* 24, no. 1 (1981): 83–98.

Van Bueren, Ellen M., Erik-Hans Klijn, and Joop F. M. Koppenjan. "Dealing with Wicked Problems in Networks: Analyzing an Environmental Debate from a Network Perspective. *Journal of Public Administration Research and Theory* 13, no. 2 (2003): 193–212.

Van Slyke, David M. "The Mythology of Privatization in Contracting for Social Services." *Public Administration Review* 63, no. 3 (2003): 296–315.

———. "Agents or Stewards: Using Theory to Understand the Government–Nonprofit Social Service Contracting Relationship." *Journal of Public Administration Research and Theory* 17, no. 2 (2007): 157–87.

Verkuil, Paul R. *Outsourcing Sovereignty: Why Privatization of Government Functions Threatens Democracy and What We Can Do About It.* Cambridge University Press, 2007.

Weber, Edward P. *Pluralism by the Rules: Conflict and Cooperation in Environmental Regulation.* Georgetown University Press, 1998.

———. *Bringing Society Back In: Grassroots Ecosystem Management, Accountability, and Sustainable Communities.* MIT Press, 2003.

Weber, Edward P., and Anne Khademian. "From Agitation to Collaboration: Clearing the Air through Negotiation." *Public Administration Review* 57, no. 5 (1997): 396–410.

———. "Wicked Problems, Knowledge Challenges, and Collaborative Capacity Builders in Network Settings." *Public Administration Review* 68, no. 2 (2008): 334–49.

Weber, Edward P., Nicholas P. Lovrich, and Michael Gaffney. "Collaboration, Enforcement, and Endangered Species: A Framework for Assessing Collaborative Problem Solving Capacity." *Society and Natural Resources* 18, no. 8 (2005): 677–98.

Weber, Edward P., Nicholas P. Lovrich, and David Nice. "Understanding Urban Commuters: How Are Non-SOV [single-occupancy-vehicle] Commuters Different from SOV Commuters?" *Transportation Quarterly* 54, no. 2 (2000): 105–16.

Weihe, Guorio. "Public-Private Partnerships and Public-Private Value Trade-Offs." *Public Money and Management* 28, no. 3 (2008): 153–58.

Williams, Jennifer, Cristina Losito, and Joanna Cottingham. *Creative Community Building through Cross-Sector Collaboration—A European Mapping and Consultation Initiative: Final Report.* Athens: Programma Melina, General Secretariat for Adult Education, 2006.

Yanow, Dvora. "Translating Local Knowledge at Organizational Peripheries." *British Journal of Management* 15, no. S1 (2004): S9–S25.

Yescombe, Edward R. *Public-Private Partnerships: Principles of Policy and Finance.* Boston: Butterworth-Heinemann, 2007.

Contributors

WILLIAM G. BERBERICH is a Ph.D. student at the Center for Public Administration and Policy at Virginia Tech's Alexandria, Virginia, campus. His research interests include homeland security, networks, and risk management. He is a civilian engineer in the U.S. Navy's Surface Ship Design Group, where he is responsible for new technology integration and maintenance policy on patrol ships. He has completed master's programs in public affairs and mechanical engineering and is a graduate of the U.S. Naval War College and a retired officer in the U.S. Naval Reserve.

TIM BURKE is research coordinator at the Ash Institute for Democratic Governance and Innovation at the Harvard University's Kennedy School of Government, where in his work with Stephen Goldsmith, he explores the role of public-private partnerships in social services. Burke's professional and volunteer experiences include both domestic and international work in the areas of affordable housing, youth development, and community relations. He has an M.S. in public affairs from the John J. McCormack Graduate School of Policy Studies at the University of Massachusetts, Boston, and a B.S. in public health from the University of North Carolina at Chapel Hill. His publications include *Democracy on Trial: Evaluating Democracy Promotion in U.S. Foreign Policy*, a 2006 occasional paper from the McCormack Graduate School, and he has received research credit in numerous articles.

G. EDWARD DESEVE, chairman of Strategy and Solution LLP, is a senior lecturer at the University of Pennsylvania's Fels Institute of Government and a senior fellow in the University of Maryland's Academy of Leadership. He served as chief financial officer of the Department of Housing and Urban Development and as controller then deputy director for management at the Office of Management and Budget. DeSeve was the director of finance for the city of Philadelphia and served as special assistant to the governor of Pennsylvania. In the private sector, he was a senior vice president for Affiliated Computer Services and was a managing director of Merrill Lynch Capital Markets. He founded Public Financial Management Inc., which serves states and localities.

WILLIAM D. EGGERS is the executive director of Deloitte's Public Leadership Institute and is the global research director for the company's public sector industry. A recognized expert on government reform, he is the author of numerous books on transforming government, including *Governing by Network: The New Shape of the Public Sector* (Brookings, 2004; it won the National Academy of Public Administration's 2005 Louis Brownlow award for best book on public management) and *Government 2.0: Using Technology to Improve Education, Cut Red Tape, Reduce Gridlock, and Enhance Democracy* (Rowman and Littlefield, 2005). A former manager of the Texas Performance Review, Eggers has advised numerous governments around the world. His commentary has appeared in dozens of major media outlets, including the *New York Times* and the *Wall Street Journal*. A volume on how government can improve its ability to execute big initiatives is forthcoming.

STEPHEN GOLDSMITH is the Daniel Paul Professor of Government and the director of the Innovations in American Government Program at the Ash Institute for Democratic Governance and Innovation at Harvard University's Kennedy School of Government. He is also the chair of the Corporation for National and Community Service. He previously served two terms as mayor of Indianapolis, where he earned a reputation as one of the country's leaders in public-private partnerships, competition, and privatization. As mayor he conducted more than eighty public-private competitions, which resulted in savings of more than $400 million, investment in infrastructure of more than $1 billion, and a transformation of downtown Indianapolis that has been singled out as a national model. The *Wall Street Journal* has called Mayor Goldsmith a "pioneering privatizer of city services." His publications include the award-winning *Governing by Network: The New Shape of the Public Sector* (Brookings, 2004) and *The Twenty-First Century City: Resurrecting Urban America* (Regnery Publishing Inc., 1997).

DONALD F. KETTL is the Robert A. Fox Leadership Professor in the Department of Political Science at the University of Pennsylvania and also serves as a nonresident senior fellow at the Brookings Institution. He is the author of *The Next Gov-*

ernment of the United States (W. W. Norton, 2009) and *The Global Public Management Revolution* (Brookings, 2005), among others. He has twice won the Louis Brownlow Book Award of the National Academy of Public Administration for the best book published in public administration, and in 2008 he was the recipient of the American Political Science Association's John Gaus lifetime achievement award in political science and public administration.

ANNE M. KHADEMIAN is the associate chair for the Center for Public Administration and Policy at Virginia Tech and the director of the Center in Alexandria, Virginia. Her research interests focus on inclusive management, organizations involved in homeland security, and financial regulation. She is the author of numerous articles on public management and public policy and of *Working with Culture: The Way the Job Gets Done in Public Programs* (CQ Press, 2002), *Checking on Banks: Autonomy and Accountability in Three Federal Agencies* (Brookings, 1996), and *The SEC and Capital Market Regulation: The Politics of Expertise* (University of Pittsburgh Press, 1992).

H. BRINTON MILWARD has studied organizational networks for his entire career and is the Providence Service Corporation Chair in Public Management at the University of Arizona. His work has focused on understanding how to efficiently and effectively manage networks of organizations that jointly produce public services such as health care. Since 2001 he has studied illegal and covert networks whose missions are predicated on redress of grievances or on pure greed. His articles on dark networks have been widely cited for their application of network analysis and management theory to terrorist networks, human trafficking, drug smuggling, and other illegal activities.

MARK H. MOORE is the Hauser Professor of Nonprofit Organizations and faculty chair of the Hauser Center for Nonprofit Organizations at Harvard University and a visiting professor at the Harvard Business School. Previously he was the Guggenheim Professor of Criminal Justice Policy and Management and faculty chair of the Program in Criminal Justice Policy and Management at Harvard University's Kennedy School of Government. He served as the founding chair of the Kennedy School's Committee on Executive Programs and served in that role for more than a decade. His research interests are public management and leadership, civil society and community mobilization, and criminal justice policy and management. His publications include *Creating Public Value: Strategic Management in Government* (Harvard University Press, 1995) and (with Malcolm Sparrow and David Kennedy) *Beyond 911: A New Era for Policing* (Basic Books, 1990). Moore's work focuses on the ways in which leaders of public organizations can engage communities in supporting and legitimatizing their work and in the role that value commitments play in enabling leadership in public sector enterprises.

PAUL POSNER is the director of the Public Administration Program at George Mason University, after serving for thirty years in the Government Accountability Office, including thirteen years as director of the federal budget and intergovernmental work. He is chair of the Federal Systems Panel of the National Academy of Public Administration and president-elect of the American Society for Public Administration. He has published widely on budgeting and federalism. He was recognized as the Outstanding Scholar on Federalism and Intergovernmental Relations in 2008 by the American Political Science Association, and his book, *The Politics of Unfunded Mandates* (Georgetown University Press, 1998), was honored by the association as the best book on federalism in 2008. With Tim Conlan, he edited *Intergovernmental Management for the 21st Century*, recently published by Brookings.

JÖRG RAAB is assistant professor of policy and organization studies at the University of Tilburg in the Netherlands. He received his Ph.D. from the University of Konstanz, Germany, in 2000. His research focuses mainly on topics in organization theory (especially interorganizational networks); quantitative network analysis; and governance mechanisms in the state, economy, and society. He is currently conducting research on the management and effectiveness of interorganizational networks, networks and teams, and temporary organizations. With H. Brinton Milward, he is pursuing a research program on dark networks as organizational problems.

BARRY G. RABE holds appointments in the Gerald Ford School of Public Policy and the School of Natural Resources and Environment at the University of Michigan and is also a nonresident senior fellow at the Brookings Institution. His most recent book, *Statehouse and Greenhouse* (Brookings, 2004), received the 2005 Caldwell Award from the American Political Science Association as the best book published on environmental policy over a three-year period. In 2006 Rabe became the first social scientist to receive a Climate Protection Award from the U.S. Environmental Protection Agency. He is currently editing books on climate change policy and transborder environmental governance in Canada and the United States.

Index